TABLE OF CONTENTS

Top 20 Test Taking Tips

1. Carefully follow all the test registration procedures
2. Know the test directions, duration, topics, question types, how many questions
3. Setup a flexible study schedule at least 3-4 weeks before test day
4. Study during the time of day you are most alert, relaxed, and stress free
5. Maximize your learning style; visual learner use visual study aids, auditory learner use auditory study aids
6. Focus on your weakest knowledge base
7. Find a study partner to review with and help clarify questions
8. Practice, practice, practice
9. Get a good night's sleep; don't try to cram the night before the test
10. Eat a well balanced meal
11. Know the exact physical location of the testing site; drive the route to the site prior to test day
12. Bring a set of ear plugs; the testing center could be noisy
13. Wear comfortable, loose fitting, layered clothing to the testing center; prepare for it to be either cold or hot during the test
14. Bring at least 2 current forms of ID to the testing center
15. Arrive to the test early; be prepared to wait and be patient
16. Eliminate the obviously wrong answer choices, then guess the first remaining choice
17. Pace yourself; don't rush, but keep working and move on if you get stuck
18. Maintain a positive attitude even if the test is going poorly
19. Keep your first answer unless you are positive it is wrong
20. Check your work, don't make a careless mistake

Fitness and Wellness and Stress Management

Health and fitness

Physical fitness depends on speed, power, agility, flexibility, cardiovascular endurance, muscular endurance, and muscular strength. A law enforcement officer must have excellent physical fitness in order to perform his or her duties without suffering from fatigue. Wellness is slightly different from physical fitness: it is the measure of the individual's illness or risk of illness. It is possible to be physically fit but not well, while it is difficult to be well without being physically fit. Physical fitness is often divided into functional or health-related fitness (more general) and motor fitness (performance-oriented). In order of decreasing importance, the factors that influence fitness and wellness are regular exercise, proper nutrition, weight control, tobacco cessation, stress management, and personal responsibility. Physical fitness is extremely important for law enforcement officers, who may be required to lift heavy objects, run quickly, jump over obstacles, or climb at a moment's notice. Unfortunately, even though new recruits typically have average or above-average fitness, officers of longer standing have an average level of fitness inferior to that of the general population.

Safe exercise programs

Before beginning an exercise program, it is a good idea to become familiar with the basic principles of safe activity. Aspiring officers who have medical problems should see a doctor or use the Par-Q checklist before initiating an exercise program. The basic characteristics of a safe exercise program are balance, specificity, regularity and recovery, and progressive overload. Balance is attention to various parts of the body, through both exercises that work opposing muscle groups and exercises that focus alternately on cardiovascular, flexibility, and strength training. Specificity is awareness of the particular improvements likely to be gained from certain activities. In other words, an effective exercise program is composed of activities that are designed to improve the targeted areas of fitness. The concept of regularity and recovery means that exercise should be consistent and frequent, but also should be interrupted by periods of rest. For instance, there should be at least 48 hours between heavy exercises that use the same muscle groups. However, research suggests that fitness levels begin to diminish after only 96 hours of rest. Finally, progressive overload is the concept that exercise must be more demanding than daily activity in order to be effective.

FITT

Exercise professionals often refer to the basic elements of an exercise program with the initials FITT, which is short for frequency, intensity, time, and type. With respect to cardiovascular training, it is important for the frequency to be at least three days a week. The intensity of exercise should be within the target heart rate zone, which is between 60 and 80 percent of the predicted maximum heart rate.

Cardiovascular exercise should begin with a five-minute warm-up period, and should include at least 20 minutes of exercise at the target heart rate. The best type of exercise for cardiovascular training is a rhythmic aerobic exercise like swimming, cycling, or running. Strength training should occur between two and four days a week, with a minimum of 48 hours between exercises that work the same muscle groups. These exercises should begin at 13 RPE and progress to 16 RPE. Time is somewhat flexible with strength training, though there should be enough time to finish between one and three sets. Calisthenics and weight training are the most common types of strength exercise.

Flexibility and anaerobic training

Flexibility training should be performed between three and seven days a week. It is important to identify and maintain proper intensity during flexibility exercise; there should be some tension but not so much that the exercise is painful. Each stretch should be held for between 10 and 20 seconds, and the entire stretching session should last at least three minutes and should be performed at the end of cardiovascular or strength training. Indeed, stretching is more beneficial when it is performed after cardiovascular exercise.

Anaerobic training involves activities that require more oxygen than the muscles have in store. These are activities, like sprinting or lifting heavy objects, that a person cannot perform for an extended time. Aspiring officers should practice anaerobic exercise once or twice a week, if possible, during a cardiovascular workout. The exercise should require 90 percent of the maximum heart rate. These exercises should be performed for at least 20 seconds, but for no more than a minute, and should be followed by an interval of rest.

Exercise program

The basic exercise program has three components: warm-up, workout, and cool-down.

The warm-up should last from five to 10 minutes, and should include some low-level cardiovascular exercise to improve circulation and joint movements. Light stretching is also a good activity during the warm-up. This part of exercise is important for reducing the risk of injury.

Next, the main part of the workout should last at least 20 minutes. It should focus on a

particular area of fitness, and should be performed at a high level of intensity. Finally, the cool-down consists of at least five minutes of moderate cardiovascular exercise and a great deal of stretching. These stretches should be performed slowly and build for a sustained period. It is important to stretch the muscles that were the focus of the workout.

Fitness training

Exercising during intense heat can be very dangerous. If the heat index, which takes into account both air temperature and humidity, is above 100, then the body is very likely to endure heat stress and even heat stroke during vigorous and prolonged exercise. One should not exercise in such heat. No matter what the heat index is during exercise, one should drink at least a gallon of water every day, including before, during, and after exercise. If pain develops during a workout, one should stop immediately and seek medical attention. This is especially true if symptoms include irregular and short breath and chest pain. Even the most advanced athletes should receive regular checkups to ensure that a regular and vigorous exercise program is appropriate.

Proper diet components

The essential components of a human diet are carbohydrates, fats, proteins, vitamins, minerals, and water. Carbohydrates are the best source of energy for the body and brain. They also include fiber, which aids in digestion. Carbohydrates can be either simple or complex. Simple carbohydrates, like white flour and soft drinks, provide only empty calories and excessive sugar. Complex carbohydrates, like potatoes and vegetables, provide energy as well as nutrients and fiber. Carbohydrates should make up between 55 and 60 percent of total daily calories. Protein is important for building and maintaining the tissues of the body. It is obtained from beans, meat, eggs, and dairy products. Protein should make up between 12 and 15 percent of daily calories.

Fats, vitamins, minerals, and water

Fats provide the most calories per serving. They also help the function of the nerves and protect the organs. Fats should not make up more than 30 percent of total calories. Fats can be either saturated, as in butter and meat, or unsaturated, as in avocados, nuts, and lighter oils. The body also needs vitamins and minerals to thrive. For aspiring law-enforcement professionals, the most important of these are vitamin C, vitamin E, and beta carotene. The most important mineral for the body, however, is water. Everyone should drink at least six eight-ounce glasses of water every day, and active people should drink more. Water should be consumed before, during, and after exercise.

Law enforcement stress

People often incorrectly assume that all stress is bad. However, some stress is necessary to stimulate top performance. Stress is not only a mental state, but a set of biochemical and hormonal responses to stimuli. Positive stress and negative stress are referred to as eustress and distress, respectively. An acute stress lasts for a short amount of time, and is typically easy for the body to handle. Chronic stress, on the other hand, lasts for a prolonged interval and can be very damaging to health.

For law enforcement professionals, critical incident stress is of particular concern. This occurs in response to a specific incident, and may last for days or months. A prolonged response to a severely stressful incident is not considered abnormal. Indeed, many law-enforcement officers must grapple with posttraumatic stress disorder, which is a painful and traumatic response to stress that lasts for longer than a month.

Symptoms of stress

Stress has all kinds of emotional and physical effects on the body, both positive and negative. Stress increases breathing rate, heart rate, consumption of oxygen, and blood pressure. It also increases alertness and muscle tension, which can be fatiguing over time. Stress directs blood to the brain and the peripheral organs, so that other organs receive less blood than they require. All of these reactions to stress are healthy, so long as they do not persist over a long period of time. Stress also triggers the release of hormones, like adrenaline, which are in limited supply. People who suffer from chronic stress eventually see their internal response systems diminish in performance, so that they become less able to respond to short and long-term stresses.

Peace officer stress

Peace officers must deal with a host of stressors. The job can be boring for long stretches, only to be suddenly punctuated by intense and traumatic activity. Some cases and incidents never achieve a satisfying conclusion. Peace officers must work at odd times, which can take a toll on the body. Many peace officers report feeling distressed by their interactions with the judicial system and the news media. Some officers even complain about receiving inadequate support from the general population and politicians. Peace officers must deal with a large amount of paperwork and, in some cases, poor training and leadership. Peace officers deal with all of the usual stressors associated with bureaucracy: unfair promotions and assignments, irregularly enforced rules, and varying support from management. Moreover, peace officers are usually motivated by idealism, and may become frustrated by their inability to improve the community quickly.

Managing stress

The work of a peace officer can be extremely stressful, so it is important for officers to develop strategies for managing stress. The simplest way to deal with stress is to eliminate or reduce exposure to stressful

- 7 -

situations and events. Of course, this is not always possible. Many officers report that their level of stress diminishes when they implement time management strategies.

It is important to take time away from the job to refresh. Officers should have hobbies and interests besides law enforcement. More generally, officers should take time to rest their bodies when they are not at work. For many officers, spirituality and religious practice are an effective way to manage stress. Also, social interaction outside of the job can be a good way to mitigate the effects of stress.

Survival stress

When a peace officer encounters an extremely stressful situation in the line of duty, his or her performance improves at first. Small increases in heart rate enhance the ability to act and process information. However, once the heart rate reaches 115 beats per minute, fine motor skills decline. At 145 beats per minute, complex motor skills begin to deteriorate as well. If the heart rate reaches 200 beats per minute, the officer will be practically incapable of performing his or her duties. During an extremely stressful episode, an officer may experience tunnel vision and a lack of depth perception. There are also effects on memory: officers have difficulty remembering stressful events immediately after they happen. Usually, an officer is able to recollect events better one or two days after the incident. Stressed officers also report alterations in their hearing and perception of time.

Traumatic event response

Officers who undergo an extremely stressful or traumatic event typically respond in similar ways. The five stages of response are denial, anger, bargaining, depression, and acceptance.

At first, the officer denies that the event occurred at all, or downplays his or her role

in it. Then, he or she feels resentful or bitter at being involved in the situation. Next, the officer enters the bargaining phase, in which he or she acts as if it is possible to negotiate the undoing of the traumatic event. The fourth and longest phase is depression, in which the officer slowly comes to grips with his or her role in the traumatic event. Finally, the officer enters the acceptance phase, in which the traumatic event ceases to be the most important thing in his or her life, and the officer is able to resume his or her routine. The speed with which an officer progresses through these stages of response depends on his or her temperament and level of support from the department and community.

PTSD

Law enforcement officials are increasingly aware of the prevalence of posttraumatic stress disorders among officers who have endured a traumatic event. Posttraumatic stress disorder (or PTSD) is like critical incident stress, only more severe and long-lasting. An officer with PTSD does not only remember the traumatic event, but rather feels as if he or she is reliving it over and over again. These officers are capable of exaggerated and highly inappropriate responses to stimuli that remind them of a stressful event. For instance, an officer who survived a horrific gun battle might become unhinged by a display of fireworks. On the other hand, an officer suffering from PTSD will have almost no response to other stimuli. PTSD disrupts sleep and interpersonal relationships. It is extremely difficult to manage this condition alone or without professional intervention.

Suicidal ideation or behavior

Officers who undergo extreme stress or trauma in the line of duty may be at greater risk of committing suicide. Males, especially those between the ages of 15 and 34 or older than 65, are more likely to commit suicide. Also, officers who abuse alcohol or drugs or who are unmarried are more likely to commit suicide. When officers believe a colleague may be contemplating suicide, they should immediately step into action. This means discussing concerns both with the at-risk individual and with the department's mental health advisors. If the person is believed to be at significant risk, he or she should not be left alone. Announcing plans to commit suicide, however casually or seemingly in jest is an immediate call for intervention.

Drug and alcohol abuse signs

Drug and alcohol abuse is especially dangerous for peace officers, whose work is stressful and whose responsibilities are great. A person may be abusing alcohol if he or she is frequently hung over, is unable to quit using, or feels guilty about his or her consumption. Alcoholics tend to use drinking as a crutch or as an escape from the stresses of their life. An alcoholic will have a hard time enjoying social events without drinking, and may feel the need to drink in order to prepare for social interaction. Alcoholics may suffer from blackouts and may have impaired short-term memory. All peace officers should frequently self-evaluate their own use of alcohol and drugs. Also, they should be vigilant about making sure their coworkers steer clear of substance abuse.

Steroid abuse

Many people are surprised to find that steroids are among the most commonly abused substances by law enforcement officials. Officers may decide to use these illegal drugs for ostensibly altruistic reasons, namely to improve their performance. However, long-term use of steroids can have damaging effects on the body and mind. The most famous negative effect of steroids is so-called "roid rage," or an increase in aggression and violent behavior. Steroid abusers are also at greater risk of developing diabetes, arthritis, high blood pressure, and some forms of cancer. Males who abuse steroids often have acne on their backs. All

steroid abusers suffer from violent mood swings and alterations to the secondary sex characteristics. If an officer gains muscle mass rapidly and his or her behavior becomes erratic, steroid abuse may be suspected.

Professional Policing

Historical development of police service

The role and methodology of police service has changed a great deal in the past century. With the introduction of radio communication, it became possible for officers to work at a greater distance from the precinct office. At the same time, however, technology created distance between police and the community, as officers began to drive more often than walk. It became possible for police to respond quickly, but for a long time law enforcement leaders failed to self-critique their service. In the first part of the 20th century, there were strong social connections between police officers and the areas in which they worked. In the past few decades, however, computers and officer rotations have severed many of these connections. To combat this trend, the most recent changes in police service have been an increase in evaluation research and community outreach.

Policing in Texas and the Commission Rules

Until the Battle of San Jacinto in 1836, the land that would become Texas was a province of Mexico and as such was policed by the Spanish military officers. When Texas became an independent republic, police work was handled by a militia organized by Stephen F. Austin, a militia that eventually evolved into the Texas Rangers. It was necessary for Texas to develop a unique model of police service because it was so vast and the population was so diffuse. In Texas, constables and sheriffs are elected officials. According to state law, licensed law enforcement officials must meet certain requirements, for instance with regard to firearms proficiency. These requirements are outlined in the Commission Rules.

Traditional police service model

In the traditional model of police service, officers react to events after they happen. The officer's job is focused on handling individual situations and events, and all of the statistics that are used to evaluate departmental performance are based on information obtained after police action has been performed. In the traditional model, the police department judges its performance on crime and arrest rates. For the most part, decisions are made by middle and upper management within the department, rather than by the community or by political leaders. Departments that follow the traditional model of police service are likely to be subdivided into specialized units. In general, these specialized units are quite good at accomplishing their limited objectives.

Community policing

Community policing represents a departure from the traditional model of police service insofar as it focuses on frequent and profitable communication with citizens and local leaders. Departmental decisions are made in cooperation with the external parties. In community policing, there is an emphasis on maintaining the same officers in the same districts for a long time, so that relationships may be built. The department management frequently solicits the opinions of the community with regard to police service. In community policing, the officer aspires to be a role model, especially for young people. Whenever possible, the officer tries to enable members of the community to solve their own problems. Rather than depending on crime and arrest rates as indicators of departmental success, a community-based police force will concentrate on improving cleanliness and morale in the community.

Professionalism and Ethics

Law enforcement profession

There is some controversy over whether law enforcement should be considered as a profession. In general, police service is better when officers adopt the major tenets of professionalism: attention to research in their chosen field, adherence to agreed-upon standards, willingness to continue training, and obedience to established ethical precepts. Law enforcement officers who think of themselves as professionals are more likely to provide excellent service and develop a stronger commitment to their work. However, establishing law enforcement as a profession has some drawbacks. Officers must receive long and expensive training, and their salaries must be paid by communities that may have financial problems. Also, the establishment of law enforcement as a profession may limit entry by people from certain socioeconomic backgrounds.

Law Enforcement Code of Ethics

The Law Enforcement Code of Ethics begins by declaring that the core duty of an officer is to protect citizens, promote peace, and respect the rights outlined by the Constitution. To do so, an officer must maintain excellent moral conduct and must obey the laws and the rules of the department. An officer should never allow personal prejudice or bias to influence his or her work. An officer must recognize that the public has placed its trust in him or her, and that honoring this trust is of paramount importance. An officer should seize every chance to improve his or her performance, whether through more education or advanced training. In general, the law enforcement officer must subjugate his or her own desires to the goal of providing top-quality service to the community.

Bribery and coercion of a public servant or voter

Section 39.02 of the Texas Penal Code states that it is illegal for a public servant to violate a law related to his or her office intentionally or to misuse government property. When this behavior is done with the intent of receiving a benefit, it is classified as an abuse of official capacity. Breaking a law related to public office is a Class A misdemeanor, while misusing government property ranges from a Class C misdemeanor to a first-degree felony, depending on the value of the property. According to Section 39.03 of the Texas Penal Code, public servants may not subject other people to an unlawful arrest, mistreatment, search, detention, or lien. It is also illegal for public servants to harass sexually or to infringe on the rights of other people in their official capacity. These offenses are known collectively as official oppression, and are designated as Class A misdemeanors.

Improper influence, and tampering with a witness

Section 39.04 of the Texas Penal Code states that peace officers and employees of correctional facilities may not deny other people their rights unlawfully or engage in any sexual contact with people in custody. The denial of rights is a Class A misdemeanor, while sexual contact with a detainee is a state jail felony unless the detainee is a minor, in which case the crime is a second-degree felony. According to Section 39.05 of the Texas Penal Code, it is illegal to fail to investigate or fully report the death of a prisoner. This offense is a Class B misdemeanor.

Obstruction or retaliation

Section 39.06 of the Texas Penal Code states that it is illegal to use information obtained in one's capacity as a public servant to receive money or to facilitate another person's profit. Also, it is illegal to suppress information or coerce other people to suppress official information. It is illegal for public servants to use official information that has not been made public for a non-governmental purpose. It is also illegal to obtain this information from a public servant with the intent to gain a benefit or to defraud. All of these offenses, except for the suppression of information, are third-degree felonies. The suppression of information is a Class C misdemeanor.

Behavior of officers

In some situations, the conduct of police officers may make them subject to prosecution under federal law. A peace officer may be subject to federal prosecution because of violations of USC 241 or 242. USC 242 pertains to conspiracy against rights: it declares that peace officers (and others) may not conspire to restrict the rights laid out by the laws and Constitution of the United States. The punishment for this crime is a fine of up to $10,000 and imprisonment for up to 10 years. If the criminal acts resulted in a death, the violator may be jailed for life. USC 242 addresses the deprivation of rights under color of law. A peace officer who uses his or her status to take away or diminish the rights of another person because of that person's being an alien, or because of his or her race or color, may be subject to a fine of up to $1000 and imprisonment for a maximum of 10 years. Again, these penalties may be raised if the misconduct results in death. When peace officers may have violated the law, the investigation is led by the FBI.

Civil penalties for sexual harassment

Officers are subject to significant penalties for sexual harassment and inappropriate conduct. Section 39.03 of the Penal Code states that it is illegal for any person who is performing in his or her capacity as a public servant to intentionally mistreat, detain, search, dispossess, or exercise a lien unlawfully. It is also illegal for public servants to intentionally deny another person the exercise or enjoyment of any power, right, or privilege, when this denial is unlawful.

Finally, it is illegal for public servants to intentionally subject another person to sexual harassment. Sexual harassment consists of unwelcome sexual advances, requests for sexual contact, or any other verbal or physical conduct of a sexual nature, so long as it is implied that tolerating this unlawful behavior is a condition of employment. All of these offenses, collectively known as official oppression, are Class A misdemeanors.

U.S. and Texas Constitutions, Bill of Rights, and Criminal Justice System

United States Constitution and Bill of Rights, and Writ of Habeas Corpus

The United States Constitution is composed of a Preamble followed by a Writ of Habeas Corpus. This writ is necessary for a person to be brought before a court or judge. Writs became mandatory to prevent people from being detained indefinitely without cause. The writ indicates the reason for detention or the charges to be brought against the detained, but is not meant to be the central document in prosecution.

Articles 2 and 3 of the United States Constitution

Article 2 of the United States Constitution outlines the procedure for electing the President and Vice President. This includes the people who are eligible to serve, the operations of the Electoral College, and the organization of voting protocols.

Article 3 establishes the composition and the jurisdiction of the Supreme Court. This article also distinguishes original and appellate jurisdiction. A court that has original jurisdiction is the first to hear some cases. The Supreme Court has appellate jurisdiction, on the other hand, which means that it only hears cases that have already been tried in lower courts and then appealed. According to

Article 3, all trials must be held in the state in which the alleged crime was committed. This article also defines treason as a crime. Indeed, treason is the only crime listed in the United States Constitution.

Constitutional Amendments I, IV, V, VI, VIII, IX, X, and XIV

Constitutional Amendment I establishes freedom of speech, religion, press, assembly, and petition.
The Fourth Amendment places restrictions on search and seizure and requires probable cause. Constitutional Amendment V declares that a person cannot be tried twice for the same crime (double jeopardy). This amendment also lays out the procedures for due process and makes it illegal to require a person to be a witness against him or herself. The Sixth Amendment guarantees the right to trial, the right to legal counsel, and the right to confront one's accusers. This amendment also guarantees that a person must receive information about the offense of which he or she has been accused. The Eighth Amendment outlaws excessive bail, excessive fines, and cruel and unusual punishment. The Ninth Amendment establishes the individual's rights, and the Tenth Amendment establishes the rights of states. The 14th Amendment declares that federal law takes precedence over state law.

Role of police defined in the United States Constitution and Bill of Rights

The United States Constitution and Bill of Rights have a particular view of the role of police. These documents declare that it is the job of police officers to create conditions of fairness and equality for all citizens. Police officers are charged with recognizing prejudice and taking whatever steps are necessary to eliminate it. Police officers are responsible for learning the rights of citizens and working to protect those rights. Police officers are responsible for staying informed about new legislation and changes in the culture that affect police methods. The

Constitution is an incredibly durable document, but the intent of its authors is debated continuously. Police officers must stay abreast of this debate so that they can provide excellent service. Too often, citizens see police officers as taking away their rights. In the view of the Constitution, police officers are there to safeguard the inalienable rights of the citizens.

Rights of the individual defined in Article 1 of the Constitution of the State of Texas

Article 1 of the Texas State Constitution is a Bill of Rights. It makes some key assertions about individual rights. Section 2 declares that political power resides in the people. Section 3 declares that all citizens have equal rights, and Section 4 states that all citizens are entitled to equal treatment by the law. Section 6 asserts the freedom of worship, and Section 8 asserts the freedoms of speech and press. Section 9 declares that people have the right to avoid unlawful searches and seizures, and Section 10 enumerates the rights of those who are accused of a crime. These include the right to counsel, the right to be confronted by the witnesses against the accused, and right of habeas corpus. Section 23 asserts the right to keep and bear arms. Section 30 outlines the rights of crime victims.

Article 17 of the Constitution of the State of Texas

Article 17 of the Constitution of the State of Texas outlines the process for making constitutional amendments. The legislature may propose amendments if a majority of two-thirds agrees to do so. The proposed amendments are then published in the newspaper and voted upon at the next election. A proposed amendment only needs a simple majority in order to be passed by the electorate. If the amendment is approved, it will be ratified by the governor. This process is distinct from the process for amending the United States Constitution, which can be done without submitting the proposed amendment to a popular vote. Some critics charge that the Texas system makes the laws of the state more subject to the whims of the people, but in practice this system has done proven effective at regulating itself and avoiding wild reactions to major events.

Interrelationships between the three components of the criminal justice system

The three components of the criminal justice system are the police, the courts, and the correctional system. There are police forces at the city, county, state, and federal levels. There are organized courts at the municipal, county, state, and federal levels. The correctional system includes parole boards, county jails, state prisons, probation systems, and municipal fines. These three components interact constantly. When there are more arrests, there is more business for the courts to manage. When the courts are more active, there are more people participating in the correctional system. The pressures on the correctional system may lead to inmates being released ahead of schedule, which can cause problems for law enforcement. In other words, when one part of the criminal justice system becomes overburdened, it tends to pass that burden on to the other areas.

Civil and criminal law

Peace officers should know the differences between criminal and civil law. Criminal law exists to prevent harm to society. It does this by indicating the conduct that is perceived as criminal, and by recommending punishments for criminal conduct. A good body of criminal law will define clearly the nature of offenses. Criminal laws are typically set forth in criminal or penal codes. Civil law, on the other hand, addresses the person and property rights of people. It promotes the rights of people to prevent harm from being done to them, or to win compensation for harm done. A civil action, or tort, is based on an accusation of some private injury or wrong. A person who is found guilty in a civil trial will not have to go to jail, but may be held financially liable for damages.

Court of Criminal Appeals and the Courts of Appeals

Section 1 of the Code of Criminal Procedure Article 4.04 states that the Court of Criminal Appeals has the authority to issue writs of habeas corpus, mandamus, procedendo, prohibition, and certiorari. This court also has the right to issue other writs necessary to protect its jurisdiction or enforce its rulings.

Section 2 of the Code of Criminal Procedure Article 4.04 declares that the Court of Criminal Appeals has final appellate and review jurisdiction in criminal cases within Texas. This court handles all final appeals in cases involving the death penalty, and has the power to review any case at its own discretion. Code of Criminal Procedure Article 4.03 declares that the Courts of Appeals have appellate jurisdiction within their respective districts, except in cases involving the death penalty. Courts of Appeals typically do not handle cases in which the fines imposed are less than $100, except when the case bears implications for the constitutionality of a law.

Jurisdiction of district courts

The Code of Criminal Procedure Article 4.05 asserts that district courts and criminal district courts have original jurisdiction for felonies, misdemeanors involving official misconduct, and misdemeanors that have been transferred to the district court.

County court at law

The Code of Criminal Procedure Article 4.07 states that county courts have original jurisdiction for misdemeanors that will have fines of $500 or less and that have not been referred to the justice court.

Justice courts

Code of Criminal Procedure Article 4.11 states that justices of the peace have original jurisdiction in criminal cases that will not lead to imprisonment. The original jurisdiction of the justice court is not affected by the quality of the court's penalties. Also, in cases that occur in the extraterritorial jurisdiction of the municipality, the justice court has concurrent jurisdiction with the municipal court.

Municipal courts

Code of Criminal Procedure Article 4.14 states that municipal courts have original and exclusive jurisdiction within their territory for all criminal cases that pertain to municipal ordinances or are punishable by a maximum fine of $500, or $2000 for cases that involve public health and sanitation, fire safety, or zoning. Municipal courts are given concurrent jurisdiction with justice courts for all criminal cases that are only punishable by a fine.

Multiculturalism and Human Relations

Prejudice

A prejudice is a negative opinion that is not based on knowledge or fact, but rather on supposition or assumption. It is related to the word "prejudge." Although most people try to avoid prejudice, everyone has it in some respect. It is better to acknowledge prejudice and try to resolve it than to pretend that it does not exist. One reason for prejudice is the desire to believe one's own group or culture is better. This is called ethnocentrism.

Another origin of prejudice is a desire to blame other people and groups for problems. In some cases, a person will project his or her own weaknesses and failings onto members of another group. Many people resort to prejudice in the form of stereotyping because they are too lazy to investigate the true nature of another group.

Impartiality

The work of a peace officer is sensitive, so it is especially important to avoid even the appearance of prejudice or bias. Peace officers often work by themselves and may not have friendly witnesses. Also, there are many opportunities for partiality in the line of duty, and there may be situations in which acting with bias or prejudice would seem to produce a better outcome. Peace officers may be under the impression that prejudiced or biased behavior would be unlikely to be reprimanded by superiors. Nevertheless, peace officers should behave as if their every action is subject to the strictest ethical standards. They should never favor one person over another, and they should always indicate in their words and actions that no one will receive preferential treatment.

Sensitive to others

Many people view police work as cold and unfeeling, but it is actually much better when it takes into account the emotions of the citizens being served. To exercise sensitivity as a peace officer, one should acquire as much information as possible about the people with whom one is dealing, and should strive to honor their feelings. Peace officers should be nonjudgmental, and should see themselves as detached enforcers of the law. At the same time, peace officers should be friendly and empathic with others. When peace officers fail to treat others with sensitivity, they engender ill will that can result in violence or criminal behavior. On the other hand, officers who serve their communities with warmth and compassion reap the rewards of cooperation and assistance from local leaders and citizens.

Cross-cultural conflict resolution

Peace officers must be adept at communicating with and resolving conflicts between people of diverse cultures. The styles of communication used by different cultures can be quite distinct, and police behavior that would be welcomed in one area might be offensive to another. In the State of Texas, it is important to be familiar with the communication styles of the following groups: African Americans, Caucasian Americans, Arab Americans, Asian Americans, Latino/Hispanic Americans, Middle-Eastern Americans, Native Americans, and Pacific Islander Americans. For instance, in many Middle-Eastern cultures, hospitality is considered to be very important. Unless absolutely necessary, a police officer should avoid entering the home of a Middle Easterner without being invited. Also, if possible, officers should take off their shoes before entering the home. On the other hand, this formality would not be required when entering the home of a Native-American family.

Code of Criminal Procedure

Six objects

Article 1.03 of the Code of Criminal Procedure states that the Code has six objects. First, it aims to prevent the commission of crime, and to dissuade offenders. It seeks to produce quick and just trials, and it hopes to create the proper conditions for fair investigations. The fifth object of the Code of Criminal Procedure is to ensure fair and impartial trials. Finally, the Code seeks to guarantee complete execution of the sentence rendered by law.

Citizen rights

Article 1.04 of the Code of Criminal Procedure declares that no state citizen should be deprived of life, liberty, property, privileges, or should be in any way disenfranchised except by the law's due course.

Accused rights

Rights of the accusedof the Code of Criminal Procedure declares that accused people have the right to a quick trial in public before an impartial jury. The accused has the right to know the charges against him, and may not be compelled to give testimony against himself.

The accused has the right to an attorney, and has the right to confront the witnesses against him. Only after the indictment of a grand jury can a person be tried for a felony.

Right to counsel

Article 1.051 of the Code of Criminal Procedure declares that criminal defendants have the right to counsel. Those defendants who cannot afford counsel are entitled to a court-appointed attorney.

Unreasonable searches and seizures

Article 1.06 of the Code of Criminal Procedure states that the citizens of Texas are protected from all unreasonable searches and seizures of their persons, homes, and possessions. Search and seizure warrants must include a thorough description and must contain probable cause.

Elgible for bail

Article 1.07 of the Code of Criminal Procedure declares that prisoners should be eligible for bail unless they are being held for capital offenses.

Writ of habeas corpus

Article 1.08 of the Code of Criminal Procedure asserts that the citizens of Texas have a right to the writ of habeas corpus, and this right shall never be suspended.

Outlaws

Article 1.09 of the Code of Criminal Procedure outlaws excessive bail, excessive fines, and cruel or unusual punishment.

Double jeopardy

Article 1.10 of the Code of Criminal Procedure states that no person may be put on trial twice for the same offense, in what is known as double jeopardy.

Acquittal did not have jurisdiction

Article 1.11 of the Code of Criminal Procedure declares that being acquitted of a crime means a person can never be tried for the same offense again, unless the court that issued the acquittal did not have jurisdiction.

Trial by jury

Article 1.12 of the Code of Criminal Procedure declares that citizens will always have the right to a trial by jury.

Right to waive trial by jury

Article 1.13 of the Code of Criminal Procedure declares that criminal defendants, except those accused of a capital felony, have the right to waive trial by jury. This waiver must be made by the defendant in person and in writing in front of the judge and the state attorney. If a defendant in a capital felony case is assured that the death penalty will not be sought by the state, he may waive a jury trial.

Waive legal rights

Article 1.14 of the Code of Criminal Procedure declares that criminal defendants may waive any of their legal rights. The only exception to this is that the accused criminals in cases involving the death penalty may not waive their right to a jury trial. This article also asserts that defendants who do not raise an objection to an error or irregularity in the indictment forfeit the right to object on these grounds in the future.

Waive right to be accused by indictment

Article 1.141 of the Code of Criminal Procedure states that defendants, so long as they are represented by counsel, may waive the right to be accused by indictment. The only exception to this rule is for cases involving capital felonies.

Conviction by jury verdict

Article 1.15 of the Code of Criminal Procedure states that citizens can only be convicted of a felony by a jury's verdict, except in cases where the defendant waives his right to a trial by jury.

Freedoms of speech and the press

Article 1.16 of the Code of Criminal Procedure asserts the freedom to speak, write, or publish on any subject. This article forbids any law from ever restricting the freedoms of speech and the press.

Giving evidence in court on basis of religious opinion

Article 1.17 of the Code of Criminal Procedure declares that no person shall be prevented from giving evidence in court on the basis of his or her religious opinions. However, divergent religious beliefs do not exempt a person from being required to deliver accurate testimony before court.

Illegal to transport

Article 1.18 of the Code of Criminal Procedure declares that it is illegal to transport any person out of Texas who has committed an offense within the state.

Senators and representatives

Article 1.21 of the Code of Criminal Procedure declares that senators and representatives are exempt from arrest during the legislative session, except in cases of treason, felony, or breach of the peace.

Judges and justices

Article 1.23 of the Code of Criminal Procedure declares that the judges and justices of the

Supreme Court, Court of Criminal Appeals, Courts of Appeals, and district courts are charged with maintaining peace in Texas. This article goes on to assert that the style of all rights and processes shall be "the State of Texas," and all prosecutions shall be carried on "in the name and by authority of the State of Texas" and shall end "against the peace and dignity of the state."

Proceedings and trials

Article 1.24 of the Code of Criminal Procedure declares that the proceedings and trials of all courts must be public.

Defendant right

Article 1.25 of the Code of Criminal Procedure asserts that, except on rare occasions, the defendant has a right to be confronted by the witnesses against him.

Common law

Article 1.27 of the Code of Criminal Procedure declares that the common law applies to any scenarios that are not covered by the Code of Criminal Procedure.

Magistrates

Article 2.09 of the Code of Criminal Procedure identifies all of the magistrates in the State of Texas. These include the justices and judges of the Supreme Court, the Court of Criminal Appeals, Courts of Appeals, district courts, and certain judges from each county.

Magistrate duty

Article 2.10 of the Code of Criminal Procedure asserts that it is the duty of every magistrate to preserve the peace by all lawful means, as well as to arrest offenders and issue all process that aims to prevent crime.

Examining court

Article 2.11 of the Code of Criminal Procedure defines an examining court as when a magistrate inquires into a criminal accusation.

Identifies peace officers

Article 2.12 of the Code of Criminal Procedure identifies peace officers. This group includes sheriffs, deputies, constables, marshals, police officers, rangers, and a number of other law enforcement agents.

Railroad peace officers

Article 2.121 of the Code of Criminal Procedure states that the director of the Department of Public Safety is allowed to appoint no more than 250 railroad peace officers to protect railroad property, passengers, and employees. These officers are given all the powers of other peace officers with respect to protecting the railroads. However, railroad peace officers may not issue transportation citations, and are not entitled to state benefits.

Right of arrest, search, and seizure

Article 2.122 of the Code of Criminal Procedure asserts that members of the following organizations have the rights of arrest, search, and seizure in felony cases in Texas: Federal Bureau of Investigation; Secret Service; United States Immigration and Customs Enforcement; Bureau of Alcohol, Tobacco, Firearms and Explosives; federal Drug Enforcement Agency; United States Postal Service; IRS Criminal Investigation Division; United States Naval Criminal Investigative Service; United States Marshals Service; United States Citizenship and Immigration Services; and United States Department of State.

Adjunct peace officers

Article 2.123 of the Code of Criminal Procedure declares that in counties with less than 200,000 people, the head of law enforcement may appoint up to 50 adjunct peace officers. These adjuncts must be employed by a private institution of higher education. These adjunct officers will aid law enforcement agencies. They have all the rights, privileges, and immunities of peace officers, but are not entitled to state compensation and retirement benefits.

Neighboring peace officers

Article 2.124 of the Code of Criminal Procedure declares that, when they are in Texas, peace officers from neighboring states have the same powers, duties, and immunities as Texas peace officers. This is true only when the peace officer from the neighboring state is discharging an official duty, like transporting a prisoner.

Special rangers

Article 2.125 of the Code of Criminal Procedure declares that the director of the Department of Public Safety has the authority to appoint no more than 50 special Rangers to assist the investigation of livestock or related property. These officers have all the rights of a regular peace officer with respect to their duties, though they do not receive the same state benefits.

Peace officer primary duty

Article 2.13 of the Code of Criminal Procedure declares that the primary duty of a peace officer is to preserve peace in his or her jurisdiction. This is done by interfering to prevent or suppress crime, executing all lawful process issued by a magistrate or court, notifying magistrates of offenses committed within the jurisdiction, and arresting offenders lawfully.

Neglect to execute subpoena or other legal process

Article 2.16 of the Code of Criminal Procedure declares that officers may be held liable for neglecting to execute a subpoena or any other legal process. This violation may be punishable by a fine of between $10 and $200. The violation is treated as a contempt of court.

Sherrifs responsibility

Article 2.17 of the Code of Criminal Procedure states that sheriffs are responsible for maintaining the peace in their county. To this end, they are given the authority to arrest offenders and suppress crime.

Prisoners jailed by warrant from magistrate court

Article 2.18 of the Code of Criminal Procedure declares that prisoners who have been jailed by warrant from a magistrate court shall be jailed by the sheriff. Letting such a person remain free is a violation by the sheriff's office.

Deputies duty

Article 2.20 of the Code of Criminal Procedure declares that all duties imposed by the code upon sheriffs may also be performed by deputies. When the sheriff is away, the deputy assumes all the powers of the office.

Child abuse response

Article 2.27 of the Code of Criminal Procedure declares that allegations of child abuse that are assigned the highest priority by the Department of Protective and Regulatory Services should be immediately handled by a peace officer from the local law enforcement agency in cooperation with an agent of the investigating department. The peace officer and agent should begin their work as soon as possible, and no later than 24 hours after being notified.

False identification given by an arrested person

Article 2.28 of the Code of Criminal Procedure describes the responsibilities of local law enforcement agents who discover that a person's identifying information was falsely given by an arrested person. In other words, this article discusses what happens when a person is falsely identified as an accused criminal. The law enforcement department in this case must notify the falsely identified person that his information was misused by another person in the county and that the person may file a declaration and have the information expunged. The law enforcement department must also notify the Department of Public Safety of the misuse, as well as the actual identity of the arrested person and whether the law enforcement agency was able to contact the person whose identity was misused.

Racial profiling

Article 3.05 of the Code of Criminal Procedure defines racial profiling as any action by law enforcement that is based on another person's race, ethnicity, or national origin instead of on the person's behavior or on information about the person's behavior.

Outlaw racial profiling

Article 2.131 of the Code of Criminal Procedure outlaws racial profiling. Departments are required to take specific steps in order to minimize the occurrence of racial profiling. To begin with, they are required to collect information about motor vehicle stops in which citations and arrests are made. They must record the race or ethnicity of the driver, and then analyze this data to determine whether there are irregular patterns that indicate racial profiling. In some cases, racial profiling occurs below the conscious level of the officer. For this reason, departments must take specific procedural steps to identify and root out unfair police behavior.

Eliminating racial profiling

Article 2.132 of the Code of Criminal Procedure describes the law enforcement approach to eliminating racial profiling. To begin with, each law enforcement agency must define racial profiling, and then issue a prohibition against this behavior by agents. The agency must also create a process for people to complain about racial profiling incidents. The department must publicize the process for handling complaints, and must punish those officers who are found to have engaged in racial profiling. Departments should also collect information about motor vehicle stops, including the race/ethnicity of the detained individual, whether a search was conducted, whether consent was given to a search, and whether the peace officer could identify the race or ethnicity of the detainee before making the stop. The chief administrator of the law enforcement agency is required to submit an annual report of the information related to departmental racial profiling.

Motor vehicle stop

Article 2.133 of the Code of Criminal Procedure describes the required content for a report related to a motor vehicle stop. Whenever a peace officer stops a motor vehicle, his report must include a physical description of the person stopped, including gender, race, and ethnicity. The report should also describe the initial reason for the stop, and whether a search was conducted. If a search was conducted, the report should indicate whether any kind of contraband was discovered. The report should also explain the reason for the search. The report of a motor vehicle stop should indicate whether an arrest was made, or whether the officer issued a written citation. Finally, the report should include the street address or rough location of the stop.

Motor vehicle damages

Article 2.136 of the Code of Criminal Procedure declares that peace officers are not liable for the damages incurred during the collection or reporting of information required by the articles on motor vehicle stops.

Forfeiture of contraband

Article 59.02 of the Code of Criminal Procedure discusses the forfeiture of contraband. All contraband is subject to seizure and forfeiture. However, any contraband that is not evidence in an investigation or pending case, money, a negotiable instrument, or a security may be re-obtained by the owner or interest holder with a valid bond of the same value.

Notification of forfeiture

Article 59.04 of the Code of Criminal Procedure declares that when property is seized by a peace officer, the state attorney must initiate a notification of forfeiture proceeding within 30 days. This process begins when the attorney files a notice of the seizure and forfeiture with the clerk of the County District Court. This notice must include the sworn statement of the peace officer and a full inventory of the forfeited items.

Jurisdiction in criminal actions

Article 4.01 of the Code of Criminal Procedure names the courts that have jurisdiction in criminal actions: Court of Criminal Appeals, Court of Appeals, district courts, criminal district court, magistrates appointed by the district court judges in certain counties, county court, county criminal courts, justice courts, municipal court, and magistrates appointed by district court judges in Lubbock County.

Court of Appeals

Article 4.03 of the Code of Criminal Procedure declares that the Courts of Appeals have jurisdiction in their districts for all criminal cases except those involving the death penalty.

Protocol for misdemeanor trials

Article 4.12 of the Code of Criminal Procedure discusses the protocol for misdemeanor trials in justice courts. Misdemeanors should be tried in the precinct in which the offense was committed, in the precinct in which the defendant resides, or anywhere else, as long as the state and each defendant consent to the location. When a misdemeanor is committed in a precinct without a qualified justice court, trial is held in the next adjacent precinct or in the defendant's home precinct. If the justice of the peace is disqualified from handling a misdemeanor committed in his precinct, the case may be tried in the next adjoining precinct.

Power to accept forfeitures of bonds

Article 4.13 of the Code of Criminal Procedure states that a justice of the peace has the power to accept forfeitures of all bonds given for the appearance of anyone in his or her court, regardless of the amount.

Written records

Article 2.30 of the Code of Criminal Procedure states that officers must prepare comprehensive written records during the investigation of certain offenses. These records should be provided to victims at their request. Special reports must be prepared in cases of assault, aggravated assault, sexual assault, aggravated sexual assault, and terroristic threat.

Family violence

Article 5.01 of the Code of Criminal Procedure declares that family violence is a serious threat to society, and victims are entitled to maximum protection from the law. Furthermore, law enforcement and judicial officials are always required to protect the victim, regardless of the relationship between the victim and the accused.

Peace officer responsibilities

Article 5.03 of the Code of Criminal Procedure declares that the peace officer's responsibilities are not waived or mitigated by the family or household relationship between alleged violators and victims.

Peace officer family violence duties

Article 5.04 of the Code of Criminal Procedure describes the duties of peace officers with respect to family violence. It states that when investigating an allegation of family violence, the primary responsibility of the peace officer is to protect the victim, enforce the state law, and make any necessary lawful arrests. The officer is also responsible for giving adult victims advice and the means to prevent future violence.

Victim protection

Article 5.045 of the Code of Criminal Procedure states that officers may decide to remain on the scene to protect the victim, the victim's children, and the victim's property. Officers are not to be held liable for any acts, omissions, or wrongful appropriation of any property that occurs during such an event.

Family violence report

Article 5.05 of the Code of Criminal Procedure describes the mandatory content for a report of family violence. Such a report must include the names of the suspects and complainant; the date, time, and location of the incident; visible or reported injuries; and a description of the incident. Law enforcement departments must also have a departmental code for handling family violence reports. Finally, law enforcement agencies are required to provide information from a report if it is requested by the victim of family violence.

Protective order

Article 5.07 of the Code of Criminal Procedure asserts that the venue for protective order offenses is in the county in which the order was issued or the county in which the offense was committed.

Threat prevention

Article 6.05 of the Code of Criminal Procedure states that it is the duty of every peace officer who is aware of a threat to prevent it by all the means within his power. A peace officer has the right to prevent a threat by whatever measures would be taken by the person who is about to be injured.

Prevent injury to people and property

Article 6.06 of the Code of Criminal Procedure states that it is the duty of a peace officer to prevent injury to people and property. Is also the duty of a peace officer to prevent a person from harming himself. The peace officer is allowed to use as much force as necessary to prevent injury.

Preventing an imminent offense

Article 6.07 of the Code of Criminal Procedure declares that when a peace officer is preventing an imminent offense, the peace officer is governed by the same rules as the person about to be injured. A peace officer is authorized to use all necessary force to repel the aggression.

Protective order

Article 6.08 of the Code of Criminal Procedure states that when a defendant appears in court and it is alleged that the offense was committed by the defendant because of bias or prejudice; someone may request the court to render a protective order for the protection of the alleged victim. If the court determines that bias and prejudice were indeed integral to the commission of the crime, and that it is likely these factors will motivate future offenses, the court will issue a protective order. The enforcement of the protective order will be comprehensive, and will include a description of findings, contents, duration, warning, delivery, law enforcement duties, and the protocol for modification. The existence of this protective order must be entered into the statewide law enforcement information system kept by the Department of Public Safety no more than 10 days after the enforcement agency receives the order.

Resisted while executing process

Article 8.01 of the Code of Criminal Procedure states that when an officer is resisted while executing process, the officer may command as many citizens as necessary to seize and arrest the resisting parties.

Disperse a rioting crowd

Article 8.04 of the Code of Criminal Procedure states that every magistrate and peace officer has the responsibility to disperse a rioting crowd. This may be done by command or by arresting people, either with or without an arrest warrant.

Power of the county

Article 8.05 of the Code of Criminal Procedure states that an officer who is trying to disperse a riot may call upon the power of the county in the precise way he would be able to when serving process.

Suppressing riot

Article 8.06 of the Code of Criminal Procedure states that an officer who is suppressing a riot, as well as those who are assisting the officer, are authorized to use only such measures as are necessary to suppress the riot, but are not authorized to use any more force than necessary.

Unlawful assembly and other unlawful disturbances

Article 8.07 of the Code of Criminal Procedure states that all of the provisions in this chapter that relate to the suppression of riots apply in the exact same way to instances of unlawful assembly and other unlawful disturbances.

Special constables

Article 8.09 of the Code of Criminal Procedure states that special constables may exercise the powers and perform the duties of peace officers during the time of their appointment.

Juvenile victim

Article 7A.01 of the Code of Criminal Procedure states that a victim of assault or sexual assault, a parent of a child younger than 17 years who is a victim of such an offense, or a prosecuting attorney acting on behalf of such a victim may apply for a protective order irrespective of the relationship between the applicant and the alleged offender. These protective orders may be filed in district court, a juvenile court with the jurisdiction of the district court, a statutory county court, or a constitutional county court in the home county of the applicant or alleged offender.

Temporary ex parte order

Article 7A.02 of the Code of Criminal Procedure states that when the court determines, based on the information in an application for protective order, that there is a clear and present danger of sexual assault or other injury to the applicant, the court may enter a temporary ex parte order for the protection of the applicant or any member of his family or household. This may be done without notifying the alleged offender or holding a hearing.

Protective order application

Article 7A.03 of the Code of Criminal Procedure states that at the end of a hearing regarding a protective order application, the court should determine whether there are reasonable grounds to declare the applicant the victim of a sexual assault who is either younger than 18 or subject to a reasonable threat of further harm from the alleged offender. If either of these conditions is met, the court will issue a protective order including a statement of these required findings.

Protective order conditions

Article 7A.05 of the Code of Criminal Procedure describes the conditions that may be contained in a protective order issued under this chapter. To begin with, the court may order the alleged offender to take specific actions that will prevent or reduce the chances of future harm to the applicant. The court may also prohibit the alleged offender from possessing a firearm or engaging in conduct specifically directed toward the applicant or any member of his family or household. Typically, the court will describe the prohibited behavior as anything likely to harass, torment, or alarm the applicant. The court may also prohibit the alleged offender from going near the home, place of business, or school of the applicant or the applicant's family. When the court does this, it needs to specify each prohibited location and the minimum distance the alleged offender must maintain.

Protective order wording

Article 7A.06 of the Code of Criminal Procedure states the required wording for protective orders. Every protective order must contain the following language: "A person who violates this order may be punished for contempt of court by a fine of as much as $500 or by confinement in jail for as long as six months, or both. No person, including a person who is protected by this order, may give permission to anyone to ignore or violate any provision of this order. During the time in which this order is valid, every provision of this order is in full force and effect unless the court changes the order. It is unlawful for any person, other than a peace officer, as defined by Section 1.07, Penal Code, actively engaged in employment as a sworn, full-time paid employee of the state agency or political subdivision, who is subject to a protective order to possess a firearm or ammunition."

Required protective order wording

Article 7A.06 of the Code of Criminal Procedure states the required wording for protective orders. All protective orders besides temporary ex parte orders must contain the following words: "A violation of this order by commission of an act prohibited by the order may be punishable by a fine of as much as $4000 or by confinement in jail for as long as one year, or both. An act that results in a separate offense may be prosecuted as a separate offense in addition to a violation of this order."

Protective order time period

Article 7A.07 of the Code of Criminal Procedure states that protective orders may be effective for the rest of the lives of the offender and victim, or for any shorter interval stated in the order. However, the protective order may only be effective for the duration of the lives of the offender or victim if the court has reasonable cause to believe that the victim is in danger of further harm from the alleged offender. A person who is 17 or older, or the parents of a person younger than 17, may at any time file an application to rescind the protective order. When a person is the subject of a protective order and is imprisoned on the day the protective order is due to expire, the order's effectiveness is extended until the first anniversary of the person's release from confinement.

No statute of limitations

Article 12.01 of the Code of Criminal Procedure states that there is no statute of limitations on indictments for the following felonies: murder, manslaughter, sexual assault, continuous sexual abuse of a young child, indecency with a child, and leaving the scene of an accident in which there was a fatality.

The statute of limitations is 10 years from the date of commission for the following crimes: forgery, injury to an elderly or disabled individual, arson, and theft by a public servant or an estate manager.

The statute of limitations for the following felonies is seven years: securing execution of a document by deception, money laundering, fraudulent use of identifying information, credit card or debit card abuse, false statement to obtain property or credit, and misapplication of fiduciary property or the property of a financial institution.

The statute of limitations for the following felonies is five years: theft or robbery, kidnapping, abandoning or endangering a child, and insurance fraud.

Class A or B or C misdemeanor

Article 12.02 of the Code of Criminal Procedure states that indictment or information related to a Class A or B misdemeanor must be presented within two years of the date of the commission of the offense. Also, a complaint or information regarding a Class C misdemeanor must be presented within two years of the date of the offense.

Statute of limitations

Article 12.03 of the Code of Criminal Procedure states that the statute of limitations for *criminal attempt* is the same as the limit for the offense attempted.

In cases of *criminal conspiracy* or organized criminal activity, the limitation period is equal to that of the most serious offense.

The limitation period for *criminal solicitation* is equal to that of the felony solicited. Also, unless noted otherwise, any aggravated offense has the same limitation period as the primary crime.

Offense against public peace

Article 14.01 of the Code of Criminal Procedure states that a peace officer or any other person for that matter may arrest an offender without a warrant if the offense committed is either a felony or an offense against the public peace. Also, peace officers may arrest offenders for any offense committed in the sight of the officer.

Magistrate orders or presence

Article 14.02 of the Code of Criminal Procedure states that a peace officer does not need a warrant to arrest a person who has committed a felony or breach of the peace in the presence of a magistrate if the magistrate orders the arrest.

No warrant

Article 14.03 of the Code of Criminal Procedure states that a peace officer does not need a warrant to arrest a person who is found in a suspicious place or in circumstances that reasonably suggest the commission of a felony. A peace officer does not need a warrant to make an arrest if he has probable cause that the person has committed assault and a desire to commit further assaults. A peace officer does not need a warrant to arrest a person who has violated a protective order, or who the peace officer has probable cause to believe has committed family violence. A peace officer does not need a warrant to arrest somebody who has interfered with an emergency call.

Public intoxication

Article 14.031 of the Code of Criminal Procedure states that when a peace officer detains someone for public intoxication, the officer may choose to release the person if he believes that detention is not required to protect the person or others, and the detainee is released to a responsible adult or verbally consents to be admitted to a voluntary treatment program for chemical dependency.

Pursue and arrest

Article 14.04 of the Code of Criminal Procedure states that when a peace officer has satisfactory proof from a credible person that a felony has been committed and the offender is going to escape, the peace officer may pursue and arrest the accused without a warrant.

Warrantless arrest

Article 14.05 of the Code of Criminal Procedure states that in every case in which a warrantless arrest is allowed, the officer is allowed to use all the necessary measures to make the arrest, with the exception of entering a home without consent or without exigent circumstances.

Peace officers from other states

Article 14.051 of the Code of Criminal Procedure states that peace officers from other states may enter Texas while in pursuit of a person, and may continue to perform their authorized duties until the completion of this task.

Arrest without warrant

Article 14.06 of the Code of Criminal Procedure states that whenever a person is arrested without a warrant, he must be taken before a magistrate as soon as possible, and no later than 48 hours after being arrested.

Subpoena

Article 24.01 of the Code of Criminal Procedure declares that a subpoena may require one or more persons to appear at a specified court term or a specified day to testify in a criminal action. It may also require one or more persons to appear before a grand jury, at a habeas corpus hearing, at a coroner's inquest, or at another official proceeding.

Juvenile subpoena

Article 24.011 of the Code of Criminal Procedure states that when a subpoena summons a person younger than 18, the document may instruct the child's parent or guardian to produce the child in court. Failure to do so is a contempt of court.

Subpoena duces tecum

Article 24.02 of the Code of Criminal Procedure states that a subpoena may require a person to bring a particular object to court as evidence. This is known as a subpoena duces tecum.

Procedure for serving a subpoena

Article 24.04 of the Code of Criminal Procedure describes the procedure for serving a subpoena. A subpoena may be served by being read in front of the witness, being delivered in paper form to the witness, being electronically transmitted to the witness, or being sent by certified mail to the witness. The method of delivery must include some provision for confirming that the subpoena was received.

Refusal to obey a subpoena

Article 24.05 of the Code of Criminal Procedure states that a witness who refuses to obey a subpoena may be fined by the court. In a misdemeanor case, a refusing witness may be fined up to $100, while in a felony case the refusing witness may be fined up to $500.

Attachment

Article 24.11 of the Code of Criminal Procedure defines an attachment as a writ issued by the foreman of a grand jury, the clerk of a court, or a magistrate that orders a peace officer to bring a witness before a court or a magistrate.

Officer who receives a subpoena procedure

Article 24.17 of the Code of Criminal Procedure states that an officer who receives a subpoena must deliver a copy of it to each witness and then return the subpoena with an indication of the time and manner of its execution or, if the subpoena was not executed, the reason for this failure.

Bail

Article 17.01 of the Code of Criminal Procedure defines bail as the security given by a person that he will appear in court to answer the charges against him. Bail may include a bail bond or a personal bond.

People arrested without a warrant

Article 17.033 of the Code of Criminal Procedure states that people who are arrested without a warrant must be released within 24 hours on bond of no more than $5000 if they were arrested for a misdemeanor and probable cause has not yet been established by a magistrate. Those who cannot obtain surety for the bond must be released on personal bond. Those who are arrested without a warrant on a felony charge must be released on bond of no more than $10,000 within 48 hours if probable cause has not been established. Again, those who cannot obtain surety for the bond must be released on personal bond. A state attorney may apply to the magistrate to postpone the release for no more than 72 hours after the arrest.

Setting bail amount

Article 17.15 of the Code of Criminal Procedure states that the court, judge, magistrate or officer taking the bail is responsible for setting the amount. When doing so, the official should be aware that bail must be high enough to ensure compliance. However, bail is not supposed to become an instrument of oppression, and the official should take into account the ability of the accused to make bail. The official should consider the future safety of alleged victims and the community at large, as well as the nature of the alleged offense.

Bail bonds

Article 17.20 of the Code of Criminal Procedure states that sheriffs and police officers may accept bail bonds from people being held on misdemeanor charges.

Felony trial bail

Article 17.21 of the Code of Criminal Procedure declares that when the court in which a felony trial is to be held is in session, the court shall fix the amount of bail. The court will also determine whether the accused is eligible for a personal bond in this situation. Sheriffs and peace officers are authorized to accept bail bonds in the amount established by the court.

Felony trial is to be held is not in session

Article 17.22 of the Code of Criminal Procedure states that when the court in which a felony trial is to be held is not in session, the sheriff or peace officer who has the defendant in custody may accept a bail bond in the amount fixed by the court or magistrate.

Victim notice of releasing accused

Article 17.29 of the Code of Criminal Procedure states that once an accused person has delivered the required bond to the magistrate or the officer with custody he must be liberated immediately. However, in cases of assault or family violence, law-enforcement agencies should attempt to give notice to the victim before releasing the accused.

After bond posted

Article 17.291 of the Code of Criminal Procedure declares that law enforcement agents may continue to detain a person who has posted bond for up to four hours if there is probable cause to believe that the detainee will commit violent acts once released. The detention period may be extended for 48 hours with the approval of the magistrate.

Order for emergency protection

Article 17.292 of the Code of Criminal Procedure states that a magistrate may issue an order for emergency protection (which prevents a person who has posted bond from being released) at the request of the victim, the victim's guardian, a peace officer, or state attorney.

Sex offender registration

Article 62.051 of the Code of Criminal Procedure states that those who are required to register as sex offenders must do so in any municipality or county where they reside or intend to reside for more than a week. This must be done within a week of arriving in the municipality or county, or on the first day possible. This registration form should include the person's full name, aliases, date of birth, gender, race, height, weight, eye color, hair color, Social Security number, driver's license number, shoe size, and address. It should also include a recent color photograph and complete set of fingerprints. It should list the type of offense of which the person was convicted, age of the victim, punishment, and date of conviction. It should indicate whether the person has been discharged, paroled, or placed on probation. It should indicate whether the person has a job, is a student, or is pursuing a vocation.

Warrant of arrest

Article 15.01 of the Code of Criminal Procedure defines a warrant of arrest as a written order from a magistrate ordering a peace officer to detain a person who has been accused of a crime.

Requisites of an arrest warrant

Article 15.02 of the Code of Criminal Procedure lists the requisites for an arrest warrant. First, an arrest warrant must either specify the name of the person to be arrested, or, if the person's name is unknown, must contain a reasonably accurate description. Second, the arrest warrant must describe the offense of which the person is accused. Finally, the arrest warrant must be signed by the magistrate, and the magistrate's office must be named somewhere on the document.

Magistrate may issue a warrant or summons

Article 15.03 of the Code of Criminal Procedure outlines the scenarios in which a magistrate may issue a warrant or summons. The magistrate is allowed to do so whenever he is authorized by law to order an arrest, whenever a person swears under oath before the magistrate that another person has committed a crime, and whenever specially authorized by the Code of Criminal Procedure to issue such a document. The issuing of a summons has the same requisites as the issuing of a warrant, except the summons merely enjoins the defendant to appear before the magistrate at a particular time and place. A summons should be delivered in person. When a summons is ignored, a warrant for arrest may be issued.

Warrant ever part of the state

Article 15.06 of the Code of Criminal Procedure declares that arrest warrants issued by the magistrate or any county or district clerk extend to every part of the state. Moreover, a peace officer who has been charged with carrying out the warrant has the authority to do so in any part of the state.

Warrant cannot be executed outside of the county

Article 15.07 of the Code of Criminal Procedure states that arrest warrants issued by the mayors of incorporated cities or towns cannot be executed outside the boundaries of the county in which they were issued. The only exception to this rule occurs when the warrant is endorsed by a judge of the court of record, or when the warrant is endorsed by a magistrate in the county in which the warrant is to be executed.

Warrant or complaint must be kept sealed

Article 15.12 of the Code of Criminal Procedure declares that a warrant or complaint must be kept sealed, and that no telegraph officer should transmit or receive a warrant unless it has been certified by a court of record or justice of the peace.

Executing an arrest warrant

Article 15.16 of the Code of Criminal Procedure describes the procedure for executing an arrest warrant. As soon as possible, the officer or the person who executes the arrest warrant should take the arrested person before the magistrate named in the warrant. If the magistrate named in the warrant is in a different county, the arrested person should be taken before a magistrate in the county in which he was arrested.

Duties of peace officer and magistrate during serving of warrant

Article 15.17 of the Code of Criminal Procedure describes the duties of the peace officer and the magistrate during the serving of an arrest warrant. First, the peace officer must take the arrested person before a magistrate as soon as possible. At this time, the magistrate will describe the accusations made against the person. The magistrate will also advise the arrested person of his right to counsel, his right to remain silent, his right to have an attorney present during interviews, his right to end interviews at any time, and his right to have an examining trial. The person should be told that if he cannot afford counsel, then counsel will be appointed. In some cases, the magistrate may appoint counsel at this time. The magistrate will then determine whether the arrested person is out on bail for another offense and, if not, whether to set bail. The substance of the conversation between the magistrate and the arrested person should be recorded. If the arrested person is only charged with a misdemeanor punishable by fine, then he or she may be released by the magistrate without bond.

County warrant was originated

Article 15.18 of the Code of Criminal Procedure states that a person who is arrested according to a warrant issued in a different county should be taken before a magistrate of the county in which the arrest occurred or, if it is more convenient, another magistrate. The magistrate should set bail and, if he does not have jurisdiction, send the bond to the court that has jurisdiction of the offense. If the person has been arrested for an offense that is only punishable by fine, the magistrate may accept a written plea of guilty or no contest, establish and receive a fine, and discharge the defendant. In this case, the presiding magistrate is required to transmit the following information to the court with jurisdiction of the offense: the written plea, all orders entered in the case, and the costs collected in the case. This information must be submitted before the 11th business day after the acceptance of the plea.

Refuses to give bail

Article 15.19 of the Code of Criminal Procedure states that when an arrested person either does not or refuses to give bail, he shall be committed to the jail in the county of his arrest. At this point, the presiding magistrate must provide notice to the sheriff in the county in which the alleged crime was committed. When a person is arrested and taken to a magistrate in a county besides the one in which he was arrested, and the person has been remanded to custody, he may be confined for no more than 72 hours in that county jail before being transferred to the jail of the county in which the arrest occurred.

Notice of arrest procedures

Article 15.20 of the Code of Criminal Procedure declares that when the sheriff receives the notice of an arrest from a magistrate in a different county, the sheriff should arrange for the arrested person to be conveyed before the proper court or magistrate. This should occur before the 11th business day after the person has been committed to the jail in the county in which he was arrested.

Accused not taken charge of

Article 15.21 of the Code of Criminal Procedure states that when the office of the county in which the offense was alleged to have been committed does not request to take charge of the accused before the 11th day after he or she is committed to jail in the county of his or her arrest, the accused must be discharged from custody.

Under arrest

Article 15.22 of the Code of Criminal Procedure states that a person is under arrest when he or she is restrained or taken into custody by a person with or without an arrest warrant.

Time of arrest

Article 15.23 of the Code of Criminal Procedure asserts that arrests may occur at any time of day or night.

Secure the arrest

Article 15.24 of the Code of Criminal Procedure declares that all reasonable means short of excessive force may be used in order to secure the arrest and detention of an accused person.

Arrest warrant for felony

Article 15.25 of the Code of Criminal Procedure declares that when executing an arrest warrant for a felony, an officer may break down the door of the house or residence should he be denied entrance after stating his identity and purpose.

Authority to arrest

Article 15.26 of the Code of Criminal Procedure declares that the authority to arrest must be made known to the accused. Although the officer is not required to have a warrant at the time of the arrest, he must show it to the accused as soon as possible. It is necessary for an officer to tell the accused that a warrant has been issued and, if possible, to name the charges against the accused.

Search Warrant

Article 18.01 of the Code of Criminal Procedure defines a search warrant as an order written by a magistrate directing a peace officer to search for and seize a piece of property or to find and photograph a child and deliver the film to the magistrate. Magistrates must receive probable cause before issuing a search warrant. Substantial facts must be set forth in a sworn affidavit which, if executed, becomes public information.

Court to seal an affidavit

Article 18.011 of the Code of Criminal Procedure declares that a state attorney prosecuting a felony may request the court to seal an affidavit. The court will agree to do so if it can be proved that public disclosure of the affidavit would endanger a victim, witness, or confidential informant, or that it could reasonably motivate the destruction of evidence. The court may also decide to seal an affidavit if it contains information from a wiretap that has not yet expired. The sealing of an affidavit expires on the 31st day after the execution of the search warrant for which the affidavit was presented.

Search warrant grounds

Article 18.02 of the Code of Criminal Procedure lists the grounds upon which a search warrant may be issued. A search warrant may be issued for property acquired by theft or other means that make its acquisition an offense. Search warrants may be issued for property that has been specially designed or adapted for the commission of the offense. Search warrants may be issued for arms and munitions intended or used for insurrection, weapons used in the commission of a crime, and weapons prohibited by the Penal Code. Search warrants may be issued for gambling devices, equipment, or paraphernalia. Warrants may be issued for obscene materials, whether they are possessed or prepared for distribution. Search warrants may be issued for controlled substances, drug paraphernalia, and any other property prohibited by law. Warrants may also be issued for any property or items that contain evidence of an offense. The only exception to this is the personal writings of the accused individual.

Search warrant to photograph a child

Article 18.021 of the Code of Criminal Procedure states that a search warrant may be issued to photograph a child who is alleged to have been the victim of an offense. In such a case, the peace officer charged with executing the warrant may be joined by an authorized photographer. Such a warrant should describe the child as closely as possible. The search warrant should always be executed by a peace officer of the same gender as the alleged victim. The exposed film should be delivered to the magistrate immediately by the peace officer.

Search warrant may also order the arrest

Article 18.03 of the Code of Criminal Procedure states that a search warrant may also order the arrest of a person, if the facts laid out to the magistrate also indicate probable cause that the person has committed an offense.

"the State of Texas"

Article 18.04 of the Code of Criminal Procedure states that a search warrant must run in the name of "the State of Texas," and it must identify as closely as possible the property and people to be located and searched. It should enjoin any peace officer of the relevant county to search the named person or property immediately, and it should be dated and signed by the magistrate.

Search warrants to inspect buildings for fires and health hazards

Article 18.05 of the Code of Criminal Procedure declares that fire marshals, health officers, and code enforcement officials may receive search warrants so that they may inspect building for fire and health hazards. However, such a search warrant may not be issued except upon the presentation of evidence of probable cause. In his consideration of probable cause, the magistrate may consider the age and general condition of the premises, its history of violations, and the purposes for which it is used.

Peace officer execute search warrant

Article 18.06 of the Code of Criminal Procedure asserts that a peace officer must execute a search warrant without delay, and within three days of its being issued. When executing the warrant, the officer should present a copy of the warrant to the owner. If the owner is not present, the officer should present a copy of the warrant to whoever is in possession of the place. Before removing property, officers should prepare a written inventory of what they are taking. The officer should endorse his name on the inventory and present it to the owner or current occupant. If there is no one attending the scene of the search, the officer should leave behind a copy of the warrant and the inventory.

Warrant for DNA analysis

Article 18.07 of the Code of Criminal Procedure asserts that a warrant remains active for 15 whole days if it is issued to seize blood and saliva specimens for DNA analysis. However, warrants issued for other purposes must be executed within three days.

Officer aid during search warrant

Article 18.08 of the Code of Criminal Procedure states that an officer may call to his or her aid any number of citizens during the execution of a search warrant.

Property seized during warrant

Article 18.09 of the Code of Criminal Procedure declares that the officer must immediately deliver to the magistrate any property that has been seized during the execution of a search warrant. Also, anyone who was arrested during the execution of a search warrant must immediately be taken to the magistrate.

Returning a search warrant

Article 18.10 of the Code of Criminal Procedure outlines the procedure for returning a search warrant. When the officer returns the warrant, he or she should indicate on the back or on another sheet of paper the manner in which the warrant was executed. The magistrate should also receive a copy of the inventory of seized property. The property remains in the custody of the officer until the magistrate issues an order directing where it should be placed for safekeeping.

Property seized pursuant to a search warrant

Article 18.11 of the Code of Criminal Procedure declares that property seized pursuant to a search warrant must be kept according to the terms issued by the magistrate's order.

Misdemeanor or felony arrest

Article 18.22 of the Code of Criminal Procedure states that any person who is arrested for a misdemeanor or felony, and who at some time during the commission of the offense or arrest had his or her body fluids exposed to a peace officer, must undergo a communicable disease tests. The peace officer may request this test, or it may be ordered by the court. The accused may not decline the test. The test results should be made available to the local health authority, who in turn will notify the peace officer. These test results should not bear on any criminal proceeding arising out of the alleged offense.

Complaint as an affidavit

Article 15.04 of the Code of Criminal Procedure defines a complaint as an affidavit made before either the magistrate or the district or county attorney who charges the commission of the offense.

Requisites for a complaint

Article 15.05 of the Code of Criminal Procedure identifies the following requisites for a complaint: name of the accused or reasonably definite description, evidence for believing that the accused has committed a crime, the time and place of the crime, and the signature of the affiant.

Polygraph

Article 15.051 of the Code of Criminal Procedure forbids peace officers or state attorneys from requiring a polygraph examination by a person who seeks to make a complaint. When a peace officer or state attorney wants to request a polygraph examination, he or she must inform the complainant that this examination is not required, and that the failure to take a polygraph or the results of a polygraph cannot justify dismissal of a complaint. Indeed, the complainant must sign a statement indicating that this information has been conveyed.

Receive and confine committed individual

Article 16.20 of the Code of Criminal Procedure defines a commitment as a magistrate's order that directs a sheriff to receive and confine the committed individual. A commitment is sufficient if it runs in the name of "the State of Texas," if it is addressed to the appropriate sheriff, if it states the offense for which the person is to be committed, if it states the time and place for the defendant to appear in court, and if it states the amount of bail.

Indictment

Article 21.01 of the Code of Criminal Procedure defines an indictment as a grand jury's written statement accusing a person of an act or omission that has been designated as an offense.

Information

Article 21.20 of the Code of Criminal Procedure defines "information" as a written statement, filed and presented by the district or county attorney on behalf of the state, in which a defendant is charged with an offense.

Credible person affidavit

Article 21.22 of the Code of Criminal Procedure declares that no information may be presented until an affidavit charging the defendant with the offense has been made by a credible person. This affidavit must be filed alongside the information. It may be rendered before any officer authorized to administer oaths, or before the district or county attorney.

Multiple offenses

Article 21.24 of the Code of Criminal Procedure states that multiple offenses arising from the same criminal episode may be joined in a single indictment, information, or complaint. Each offense should be stated in a separate count.

Capias

Article 23.01 of the Code of Criminal Procedure defines a capias as a writ that is issued either by a clerk at the behest of a judge or by a judge of the court with jurisdiction after commitment or bail but before trial.

Requisite elements of a capias

Article 23.02 of the Code of Criminal Procedure outlines the requisite elements of a capias. A capias must run in the name of "the State of Texas," and it must either name or describe the person whose arrest is ordered. It must specify the offense of which the person is accused, and it must name the court and time at which it is returnable. Finally, it must be dated and officially attested by the issuing authority.

Autopsy

Article 49.01 of the Code of Criminal Procedure defines an autopsy as a postmortem examination of a body. An autopsy may include x-rays and an examination of internal organs and structures after dissection. The intention of autopsy is to determine the cause of death or the nature of any factors that contributed to death. This article also defines an inquest as an investigation into the cause or circumstances of death, as well as a determination as to whether the death was caused by an unlawful act or omission. This determination may be made with or without a formal court hearing. An inquest hearing may include the gathering of evidence to form the basis of a criminal prosecution.

Inquests

Article 49.02 of the Code of Criminal Procedure declares that this part of the Code applies to inquests in counties that do not have a medical examiner's office or that are not part of a medical examiner's district.

Justice of the peace to conduct inquest scenarios

Article 49.04 of the Code of Criminal Procedure establishes the scenarios that require a justice of the peace to conduct an inquest into the death of a person who dies in the justice's county. A justice must perform an inquest if a person dies an unnatural death, dies in prison, or possibly commits suicide. Justices must also perform an inquest if the circumstances suggest that the cause of death may have been unlawful behavior, or if a body or body part is found and the cause of death is unknown. Physicians are required to ask for an inquest when they attend the death of a person and are unable to certify the cause of death. When a person dies of unknown causes in a hospital or other institution, the superintendent or general manager of the institution must report the death to the justice of the peace.

Law enforcement agency notified of a death that requires an inquest

Article 49.05 (d) of the Code of Criminal Procedure states that when a law enforcement agency is notified of a death that requires an inquest, the agency must begin investigating immediately or as soon as possible.

Investigating peace officer procedures

Article 49.05 (e) of the Code of Criminal Procedure states that an investigating peace officer must not move the body or any part of the environment around the place of death without authorization from a justice of the peace.

Illegal to move a dead boy or manipulate surroundings

Article 49.05 (f) of the Code of Criminal Procedure states that it is illegal for unauthorized people to move a dead body or manipulate any part of the physical surroundings of a dead body. This offense is punishable by a fine of no more than $500.

Illegal to obstruct intentionally or knowingly crime scene

Article 49.06 of the Code of Criminal Procedure asserts that it is illegal to obstruct intentionally or knowingly the entrance of the justice of the peace to a place where a death has occurred or a body has been found. This offense is a Class B misdemeanor.

Requires inquest procedures

Article 49.07 of the Code of Criminal Procedure asserts that a physician or any other person who has a body or body part that requires an inquest must immediately contact the local justice of the peace. Similarly, a peace officer who was notified of a death requiring an inquest must immediately notify the justice of the peace. If

for some reason the local justice of the peace is not available, the nearest available justice of the peace should be contacted. If no justice of the peace is found, a county judge may initiate the inquest. The county judge is authorized to handle all aspects of an inquest, but must transfer all information to the appropriate justice of the peace no later than five days after the inquest is initiated. Failure to give notice to an official charged with initiating inquests is a Class C misdemeanor.

Preserve all the tangible evidence

Article 49.17 of the Code of Criminal Procedure asserts that a justice of the peace must preserve all the tangible evidence that indicates the real cause of death or identifies a person who caused the death. The justice is required to either deliver this evidence to the district clerk for safekeeping or deposit it with the proper law enforcement agency.

Prisoner death

Article 49.18 of the Code of Criminal Procedure states that the sheriff or other senior administrator in a penal institution must contact the local justice of the peace whenever a prisoner dies. If the prisoner dies while in custody or as a result of an officer's use of force, or if a prisoner dies while incarcerated in a jail, correctional facility, or state juvenile facility, the director of the relevant institution must investigate the death and file a written report with the attorney general no more than 30 days after the death. This report should be made available to any member of the public by the attorney general. The director who assembles the report must make a good-faith effort to obtain all relevant facts.

Suspect of causing a death under inquest

Article 49.19 of the Code of Criminal Procedure states that a justice of the peace may issue a warrant for the arrest of a person suspected of causing a death under inquest if the justice knows of the person's involvement, received an affidavit indicating this involvement, or receives evidence at an inquest hearing that creates probable cause. This article also declares that when a justice of the peace issues an arrest warrant, the peace officer must execute it immediately and detain the person named until ordered otherwise by the justice of the peace. Such a prisoner may not be removed from the peace officer's custody by a warrant from another magistrate.

County Commissioners' Court

Article 49.23 of the Code of Criminal Procedure asserts that a County Commissioners' Court may establish the office of death investigator, and may employ multiple people to assist the county employees charged with conducting inquests. These death investigators will receive compensation amounts set by the Commissioners' Court. In order to fill this position, a person must have experience or training in investigating deaths. Death investigators may investigate the time, place, and manner of death, and may seal the premises of the deceased. Death investigators are required to submit a full report of their activities and findings to the justice of the peace no more than eight hours after finishing the investigation.

Sex offender

Article 62.102 of the Code of Criminal Procedure states that it is illegal for a person who is required to register as a sex offender fails to do so. Failure to comply with registration requirements is a state jail felony, third-degree felony, or second-degree felony, depending on the severity of the restrictions placed on the offender.

Sexually violent predator

Article 62.203 of the Code of Criminal Procedure states that: it is a second-degree felony to fail to comply with all requirements of the civil commitment process after commitment as a sexually violent predator.

Under arrest

Article 15.22 of the Code of Criminal Procedure states that: a person is technically arrested, when he has been restrained, or taken into custody by an officer or another person with or without a warrant.

Constructive custody

Article 11.21 of the Code of Criminal Procedure states that: a person may be held in constructive custody not only through actual, physical, and forcible detention, but also through any coercive measures, such as threats of injury.

Arrest, Search, and Seizure

Probable cause

Probable cause is the reasonable suspicion that a crime has been committed, is being committed, or will be committed. Probable cause can also be used to justify police officers entering an area in which there are specific objects believed to have been used in a crime. The amount of evidence required for probable cause does not need to be sufficient to guarantee a conviction in trial, but it does need to exceed simple suspicion on the part of the officer. The Fourth Amendment of the United States Constitution declares that officers must demonstrate probable cause before receiving an arrest warrant or search warrant. In other contexts, probable cause may be referred to as sufficient cause, reasonable grounds, or reasonable cause. It is important to note that the courts view probable cause as subject to an objective standard rather than to the opinion of the officer. Probable cause only exists when a reasonable person would agree that there is sufficient evidence. However, the definition of what constitutes a "reasonable person" or sufficient evidence is continuously refined by the courts.

<u>Building and applying</u>
Probable cause can be based on a number of factors. A peace officer who witnesses a suspect committing a furtive or secretive act may use this as probable cause. Probable cause may be based on the crime rate in the area or the time at which an observation is made. An officer may also base probable cause on the appearance of the suspect. Probable cause may be based on an officer's prior knowledge of a suspect, or on information obtained from an informant. Probable cause may be based on possession of or proximity to contraband or objects related to a crime. Any arrests made subsequent to an assertion of probable cause should only relate to the crimes for which probable cause was obtained.

Reasonable suspicion and temporary detention

Peace officers must be careful before confronting a suspect based on mere suspicion. A suspicion is based on a perception (such as a sight, sound, or smell) that suggests possible criminal activity. A suspicious peace officer may investigate further, and may approach people to ask questions. However, these people may not be detained, may not be forced to identify themselves, and may refuse to answer questions.

If an officer has a reasonable suspicion that a crime has taken place, he or she may temporarily detain a suspect. In order to do so, the officer must have a reason to believe that a crime has been committed and that the detained individual is in some way connected. A person being temporarily detained is not required to identify him or herself. Also, if the officer believes that the person may be carrying a weapon, he or she is allowed to frisk the person.

Frisking

Frisking is permissible whenever an officer feels his or her safety may be threatened. A frisk is just a careful patting of the outer clothing of the detained person. A frisk should not include going into the person's pockets or possessions. An officer should be able to describe the reasons for the frisk. A frisk may extend over the entire body of the suspect. In some situations, the detained person may resist being frisked. Officers are only allowed to use the minimum force necessary to complete the frisk. If illegal weapons are found during a frisk, officers should seize them and file the appropriate charges. A frisk must respect the rights of the detainee as much as possible, without compromising the safety of the officer or of others.

Lawful searches

A search may be conducted if an officer has a reasonable expectation of discovering the fruits of a crime, the tools of a crime, evidence, or contraband. A search may be justified either by a search warrant or as part of a lawful arrest. A search that is incidental to a lawful arrest should not extend beyond the area within the immediate control of the suspect. The search should be conducted at the same time as the arrest. A search may be conducted of people, vehicles, places, and open fields. The search of an area outside of a house or building should begin where the curtilage (area immediately adjacent to the house and that can be considered part of the house) ends.

Exclusionary rule

The exclusionary rule states that evidence obtained through illegal searches or other illegal government actions cannot be included in a trial. It is important to note that this rule applies not only to physical pieces of evidence, but also to confessions or other testimony received subsequent to an illegal search. All of this evidence is referred to as "fruit of the poisonous tree," and must be excluded.

Code of Criminal Procedure's

Preventing the consequences of theft and the Uniform Criminal Extradition Act's discussion of warrantless arrest:
Article 18.16 of the Code of Criminal Procedure states that citizens have the right to prevent the consequences of theft by seizing stolen personal property and bringing it before a magistrate. If possible, they can also present the person who committed the theft to a magistrate. Another option is to take the person and the property to a peace officer. This must be done immediately and there must be reasonable grounds to believe the property has been stolen.

Article 51.13 of the Code of Criminal Procedure is also known as the Uniform Criminal Extradition Act. Section 14 of this document states that peace officers and private citizens may arrest a person without a warrant so long as there is reasonable information to believe that the accused is guilty of a crime punishable by at least one year in prison. It is necessary for the accused to be taken before a judge or magistrate as soon as possible.

Complaints, including their contents, and the dismissal of charges:
Article 15.04 of the Code of Criminal Procedure states that an affidavit made before the magistrate or district or county attorney is referred to as a complaint when it charges the commission of an offense.

Article 15.05 of the Code of Criminal Procedure states a complaint must have the following components: name of the accused or a reasonable description of him, reasons to believe the accused has committed some offense, time and place of the commission of the offense, and the signature or mark of the affiant.

Article 24.13 of the Code of Criminal Procedure states that if a person is released on bail or has his charges dismissed after being transferred to a county but before being returned to the department, the county must notify the department.

Penal Code

Objectives and the applicability

Section 1.02 of the Penal Code describes the objectives of the code. In general, the intention of the Code is to establish a series of penalties to handle behavior that causes or threatens harm to individual or public interests. The Penal Code seeks to ensure public safety by deterring crime, rehabilitating violators, and preventing recidivism. The Penal Code also endeavors to provide clear definition and gradation of offenses, as well as to prescribe penalties that are appropriate to the offenses. One of the other goals of the Code is to protect behavior that should not be classified as criminal. The Penal Code should also inform and restrict the activities of law enforcement officials, as well as define the scope of law enforcement officers with respect to particular offenses. Section

1.03 of the Penal Code states that no act or emission is an offense unless it is defined as such by a statute, municipal ordinance, order of the County Commissioners Court, or rule adopted under a statute. The Penal Code impacts the right or liability to damages, penalty, or other remedy authorized by a civil suit.

Territorial jurisdiction

Section 1.04 of the Penal Code declares that the state has jurisdiction over offenses that occur inside the state, that occur outside the state but constitute an attempt to commit an offense inside the state, or occur inside the state and constitute an attempt to commit an offense in another jurisdiction. With regard to criminal homicide, the Penal Code covers both the physical acts that caused the death and the death itself. When the victim of a homicide is found in Texas, the law presumes that the death occurred in the state. The Penal Code considers all of the land, water, and air space within the state boundaries to be part of Texas. If an offense is based on an omission of a duty imposed by a statute of the state, and the adverse event occurs inside the state, Texas has jurisdiction no matter where the offending individual was at the time of the event.

Age

Regarding age, section 1.06 of the Penal Code states that a person reaches a particular age on the day of the anniversary of his or her birthday.

Burden of proof

Section 2.01 of the Penal Code declares that all persons are presumed innocent and may not be convicted of an offense unless guilt is proved beyond a reasonable doubt. The mere fact of a person's arrest or indictment does not imply guilt.

Exceptions

Section 2.02 of the Penal Code describes the exceptions, and the prosecuting attorney has the burden of demonstrating beyond a reasonable doubt that the defendant's conduct does not fall within those exceptions.

Defenses to prosecution

Section 2.03 of the Penal Code describes defenses to prosecution. The prosecuting attorneys are not responsible for disproving defenses. Indeed, the possibility of the defense will not be submitted to the jury unless evidence supporting the defense is admitted. If the defense is submitted to the jury, the court may assert that a reasonable doubt requires acquittal.

Affirmative defenses to prosecution

Section 2.04 of the Penal Code declares that prosecutors are not required to negate the existence of an affirmative defense, and information regarding a possible affirmative defense will not be submitted to the jury unless evidence in support of the defense has been admitted. When the issue of the existence of an affirmative defense is submitted to the jury, the court will require the defendant to prove the affirmative defense with a preponderance of evidence. There are also unique defenses that only apply in very limited circumstances, and which are detailed in the section of the Penal Code related to the offense.

Consequences of presumption

Section 2.05 of the Penal Code describes the consequences of presumption. When the Penal Code or any other law establishes a presumption regarding any fact, it must be submitted to the jury, unless the court is convinced that the entire body of evidence clearly precludes a finding beyond a reasonable doubt of the presumed fact. When the existence of the presumed fact has been submitted to the jury, the court will inform the jury that the facts supporting the presumption must be proved beyond a reasonable doubt and that, even if the facts are proven beyond a reasonable doubt, the jury is not bound to find that the corresponding element of the offense exists. The court will also inform the jury that the state must prove beyond a reasonable doubt the truth of the other elements of the offense and that, if the jury has reasonable doubt about the facts supporting a presumption, the presumption fails and should not be considered at all.

In favor of the defendant
Section 2.05 of the Penal Code also describes the consequences of establishing a presumption in favor of the defendant with respect to any fact. When the presumption is supported by sufficient facts, the issue of the

existence of the presumed fact is submitted to the jury, unless the court is content that the entire body of evidence precludes a finding beyond a reasonable doubt of said presumed fact. If the existence of the presumed fact is submitted to the jury, the court shall tell the jury that the presumption is true unless the state proves beyond a reasonable doubt that the facts supporting the presumption do not exist. The jury must also be informed that if the state fails to prove beyond a reasonable doubt that the facts giving rise to the presumption do not exist, then the jury must find that the presumed fact exists. However, even if the jury finds that the presumed fact does not exist, the state still must prove beyond a reasonable doubt each of the elements of the offense. Finally, if the jury has reasonable doubt about the existence of the presumed fact, the presumption continues to apply and the jury must consider the presumed fact to exist.

Criminal episode

Section 3.01 of the Penal Code defines a criminal episode as the commission of two or more offenses, so long as the offenses are committed as part of the same transaction or as part of multiple transactions connected by a common scheme or plan. A criminal episode may also include multiple commissions of the same offense.

Section 3.02 of the Penal Code asserts that a defendant may be prosecuted in a single criminal action for all of the offenses devolving from a single criminal episode. When a single criminal action is based on more than one charging instrument, the state must file written notice of the action at least 30 days before the trial. Whenever a guilty verdict is reversed, set aside, or vacated and a new trial is ordered, the state may not add offenses to a single criminal action unless evidence establishing probable guilt for that offense was not known by the prosecutor on the initiation of the first prosecution.

Consecutive and concurrent sentences

Section 3.03 of the Penal Code declares that when a person is found guilty of more than one offense from the same criminal episode, the sentences for each offense will be pronounced separately but may be served concurrently, except in certain circumstances. For particularly heinous crimes, the court may indicate that sentences are to be served consecutively.

Severance of multiple offenses

Section 3.04 of the Penal Code states that the defendant has a right to sever multiple offenses joined for trial. When severance occurs, individual sentences may be served either concurrently or consecutively, at the discretion of the court. Severance is not available for defendants in all cases.

Voluntary act or omission

Section 6.01 of the Penal Code states that an offense is committed only if a person voluntarily engages in the offending conduct, though this may include action, omission, or possession. Possession is considered a voluntary act when the possessor knowingly obtains or receives something, and has sufficient time to terminate this control.

Culpability

Section 6.02 of the Penal Code declares that in order to be culpable, a person must intentionally, knowingly, recklessly, or with criminal negligence commit the offense. The range of culpability in mental states proceeds as follows, from highest to lowest: intentional, knowing, reckless, and criminally negligent. If a person is proven culpable to a higher degree than he was charged, this constitutes proof of the culpability charged.

Culpable mental states and causation

Section 6.03 of the Penal Code defines the culpable mental states. A person acts

- 39 -

intentionally when it is his conscious desire to perform the action or cause the result. A person acts knowingly when he is aware of what he is doing, that the circumstances for an offense exist, or when he is aware that his conduct is reasonably certain to cause a particular result. A person acts recklessly when he is aware of but consciously ignores a substantial risk that would be considered a gross deviation from the behavior of an ordinary person. Finally, a person acts with criminal negligence when he should be aware of a significant risk.

Section 6.04 of the Penal Code declares that a person is criminally responsible if a result was the inevitable consequence of his conduct. A person is also criminally responsible if, despite his intention, a different offense was committed, a different person was harmed, or different property was damaged.

Criminal responsibility for the conduct of another

Section 7.01 of the Penal Code states that a person is criminally responsible as a party to an offense if it is either the result of his conduct or the conduct of another person for whom he is criminally responsible. Each party to an offense may be charged with commission. It is not necessary to declare whether a person acted as a principal or accomplice.

Section 7.02 of the Penal Code declares that a person is criminally responsible for another person's conduct if he intentionally solicited, directed, or attempted to help the other person commit the offense. A person is also criminally responsible if he helped or forced an innocent person to commit an offense. A person is considered criminally responsible if he has a legal duty to prevent an offense and fails to make a reasonable effort to do so. If a group of conspirators commits one felony while attempting to commit another, then they are guilty of the felony actually committed, so long as the offense was

committed with unlawful intent and could have been anticipated as a consequence of the original conspiracy.

Excluded defenses
Section 7.03 of the Penal Code declares that a person who has been charged with criminal responsibility for the conduct of another may not use the defense that he is legally incapable of committing the offense himself, or that the person who committed the act has not been prosecuted or convicted.

Criminal responsibility of a corporation or association

Section 7.22 of the Penal Code declares that corporations are responsible for any offenses committed by agents acting on their behalf within the scope of their office or employment. However, corporations are only criminally responsible for felony offenses if the offenses were authorized, requested, performed, or recklessly tolerated by a majority of the governing board or a high managerial agent.

Criminal responsibility for conduct on behalf of a corporation

Section 7.23 of the Penal Code states that individuals are just as criminally responsible for conduct performed in the name of a corporation as they are for conduct performed in their own name. This section also states that agents may be held criminally responsible for the failure to discharge a duty imposed by law on a corporation. This responsibility is the same as if the duty was imposed directly on the person. Finally, the sentence for a person who commits an offense on behalf of a corporation is the same as for a person who commits that offense on his own behalf.

Affirmative defense of mental deficiency

Section 8.01 of the Penal Code asserts it is an affirmative defense to prosecution if the offender did not realize his conduct was wrong at the time because of severe mental disease or defect. However, mental disease or defect does not include any irregularities caused only by repeated criminal or antisocial conduct.

Mistaken belief defense

Section 8.02 of the Penal Code states that it is a defense to prosecution that the accused developed very incorrect beliefs about a fact, so long as the mistaken belief negates the charged level of culpability. However, though a mistake of fact may serve as a defense, the accused may still be convicted of any lesser offense of which he might be guilty if his mistaken belief was true.

Ignorance of illegality defense

Section 8.03 of the Penal Code states that accused individuals may not defend themselves by saying they did not know their conduct was illegal. However, it may be an affirmative defense to prosecution if the person did not know his actions were illegal and based this presumption on an official statement of the law or written interpretation of the law. Ignorance of the law may constitute a defense against the violation with which the person is charged, but he may still be prosecuted for lesser offenses of which he would be guilty if the law were as he believed.

Voluntary intoxication

Section 8.04 of the Penal Code declares that voluntary intoxication is not a defense. However, a convicted person may introduce evidence of temporary insanity caused by intoxication to mitigate the penalty.

Compulsion as defenses against prosecution

Section 8.05 of the Penal Code asserts that it is an affirmative defense to prosecution that the person committed the offense because he was threatened with imminent death or serious injury to himself or another person.

This is called acting under duress. A person is only compelled if the force or threat of force would render a person of reasonable integrity incapable of resisting. If a person intentionally, knowingly, or recklessly places himself in a situation likely to result in compulsion, he may not use duress as an affirmative defense. Compulsion by a spouse is subject to the same criteria.

Entrapment

Section 8.06 of the Penal Code declares that the accused may defend against prosecution by saying he was induced by a law enforcement agent. However, the law enforcement agent must have used persuasion or some other means likely to cause commission, because simply giving a person an opportunity to commit a crime does not constitute entrapment.

Youth as defenses against prosecution

Section 8.07 of the Penal Code states that a person may not face prosecution for any offense he committed when younger than 15. There are a few exceptions to this rule: perjury, motor vehicle violations, misdemeanors punishable only by fine, penal ordinances of political subdivisions, and felony offenses for which the person has been transferred to the court under Section 54.02 of the Family Code.

Classification of felonies and misdemeanors

Section 12.02 of the Penal Code declares that all offenses are designated as either felonies or misdemeanors. Section 12.03 of the Penal Code declares that misdemeanors are classified into three categories—Class A, B, or C—according to their relative severity. Offenses designated as misdemeanors by the Penal Code without mention of punishment or category are Class C misdemeanors, which do not impose any legal disability or disadvantage.

- 41 -

Section 12.04 of the Penal Code declares that felonies are classified into five categories according to their relative severity. From most severe to least, they are capital felonies, first-degree felonies, second-degree felonies, third-degree felonies, and state jail felonies. Whenever a felony is mentioned in the Code without reference to category, it is a state jail felony.

Class A misdemeanors

Section 12.21 of the Penal Code declares that Class A misdemeanors are punishable by a fine of no more than $4000, a jail sentence of no more than one year, or both.

Class B and C misdemeanors

Section 12.22 of the Penal Code declares that Class B misdemeanors are punishable by a fine of no more than $2000, a jail sentence of no more than 180 days, or both. Section 12.23 of the Penal Code declares that Class C misdemeanors are punishable by a fine of not more than $500.

Capital felonies

Section 12.31 of the Penal Code declares that a capital felony is punishable by imprisonment for life without the possibility of parole or death in cases where the state seeks the death penalty. If the state does not seek the death penalty, a capital felony is punishable by imprisonment for life or imprisonment for life without the possibility of parole. When the state seeks the death penalty, prospective jurors must be told that either a sentence of life imprisonment without parole or the death sentence is mandatory on conviction.

First-degree felony

Section 12.32 of the Penal Code declares that a first-degree felony is punishable by life imprisonment or a prison term of between five and 99 years. Also, a person convicted of a first-degree felony may be fined up to $10,000.

Second-degree felony

Section 12.33 of the Penal Code declares that a second-degree felony is punishable by a prison term of between two and 20 years, with an optional fine of no more than $10,000.

Third-degree felony

Section 12.34 of the Penal Code declares that a third-degree felony is punishable by a prison term of between two and 10 years, with an optional fine of no more than $10,000.

State jail felony

Section 12.35 of the Penal Code declares that state jail felony is punishable by confinement in a state jail for a term of 180 days to two years, as well as an optional fine of no more than $10,000. A person who is found guilty of a state jail felony may be punished for a third-degree felony if the crime involved a deadly weapon or the person has been previously convicted of a felony.

Exceptional sentences

Section 12.41 of the Penal Code outlines the classification of convictions not obtained from a prosecution under said Penal Code. If the offense is punishable by imprisonment in the Texas Department of Criminal Justice or another penitentiary, the crime is classified as a felony of the third degree. If the crime is punishable by jail but is not a felony, it is classified as a Class B misdemeanor. If the crime is only punishable by a fine, it is classified as a Class C misdemeanor. These designations are subject to change within individual sections of the Code.

State jail and first-degree felonies

Section 12.42 of the Penal Code declares that if a person is convicted of a state jail felony, and it is found that he has previously been convicted of two state jail felonies, then his punishment will be upgraded to a third-degree felony. If a person on trial for a state jail felony has been convicted of two previous felonies, the second of which occurred after the first conviction became final, he shall be punished for a second-degree felony. If a person on trial for a first-degree felony has previously been convicted of a felony, the crime is punishable by life imprisonment or a term of between 15 and 99 years, accompanied by an optional fine of up to $10,000. There are other special circumstances in which habitual felony offenders may have their sentences augmented.

Enhancements for misdemeanors

Section 12.43 of the Penal Code declares that if a person who is being tried for a Class A misdemeanor has previously been convicted of a Class A misdemeanor or a felony, conviction is punishable by a fine of not more than $4000, a jail sentence of between 90 days and one year, or both. If a person is on trial for a Class B misdemeanor and has been previously convicted of a felony or a Class A or B misdemeanor, the conviction would be punishable by a fine of no more than $2000, a jail sentence of between 30 and 180 days, or both. If a person is on trial for a Class C misdemeanor and has been convicted of three similar violations in the two years before the date of the current offense, the crime is punishable by a fine of no more than $2000, a maximum jail sentence of 180 days, or both.

Discretionary sentence adjustment by the court

Section 12.44 of the Penal Code declares that when a court decides it is in the best interests of justice, it may punish a defendant convicted of a state jail felony by imposing the confinement penalty for a Class A misdemeanor. This action is taken when the court determines that it will best promote the ends of justice. Also, the prosecuting attorney may request that the court allow him to prosecute a state jail felony as a Class A misdemeanor.

Penalty adjustments for crimes involving bias or prejudice

Section 12.47 of the Penal Code declares that for all offenses other than first-degree felonies or Class A misdemeanors, punishment is increased to the next highest category of offense if it is found that the offense was committed because of bias or prejudice. For Class A misdemeanors, bias or prejudice increases the minimum term of confinement to 180 days. The attorney general may be asked to assist the prosecutor in cases that involve bias or prejudice.

Sentencing adjustments for acts involving controlled substances and preparatory acts

Section 12.49 of the Penal Code declares that when the court finds that a controlled substance was used to commit an offense, any offense other than a first-degree felony or Class A misdemeanor will have its punishment increased to the next highest category of offense. For Class A misdemeanors committed with a controlled substance, the minimum term of imprisonment is increased to 180 days.

Section 15.01 of the Penal Code declares that a person has committed an offense if he performs an act that is more than mere preparation but fails to affect the commission of the offense intended, if this act was performed with the specific intent to commit an offense. Also, if a person attempts a potentially aggravated offense, this act is considered as severe as the aggravated offense, assuming that some aggravating element is part of the attempt. A prosecution for criminal attempts may not be defended against by the claim that the offense was actually committed. Criminal attempts are designated one category lower than the attempted offense. If the offense attempted is a state jail felony, the attempt is a Class A misdemeanor.

Criminal conspiracy

Section 15.02 of the Penal Code declares that a person has committed criminal conspiracy if he intends to commit a felony and agrees with one or more people that they should perform the offending act, and then one or more of this group performs an act pursuant to the agreement. The presence of a conspiracy may be inferred from the offending acts. A person accused of criminal conspiracy may not defend himself by saying that one or more of the co-conspirators is not criminally responsible, or that one or more of the co-conspirators has been acquitted or not prosecuted at all. The accused criminal conspirators also may not defend themselves by demonstrating that the object offense was actually committed, or that the individual accused is a type of person who could not commit the object offense alone. Criminal conspiracy is designated one category lower than the most serious felony object offense. If the most serious felony object offense is a state jail felony, criminal conspiracy is designated as a Class A misdemeanor.

Criminal solicitation

Section 15.03 of the Penal Code defines criminal solicitation as the request, command, or attempt to persuade another to engage in specific conduct that amounts to a felony, and if it is done with the intent that a capital felony or first-degree felony be committed. A person may not be convicted of criminal solicitation based on the uncorroborated testimony of the solicited person, unless the solicitation is made in extremely prejudicial circumstances. A person accused of criminal solicitation may not defend himself by saying that the solicited person is not criminally responsible, has been acquitted, or has not

been prosecuted. It is also not a defense to argue that the solicited felony was actually committed. Criminal solicitation is a first-degree felony if the solicited offense is a capital offense, and it is a second-degree felony if the solicited offense is a first-degree felony.

Denunciation defense

Section 15.04 of the Penal Code declares that defendants may argue that they voluntarily and completely renounced their criminal objective before the commission of the offense or, if the offense was committed, that they took affirmative action to prevent its commission. This is known as the renunciation defense. A defendant may not claim that renunciation was voluntary if it came after he obtained information indicating that the crime would be more difficult and the likelihood of getting caught would be higher. The decision to postpone criminal conduct is not equivalent to renunciation. When the affirmative defense of renunciation is accepted by the court, the punishment is one grade lower.

Attempted preparatory offenses

Section 15.05 of the Penal Code states that it is not an offense to attempt or conspire to commit or solicit a preparatory offense as defined by the Penal Code.

Criminal instruments

Section 16.01 of the Penal Code declares that it is illegal to possess, manufacture, sell, or install a criminal instrument for use in the commission of an offense. The unlawful use of a criminal instrument is a state jail felony, unless charge is for possession, in which case the punishment is one category lower than the offense intended.

- 44 -

Interception of wire or electronic communications

Section 16.02 of the Penal Code asserts that it is illegal to intercept or attempt to intercept a wire or electronic communication. It is also illegal to intentionally disclose or try to disclose the contents of such a communication when the contents are known to have been obtained through interception. It is illegal to use the contents of an intercepted communication, or to take any actions that tend towards interception of a communication. Some employees of communication companies and services may be exempt from prosecution under this section. These offenses are second-degree felonies.

Pen registers, trap-and-trace devices

Section 16.03 of the Penal Code declares that it is illegal to install or use a pen register or trap-and-trace device for the purposes of identifying telephone numbers. Law enforcement officers are exempt from prosecution under this section. This offense is a state jail felony.

Improper disclosure of communications

Section 16.04 of the Penal Code declares that it is illegal to obtain, alter, or block authorized access to a wire or electronic communication in storage without authorization. Unlawful access to a stored communication is a Class A misdemeanor, unless it was performed to obtain a benefit or harm another party, in which case it is a state jail felony.

Section 16.05 of the Penal Code asserts that it is illegal to knowingly divulge the contents of a communication to a person who is not the intended recipient. There are some exceptions to this law for employees of communication services and law enforcement agencies. If this act involves a scrambled or encrypted radio communication, it is a state jail felony. If the act is performed to gain a benefit, it is either a Class A or C misdemeanor.

Installation of motor vehicle tracking devices

Section 16.06 of the Penal Code declares that it is illegal to knowingly install a tracking device on another person's motor vehicle. This is a Class A misdemeanor.

Criminal homicide and murder

Section 19.01 of the Penal Code defines criminal homicide as an intentional, knowing, reckless, or criminally negligent action that causes the death of another person. Murder, capital murder, manslaughter, and criminally negligent homicide are all forms of criminal homicide. Section 19.02 of the Penal Code declares that a person has committed murder if he intentionally or knowingly causes a death, intends to cause serious injury and instead causes death, or causes a death during the commission of a felony, so long as his actions are clearly dangerous to human life. In almost every case, murder is a first-degree felony. However, if the defendant proves that he acted under the immediate influence of passion arising from an adequate cause, murder may be downgraded to a second-degree felony.

Capital murder

Section 19.03 of the Penal Code asserts that a murder becomes defined as capital murder if the victim is a known peace officer or firefighter who is performing his duties lawfully. A crime may be designated as capital murder if the offender intentionally commits the murder during a kidnapping, burglary, robbery, arson, aggravated sexual assault, or act of terrorism. The murder becomes capital if it is committed for remuneration, or if a person employs another person to commit the murder for remuneration. Prisoners may be charged with capital murder if they kill a penal institution employee. Murders may become capital if they involve more than one

- 45 -

victim during the same criminal transaction, if the victim is less than six years of age, or if the crime has to do with the service or status of a judicial official. Capital murder is a capital felony.

Criminal homicide

Section 19.04 of the Penal Code defines manslaughter as a reckless act that causes the death of another person. Manslaughter is a second-degree felony.

Criminally negligent homicide

Section 19.05 of the Penal Code declares that a person has committed criminally negligent homicide if his criminal negligence results in the death of another person. Criminally negligent homicide is a state jail felony.

Homicide involving unborn children

Section 19.06 of the Penal Code states that the provisions related to criminal homicide do not apply to unborn children if the conduct is committed by the unborn child's mother or a physician who has the consent of the child's mother.

Illegal restraint

Section 20.02 of the Penal Code declares that it is illegal to restrain another person intentionally or knowingly. However, it is an affirmative defense to prosecution that the restrained person was younger than 14, was a relative of the accused, and was being restrained so that the accused could assume lawful control. Unlawful restraint is a Class A misdemeanor, unless the person restrained was younger than 17, in which case it is a state jail felony, or unless the restraint recklessly exposes the victim to risk, in which case it is a third-degree felony. It is also a state jail felony to restrain another person while in custody, or to restrain a known public servant who is lawfully discharging an official duty.

Kidnapping

Section 20.03 of the Penal Code declares that it is illegal to intentionally or knowingly abduct another person. The accused may attempt an affirmative defense on the grounds that the abduction was not accompanied by deadly force or the threat of deadly force, that the abductor was a relative, and that the sole intent of the abduction was to assume lawful control of the abducted. Kidnapping is a third-degree felony.

Aggravated kidnapping

Section 20.04 of the Penal Code declares that it is illegal to intentionally or knowingly abduct another person with the intent of holding him for ransom, using him as a shield or hostage, aiding the commission of a felony, abusing him, terrorizing him, or interfering with the performance of an official function. These acts are collectively known as aggravated kidnapping, and are designated as first-degree felonies. However, during the punishment stage of the trial, a defendant may prove that he voluntarily released the victim in a safe place, in which case the offense is downgraded to a second-degree felony.

Unlawful transport

Section 20.05 of the Penal Code declares that it is illegal to transport a person for pecuniary benefit in a manner that is designed to conceal the person from law enforcement and creates the likelihood that the person will be injured or killed. Unlawful transport is a state jail felony.

Trafficking of persons

Section 20A.02 of the Penal Code states that it is illegal to knowingly traffic another person with the knowledge that the person will be forced to provide labor or services. It is also illegal to receive the labor or services of trafficked people. These offenses are second-degree felonies, though they become first-degree felonies if the trafficked person is younger than 18 or the offense results in the death of a trafficked individual.

Deviate sexual intercourse
Section 21.01 of the Penal Code defines deviate sexual intercourse as contact between one person's genitals and another person's mouth or anus, or the penetration of the anus or genitals with an object.

Continuous sexual abuse of a minor

Section 21.02 of the Penal Code asserts that it is illegal to commit two or more acts of sexual abuse (aggravated kidnapping with sexual intent, indecency with a child, sexual assault, aggravated sexual assault, or burglary with the intent to commit a sex offense) over the course of 30 days if the offender is 17 years or older and the victim is younger than 14. One affirmative defense to this charge is that the offender was no more than five years older than the victim. This is a first-degree felony.

Homosexual intercourse

Section 21.06 of the Penal Code has been declared unconstitutional by the Supreme Court case *Lawrence v. Texas*, but it states that engaging in deviate sexual intercourse with another person of the same sex is a Class C misdemeanor.

Public lewdness

Section 21.07 of the Penal Code declares that it is illegal to knowingly engage in sexual intercourse, sexual contact, or deviate sexual intercourse with another person, or to engage in any sexual contact with an animal, in a public place with reckless disregard for other people. This offense, known as public lewdness, is a Class A misdemeanor.

Indecent exposure

Section 21.08 of the Penal Code defines indecent exposure as showing off the anus or any part of the genitals with the intent to arouse other people, and with reckless disregard to others. Indecent exposure is a Class B misdemeanor.

Indecency with a child

Section 21.11 of the Penal Code declares that it is illegal to have sexual contact with a child younger than 17. This is known as indecency with a child, and it is a second-degree felony, unless the offense is based on exposure rather than sexual contact, in which case the offense is a third-degree felony.

Sexual contact with a student

Section 21.12 of the Penal Code declares that it is illegal for an employee of a public or private primary or secondary school to have sexual contact with a student. This is a second-degree felony.

Improper photography or visual recording

Section 21.15 of the Penal Code declares that it is illegal to photograph or videotape an image of another person without the other person's consent and with the intent to satisfy the sexual desire of any person. The penalty for such improper photography or visual recording is a state jail felony.

Assault

Section 22.01 of the Penal Code defines assault as the intentional, knowing, or reckless injury of another person, or attempted injury to another person, or physical contact with another person that could reasonably be assumed to cause injury. Assault is a Class A misdemeanor, unless it is committed against a family member or public servant, in which case it is a third-degree felony.

Sexual assault

Section 22.011 of the Penal Code declares that a person has committed sexual assault if he intentionally or knowingly penetrates the anus or sexual organ of another person without consent, or causes that penetration, or intentionally or knowingly causes that penetration with respect to a child. Sexual assault is a second-degree felony.

Aggravated assault

Section 22.02 of the Penal Code declares that an assault is aggravated if it causes serious injury or involves the use of a deadly weapon. Aggravated assault is a second-degree felony, unless it is committed against a public servant or family member or in retaliation, in which case it is a first-degree felony.

Aggravated sexual assault

Section 22.021 of the Penal Code declares that sexual assault is aggravated if it is accompanied by serious bodily injury or attempted murder, the threats of these, or the use of a deadly weapon. Sexual assault is also aggravated if the victim is younger than 14, elderly, or disabled. Aggravated sexual assault is a first-degree felony. If the victim of the offense is younger than 6 years, the minimum term of imprisonment is increased to 25 years.

Injury to a child, elderly person, or disabled person

Section 22.04 of the Penal Code declares that it is illegal to intentionally, knowingly, recklessly, or with criminal negligence act or fail to act in a way that causes serious bodily or mental injury to a child, elderly individual, or disabled individual. These crimes are designated as felonies of different severity, depending on the circumstances of the offense.

Child abandonment

Section 22.042 of the Penal Code declares that it is illegal to intentionally abandon a child younger than 15 years in circumstances that expose him or her to an unreasonable

risk of harm. This is a state jail felony if the offender intended to return for the child, or a third-degree felony if the offender did not intend to return.

Reckless endangerment

Section 22.05 of the Penal Code declares that it is illegal to act recklessly in a way that puts another person in imminent danger of serious bodily injury. It is also illegal to knowingly discharge firearms in the direction of people, houses, buildings, or vehicles. Placing another person in imminent danger of serious injury is a Class A misdemeanor, while recklessly discharging a firearm is a third-degree felony.

Effective consent defense

Section 22.06 of the Penal Code asserts that the effective consent of the victim is a defense to prosecution for assault, so long as the conduct did not threaten or inflict serious injury or the victim knew the conduct was a risk of his job or a scientific experiment.

Threatened violence

Section 22.07 of the Penal Code declares that it is illegal to threaten to commit a violent act against any person or property if this threat is made to generate fear or the reaction of emergency response agencies. It is also illegal to threaten violence to influence the conduct of the government at any level. These offenses are designated as Class A or B misdemeanors, state jail felonies, or third-degree felonies, depending on the severity.

Assisting suicide

Section 22.08 of the Penal Code declares that it is illegal to help or attempt to help another person commit suicide. This offense is a Class C misdemeanor, unless the actions taken by the offender cause death or serious bodily injury, in which case the offense is a state jail felony.

Tampering with a consumer product

Section 22.09 of the Penal Code declares that it is illegal to knowingly or intentionally tamper with a consumer product that will be offered for sale, especially if this is done to affect sales, cause bodily injury, or frighten people. Tampering with a product is a second-degree felony or, if anyone is injured, a first-degree felony. Tampering with a product with malicious intent is a third-degree felony.

Leaving a child in a motor vehicle

Section 22.10 of the Penal Code declares that it is illegal to intentionally or knowingly leave a child under the age of 7 unaccompanied by another person who is 14 years or older in a motor vehicle for more than five minutes. Leaving a child in the vehicle is a Class C misdemeanor.

Harassing a correctional officer or public servant

Section 22.11 of the Penal Code declares that it is illegal to cause a correctional officer or public servant to contact the offender's blood, seminal fluid, vaginal fluid, saliva, urine, or feces. This is a third-degree felony.

Bigamy

Section 25.01 of the Penal Code asserts that it is illegal for a legally married person to marry a person besides his spouse or live with another person in Texas under the appearance of marriage. It is also illegal to marry or live with another person knowing that that person is already married to someone else. These offenses are called bigamy, and they are third-degree felonies, unless one of the parties is younger than 16, in which case the offense is a first-degree felony.

Prohibited sexual conduct

Section 25.02 of the Penal Code forbids people from engaging in sexual intercourse or deviate sexual conduct with a person who is known to be a relative by blood or adoption. This prohibited sexual conduct is a third-degree felony.

Interference with child custody

Section 25.03 of the Penal Code asserts that it is illegal to retain or take a child younger than 18 years old in violation of a court order. It is also illegal to take possession of a child when one has not been awarded custody or when custody is pending. Interference with child custody is a state jail felony.

Enticing a child

Section 25.04 of the Penal Code asserts that it is illegal to interfere with the lawful custody of a child younger than 18 years old by enticing, persuading, or taking the child from his or her parent or guardian. Enticing a child is a Class B misdemeanor, except when it is proven that the offender intended to commit an offense against the child, in which case it is a third-degree felony.

Failing to provide child support

Section 25.05 of the Penal Code declares that it is illegal to intentionally or knowingly fail to provide child support, regardless of whether this support has been ordered by a court. Being unable to provide support is an affirmative defense to a charge of criminal nonsupport, which is a state jail felony.

Harboring a runaway

Section 25.06 of the Penal Code declares that it is against the law to knowingly harbor a child and be criminally negligent about whether the child is older than 18 or whether the child has escaped from custody. Harboring a runaway child is a Class A misdemeanor, but it is a defense to

- 49 -

prosecution to prove that an attempt was made to notify the authorities.

Violation of court orders or conditions of bond in a family violence case

Section 25.07 of the Penal Code declares that it is illegal to violate court orders or the conditions of bond in a family violence by committing one of the following acts: violence, improper communication or approach, or possession of a firearm. Any such offense is a Class A misdemeanor, unless the defendant has been convicted of such violations twice in the past or the violations include violence or stalking, in which case the offense is a third-degree felony.

Sale or purchase of a child

Section 25.08 of the Penal Code declares that it is illegal to purchase or sell a child younger than 18 years of age. This is a third-degree felony, unless the transaction is for the purpose of performing a further crime in the future, in which case it is a second-degree felony.

Advertising for the placement of a child

Section 25.09 of the Penal Code declares that it is illegal to advertise that a child is up for adoption or that an adopted child is sought. This law does not apply to child placement services. Advertising for the placement of a child is a Class A misdemeanor, unless the defendant has been convicted in the past, in which case it is a third-degree felony.

Interference with the rights of a guardian

Section 25.10 of the Penal Code asserts that it is illegal to take, retain, or hide a guardian's ward in a way that interferes with the guardian's rights. This crime, which is called interference with the rights of a guardian, is a state jail felony. This law does not apply to situations in which the government must take control of a child.

Arson

Section 28.02 of the Penal Code declares that it is illegal to start a fire with the intent to damage or destroy vegetation, fences, structure, habitations, buildings, or vehicles. This is considered arson when the offender knows that the target is within town limits, insured, subject to a mortgage or other security interest, located on someone else's property, or when the fire endangers another person or another person's property. Arson is a second-degree felony, unless the fire causes injury or death or the target was a place of worship, in which cases the offense is a first-degree felony.

Criminal mischief

Section 28.03 of the Penal Code declares that it is illegal to intentionally or knowingly destroy or tamper with another person's tangible property. These offenses are called criminal mischief, and the classification of the offense depends on the type and value of the damaged property.

Reckless damage

Section 28.04 of the Penal Code declares that it is illegal to recklessly damage another person's property without receiving the effective consent of the owner. This is known as reckless damage or destruction, and it is a Class C misdemeanor.

No interest in property

Section 28.05 of the Penal Code states that accused individuals may not use the defense that they had no interest in the property damaged or destroyed, so long as some other person had an interest that the accused had no right to infringe.

Amount of pecuniary loss

Section 28.06 of the Penal Code declares that in offenses where property is damaged or destroyed, the amount of pecuniary loss is calculated as the fair market value of the property at the time and place of destruction or, if the fair market value cannot be determined, the replacement cost of the property. Fair market value may also be established as the cost of repairing or restoring damaged property within a reasonable time or, for documents without an obvious market value, the amount due and collectible at maturity or the greatest amount of economic loss the owner might suffer due to the document's destruction.

Interference with railroad property

Section 28.07 of the Penal Code asserts that it is illegal to damage, obstruct, tamper with, or derail a train, railroad car, or any other rail property. Throwing an object or discharging a firearm at a train is a Class B misdemeanor unless bodily injury occurs, in which case it is a third-degree felony. Trespassing on railroad property is a Class C misdemeanor. Tampering with, obstructing, or derailing railroad property is a Class C misdemeanor, though it may be upgraded all the way to a first-degree felony depending on the amount of pecuniary loss.

Graffiti

Section 28.08 of the Penal Code declares that it is illegal to intentionally or knowingly mark with paint, an engraving device, or an indelible marker on the tangible property of another person. This offense ranges from a Class B misdemeanor to a first-degree felony, depending on the pecuniary loss to the property owner.

Robbery

Chapter 29 of the Penal Code outlines the offenses against property. Section 29.02 of the Penal Code declares that a person has committed robbery, a second-degree felony, if he intentionally, knowingly, or recklessly causes or threatens bodily injury to another

person during the course of a theft and with the intent to take control of property.

Aggravated robbery

Section 29.03 of the Penal Code describes aggravated robbery as including serious bodily injury to another, the use of a deadly weapon, or the threat of bodily injury or death to a person who is older than 65 or disabled. Aggravated robbery is a first-degree felony. For the purposes of this law, a disabled person is defined as anyone who cannot defend him or herself because of mental or physical deficiencies.

Burglary

Section 30.02 of the Penal Code declares that it is illegal to, without the effective consent of the owner; enter a building with the intent to commit a felony, theft, or assault. It is also illegal to remain concealed in a building with the intent to commit a felony, theft, or assault. Burglary is a state jail felony if it is not committed in a habitation and a second-degree felony if it is. Burglary is a first-degree felony if the premises are a habitation and any person involved in the crime either committed or entered with the intent to commit a felony other than theft.

Coin-operated and coin collection machines

Section 30.03 of the Penal Code states that it is illegal to break or enter a coin-operated machine or other such device without the effective consent of the owner and with the intent to obtain property or services. The burglary of coin-operated or coin collection machines is a Class A misdemeanor.

Vehicle burglary

Section 30.04 of the Penal Code declares that it is illegal to break into or enter a vehicle or any part of a vehicle with the intent to commit any felony or theft without the effective consent of the owner. This offense is typically a Class A misdemeanor, with a minimum term of confinement of six months if it is shown that the defendant has previously been convicted of this crime. Burglary of vehicles is a state jail felony if the defendant has been previously convicted two or more times of this crime, or if the vehicle in question is a rail car.

Criminal trespass

Section 30.05 of the Penal Code declares that it is illegal to enter or remain on another person's property, without the effective consent of that person, assuming entry was clearly forbidden or the violator had been told to leave. In this section, property includes residential land, agricultural land, a recreational vehicle park, building, or an aircraft or other vehicle. Criminal trespass is a Class A, B, or C misdemeanor, depending on various circumstances

Trespass with a concealed handgun

Section 30.06 of the Penal Code declares that it is illegal for a person who holds a concealed handgun license to carry a handgun on or to fail to depart from another person's property after receiving notice that concealed handguns are forbidden and without receiving effective consent. Trespass by the holder of a license to carry a concealed handgun is a Class A misdemeanor.

Section 31.02 of the Penal Code states that theft supersedes offenses like shoplifting, swindling, embezzlement, extortion, and receiving stolen property. Section 31.03 of the Penal Code declares that a person has committed theft if he unlawfully appropriated property intending to deprive the owner of it. This appropriation is illegal when it is done without effective consent of the owner or when it is appropriated with the knowledge that it is stolen. Theft may be classified as severely as a first-degree felony if the property appropriated is sufficiently valuable.

Theft of service

Section 31.04 of the Penal Code defines theft of service as a crime committed with the intent to avoid paying for services that demand compensation. A person commits theft of service if he intentionally or knowingly secures performance by deception or fraud. Theft of service may be classified anywhere from a Class C misdemeanor to a first-degree felony, depending on the value of the stolen service.

Trade secrets theft

Section 31.05 of the Penal Code declares that it is illegal to steal, copy, or communicate trade secrets without the effective consent of the owner. This is a third-degree felony. Section 31.06 of the Penal Code declares that it is illegal for an individual to obtain a property or service by passing a bad check.

Motor vehicles theft

Section 31.07 of the Penal Code declares that it is illegal to intentionally or knowingly operate another person's motor vehicle, including boats and airplanes, without the owner's effective consent. The unauthorized use of a vehicle is a state jail felony.

Aggregating theft amounts

Section 31.09 of the Penal Code states that various amounts obtained in the course of one theft may be aggregated when determining the severity of the offense.

Section 31.10 of the Penal Code declares that a person accused of theft may not defend himself by declaring an interest in the stolen property or service, assuming some other person has the right of exclusive possession of the property.

Shielding and deactivation equipment

Section 31.15 of the Penal Code declares that it is a Class A misdemeanor to possess, manufacture, or distribute a shielding or deactivation instrument with the intent to facilitate theft.

Organized retail theft

Section 31.16 of the Penal Code declares that it is illegal to intentionally conduct, promote, or assist the appropriation, concealment, or disposal of at least $1500 of stolen retail merchandise. Organized retail theft ranges from a state jail felony to a first-degree felony, depending on the value of the stolen merchandise.

Value

Section 32.02 of the Penal Code defines value. In most cases, value is defined as the fair market value of the property at the time and place of the offense. When a fair market value cannot be determined, the value is a reasonable replacement cost. For documents that do not have an easy market value to determine, the value is the amount due at maturity minus any part that has been satisfied, or the largest economic loss that might be suffered by the owner as a result of losing the document. For property that cannot have its value estimated by either of these methods, value is set between $750 and $2500.

Aggregate value in a single criminal episode

Section 32.03 of the Penal Code states that when multiple amounts are obtained as a result of a single criminal episode, whether from the same or different sources, the violation is considered as a single offense and the amounts are aggregated to determine the grade of the offense.

Criminal simulation

Section 32.22 of the Penal Code declares that it is illegal to intentionally defraud or harm another person by fabricating or adjusting an object so that it appears to have more value.

It is also illegal to possess such an object with intent to sell it, or to certify such an object as genuine. These offenses are known as criminal simulation, and they are designated as Class A misdemeanors.

Sale of counterfeit items

Section 32.23 of the Penal Code states that it is illegal to intentionally make, distribute, sell, or possess with intent to sell a counterfeit item. This offense may be classified anywhere from a Class C misdemeanor to a first-degree felony, depending on the value of the item.

Use of unsigned checks

Section 32.24 of the Penal Code states that it is illegal to steal an unsigned check, or to receive such a check with the intent to use it or give it to someone other than the original owner. This offense is a Class A misdemeanor.

Fraudulent credit card use

Section 32.31 of the Penal Code states that it is illegal to present or use a credit card, with the intent to obtain a benefit fraudulently, knowing the card was issued to someone else who has not given consent for its use. It is also illegal to use a card knowing that it is expired, canceled, or revoked. It is illegal to use a fictitious credit or debit card to obtain a benefit. It is also illegal to receive a benefit that has been obtained in such a manner. It is illegal for a non-issuer to sell or buy a credit or debit card, and it is illegal to buy a credit or debit card from a person who is known not to be the issuer. These offenses are all state jail felonies, except if it is shown during the trial that the offense was committed against an elderly person, in which case the crime is a third-degree felony.

False written statements to obtain property

Section 32.32 of the Penal Code states that it is illegal to intentionally or knowingly give materially false or misleading written statements to obtain property or credit. This offense ranges from a Class C misdemeanor to a first-degree felony, depending on the value of the property or amount of credit.

Obstructing enforcement of interest or lien

Section 32.33 of the Penal Code states that it is illegal for a person who has signed a security agreement to reduce the value of the property intentionally with the intent to obstruct enforcement of the interest or lien. A person may be found to have committed this violation if he failed to pay the part of the debt security that had been demanded at a particular time. This offense ranges from a Class C misdemeanor to a first-degree felony, depending on the value of the property.

Vehicle fraud

Section 32.34 of the Penal Code declares that it is illegal for a person to acquire or control another person's motor vehicle as part of an agreement to transfer the vehicle to the third party and then act to defraud the owner. For instance, the temporary controller of the vehicle may know that it is subject to a security interest, lease, or lien, but may transfer it to a third party without obtaining written authorization from the secured creditor, lessor, or lien holder. The temporary controller may commit a violation by failing to disclose the location of the vehicle upon request by the owner, secured creditor, lessor, or lien holder. Finally, he may commit a violation merely by intending to defraud or harm the vehicle's owner, whether by transferring the vehicle to a third party or disposing of it in some other manner. This offense is designated as a Class A misdemeanor, state jail felony, or third-degree felony, depending on the value of the motor vehicle.

Fraudulent credit card transaction records

Section 32.35 of the Penal Code declares that it is illegal for an authorized vendor to present to a creditor, for payment, a credit card transaction record of a sale that was not made by the authorized vendor or his agent. It is also an offense for a person to cause an authorized vendor to present to a creditor, without the creditor's authorization, a demand for payment related to a credit card transaction that was not made by the authorized vendor or his agent. These offenses range from Class C misdemeanors to first-degree felonies, depending on the amount of the record of the sale.

Issuing checks despite having insufficient funds for payment

Section 32.41 of the Penal Code declares that it is illegal to issue or pass a check knowing that the issuer does not have sufficient funds for payment. The issuer's knowledge of insufficient funds may be presumed if he had no account with the bank at the time the check was issued, or if the check was refused by the bank for lack of funds on presentation within 30 days after being issued and the issuer fails to pay the holder in full within 10 days of receiving that refusal bonus. In some cases, a person who passes bad checks may be allowed to make restitution through the prosecutor's office or the court. Passing a bad check is a Class C misdemeanor, unless the check was written to pay for court-ordered child support, in which case it is a Class B misdemeanor.

Deceptive business practices

Section 32.42 of the Penal Code names deceptive business practices. It is illegal for a person in the course of business to intentionally, knowingly, recklessly, or with criminal negligence sell less than the represented quantity of a product or service. It is illegal to sell an adulterated or mislabeled commodity, and it is illegal to pass off one property or service as another. It is illegal to use, sell, or possess a false weight or measure. It is illegal to represent a commodity as new or original if it is used, altered, or depreciated. It is illegal to misrepresent the style, grade, or model of a commodity or service. It is illegal to advertise a property or service while intending to sell it in a different way or to not supply a reasonably expectable public demand, unless the advertising mentions a time or quantity limit. It is illegal to misrepresent price or the reason or amount of a price reduction. If one of these violations is committed with criminal negligence by a person who has not previously been convicted of deceptive business practices, it is a Class C misdemeanor. If the person has previously been convicted of a Class B or C misdemeanor in this section, or engages in deceptive business practices knowingly, intentionally, or recklessly, it is a Class A misdemeanor.

Improper fiduciary benefits

Section 32.43 of the Penal Code declares that it is illegal for a fiduciary to solicit or accept, without the consent of the beneficiary, any benefit from another person in exchange for particular conduct related to the affairs of the beneficiary. This offense is a state jail felony.

Tampering with a contest

Section 32.44 of the Penal Code declares that it is illegal for a person to offer benefit or threaten harm to a participant, official, or other person with the intent of altering the outcome of a contest. It is also a crime to tamper with any person, animal, or thing with the intent of altering the outcome of a contest. These crimes are known as rigging a publicly exhibited contest, and they are designated as Class A misdemeanors.

Misapplying property held as a fiduciary

Section 32.45 of the Penal Code declares that it is illegal to misapply property held as a fiduciary or property of a financial institution.

Specifically, it is illegal to use this property in a manner that entails substantial risk. This violation may be anywhere from a Class C misdemeanor to a first-degree felony, depending on the value of the property.

Inducement to sign documents

Section 32.46 of the Penal Code declares that it is illegal to induce, with the intent to defraud or harm any person to sign or execute a document that affects property or pecuniary interest. This offense may be anywhere from a Class C misdemeanor to a first-degree felony, depending on the value of the property or pecuniary interest. It is also illegal to induce a public servant to file or report a fraudulent document. This is a state jail felony.

Destruction of writings

Section 32.47 of the Penal Code declares that it is illegal to destroy or alter, with the intent to defraud or harm another person, any writing other than a governmental record. Writings may include printed matter, money (including coins and credit cards), symbols of value or identification, and universal product codes or labels. This offense is a Class A misdemeanor, unless the writing is a will, deed, mortgage, deed of trust, security instrument, or security agreement, in which case the crime is a state jail felony.

Simulated process

Section 32.48 of the Penal Code states that it is illegal to recklessly deliver a simulated summons, complaint, judgment, or other court process with the goal of inducing payment or forcing another person to take or refrain from any action. If the document declares itself not to be legal process, or if it is issued by an entity that is not authorized to do so, this cannot be used as a defense to prosecution. This crime is a Class A misdemeanor, unless the defendant has been convicted of a similar violation in the past, in which case it is a state jail felony.

Fraudulent liens or claims

Section 32.49 of the Penal Code states that it is illegal to own, with the intent to defraud or harm another person, a purported but fraudulent lien or claim against real or personal property. It is also illegal to fail to honor a request to release a fraudulent lien or claim within 21 days after receiving notice. These crimes are Class A misdemeanors.

Fraudulent academic products

Section 32.50 of the Penal Code states that it is illegal to sell or deliver, with the goal of making a profit, an academic product that will satisfy another person's academic requirements. An accused person may defend himself or herself by claiming that the alleged violation was a product of his or her service for an institution of higher learning. These offenses are designated as Class C misdemeanors.

Fraudulent use of identifying information

Section 32.51 of the Penal Code states that it is illegal to obtain, possess, transfer, or use, with the intent to harm or defraud another person, the identifying information of another person without consent. This includes information about dead people. It is also illegal to use the identifying information of a person younger than 18 years in such a way. The designation of this violation ranges from state jail felony to first-degree felony, depending on the number of items involved.

Fraudulent postsecondary degrees

Section 32.52 of the Penal Code declares that it is illegal to intentionally use or claim to use a fraudulent, fictitious, or revoked postsecondary degree. It is illegal to use such a degree in advertising, or with the intent to obtain employment, certification, or another benefit. These crimes are Class B misdemeanors.

Illegal breach of computer security

Section 33.02 of the Penal Code states that it is illegal to knowingly access a computer or network without the effective consent of the owner. If this breach of computer security is committed without the violator obtaining a benefit, damaging property, or defrauding another person, it is a Class B misdemeanor. Otherwise, it ranges from a Class A misdemeanor to a first-degree felony, depending on the value of the benefits obtained or property damaged.

Sexual communication with and solicitation of a minor over the Internet

Section 33.021 of the Penal Code states that it is illegal for a person 17 years of age or older to communicate in a sexually explicit manner with or distribute sexually explicit material to a minor over the Internet with the intent to arouse or gratify sexual desire. It is also illegal to solicit a minor over the Internet to engage in sexual contact or intercourse. A person may not defend himself against this charge by proving that the meeting did not occur or that he did not mean for the meeting to occur. These offenses are third-degree felonies, unless the minor is younger than 14, in which case they are second-degree felonies.

Section 33.03 of the Penal Code states that a person may defend himself against charges of soliciting a minor online by demonstrating that he was an employee of a law enforcement or communications agency charged with policing such activity.

Section 33.04 of the Penal Code states that the prosecuting attorney may request the assistance of the attorney general when investigating and prosecuting computer crimes.

Tampering with a direct-recording electronic voting machine

Section 33.05 of the Penal Code states that it is illegal to knowingly access a computer or network that is used as part of a voting system in order to obstruct votes, change votes, or in any way influence the outcome of an election. Tampering with a direct-recording electronic voting machine is a first-degree felony.

Unauthorized use of telecommunications services

Section 33A.02 of the Penal Code states that it is illegal for an officer, employee, agent, or independent contractor of a telecommunications service provider to willingly and without authority use or manipulate telecommunications services for his benefit or the benefit of another person. The unauthorized use of telecommunication services ranges from a Class B misdemeanor to a first-degree felony, depending on the value of the services used or diverted.

Counterfeit telecommunications devices

Section 33A.03 of the Penal Code states that it is illegal to make, process, deliver, or advertise a counterfeit telecommunications device or any materials intended for use in such a device. These offenses are third-degree felonies.

Unlawful telecommunications services

Section 33A.04 of the Penal Code states that it is illegal to knowingly obtain or attempt to obtain a telecommunications service in avoidance of lawful charges. This offense may be designated anywhere from a Class B misdemeanor to a first-degree felony, depending on the value of the telecommunication services.

Unlawful telecommunications devices

Section 33A.05 of the Penal Code declares that it is illegal to publish a telecommunications access device designed to help people avoid lawful service charges. This is a Class A misdemeanor, unless the offender has been convicted of a similar offense in the past, in which case it is a third-degree felony.

Role of the attorney general
Section 33A.06 of the Penal Code states that the prosecuting attorney in a telecommunications case may request the assistance of the attorney general.

Money laundering

Section 34.02 of the Penal Code states that it is illegal to knowingly acquire, conceal, possess, or transfer the proceeds of criminal activity. It is also illegal to supervise or facilitate transactions involving funds generated by criminal activity. It is illegal to knowingly invest or receive funds derived from criminal activity, and it is illegal to knowingly finance or invest funds for the furtherance of criminal activity. The prosecutor is not required to demonstrate that the violator had specific knowledge of the criminal activity in question in order to establish a culpable mental state. Money laundering may be designated anywhere from a state jail felony to a first-degree felony, depending on the amount of money.

Insurance fraud

Section 35.02 of the Penal Code declares that it is illegal to prepare or present a false or misleading insurance statement with the intent to defraud or deceive the insurer. Insurance fraud ranges from a Class C misdemeanor to a first-degree felony, depending on the value of the insurance claim.

Medicaid fraud

Section 35A.02 of the Penal Code describes Medicaid fraud. It is illegal to knowingly make a false statement or misrepresentation of a material fact for the purpose of receiving a Medicaid benefit. It is also illegal to knowingly conceal or fail to disclose information that results in a person receiving a large Medicaid benefit. It is illegal to apply for and receive a Medicaid payment and then use it for alternate purposes. It is also illegal to knowingly make a false statement or misrepresentation of medical care or facilities for the purpose of obtaining certification or recertification required by Medicaid. Medicaid fraud ranges from a Class C misdemeanor to a first-degree felony, depending on the value of the services obtained.

Prohibited gifts to public servants

Section 36.09 of the Penal Code states that it is a Class A misdemeanor to offer or agree to confer any prohibited benefit on a public servant.

Material statements

Section 37.04 of the Penal Code defines a material statement as one that could have affected the course or the outcome of an official proceeding, regardless of whether the statement is admissible or not. A person accused of aggravated perjury may not defend himself by saying he believed his statement to be immaterial.

Defenses for aggravated perjury

Section 37.05 of the Penal Code states that a person may defend himself against prosecution for aggravated perjury by saying that he retracted his false statement before the completion of his testimony and before it became manifest that the falseness of the statement would be discovered.

Inconsistent statements

Section 37.06 of the Penal Code states that when an information or indictment for perjury or aggravated perjury contends that the accused has made inconsistent statements, it does not need to prove which of the statements is false. Section 37.07 of the Penal Code declares that a person may not defend himself against charges of perjury or aggravated perjury by saying that the oath was delivered in an irregular way.

Impersonation of a public servant

Section 37.11 of the Penal Code states that it is illegal to impersonate a public servant with the intent of inducing another person to act in a certain way based on the impersonation. It is also illegal to knowingly exercise any function of a fictional public servant or a nonexistent public office. Impersonating a public servant is a third-degree felony.

Illegal representation of law enforcement paraphernalia

Section 37.12 of the Penal Code declares that it is illegal to make or possess any identifying object of a law enforcement agency, as for instance a badge or identification card. This law does not apply to honorary memorabilia. Is also illegal, however, to intentionally or knowingly misrepresent an object as belonging to a law enforcement agency. False identification as a peace officer and misrepresentation of law-enforcement property are Class B misdemeanors.

Fraudulent court documents

Section 37.13 of the Penal Code declares that it is illegal to make, present, or use a fraudulent court document. This is a Class A misdemeanor.

False and fictitious identifying information

Section 38.02 of the Penal Code states that it is illegal for an arrested person to intentionally refuse to give his name, address, or date of birth to a peace officer who has requested such information. It is also illegal to intentionally give a false or fictitious name, address, or date of birth. Refusing to give information is a Class C misdemeanor, and giving fictitious information is a Class B misdemeanor. In either case, if the accused is a fugitive from justice at the time of the alleged offense, the charges are upgraded one level.

Resisting arrest

Section 38.03 of the Penal Code states that it is illegal to intentionally prevent or obstruct a peace officer from arresting, searching, or transporting any person, including the obstructer. A person accused of resisting arrest may not defend himself by proving that the arrest or search was unlawful. Resisting arrest, search, or transportation is a Class A misdemeanor, unless a deadly weapon is used in the offense, in which case it is a third-degree felony.

Fleeing arrest

Section 38.04 of the Penal Code declares that it is illegal to intentionally flee from a peace officer attempting a lawful arrest or detention. This offense is typically a Class A misdemeanor, unless there are aggravating circumstances.

Assisting a fugitive

Section 38.05 of the Penal Code states that it is illegal to hinder the arrest, prosecution, conviction, or punishment of another person by concealing him, warning him, or providing aid in any other way. Interfering with apprehension or prosecution is a Class A misdemeanor.

Escaping from custody

Section 38.06 of the Penal Code states that it is illegal to escape from custody. This offense is typically a Class A misdemeanor. However, the offense is a third-degree felony if the accused was being held in connection with a felony or was confined in a secure correctional facility. Escaping is a second-degree felony if it results in bodily injury. It is a first-degree felony if it causes serious bodily injury or entails the use or threat of a deadly weapon.

Assisting an escape from custody

Section 38.07 of the Penal Code states that it is illegal for correctional facility officials or employees to knowingly allow or aid the escape of a person in custody. This offense is typically a Class A misdemeanor, but may be designated as a more severe offense if it involves the use of force or is committed in connection with a felony.

Defenses against these charges

Section 38.08 of the Penal Code states that a person may not defend against an accusation of escaping or facilitating escape on the grounds that custody was unlawful.

Providing a person in custody with an instrument of escape

Section 38.09 of the Penal Code states that it is illegal to provide a person in custody with a deadly weapon or anything that might be useful for escape. This is a third-degree felony unless the object introduced is a deadly weapon, in which case the offense is a second-degree felony.

Failure to appear in court

Section 38.10 of the Penal Code declares that it is illegal to intentionally or knowingly fail to appear in court in accordance with the terms of release from confinement. Bail jumping and failure to appear are Class A misdemeanors, unless the original sentence was only punishable by a fine, in which case they are Class C misdemeanors. However, if the appearance is related to a felony charge, bail jumping and failure to appear are third-degree felonies.

Providing inmates with contraband

Section 38.11 of the Penal Code states that it is illegal to provide alcoholic beverages, controlled substances, or dangerous drugs to the inmates of correctional facilities. It is also illegal to provide deadly weapons, cell phones, money, or tobacco products to a person in confinement. These are third-degree felonies.

False representation as a lawyer

Section 38.123 of the Penal Code declares that it is illegal to falsely represent oneself as a lawyer with an intent to obtain economic benefit. This is a third-degree felony.

Intentionally hinder an official

Section 38.13 of the Penal Code declares that it is illegal to intentionally hinder an official proceeding by making noise or behaving disruptively. It is also illegal to recklessly hinder an official proceeding after being explicitly asked to stop. These are Class A misdemeanors.

Taking a weapon from a peace officer

Section 38.14 of the Penal Code declares that it is illegal to intentionally or knowingly and with force take or attempt to take a weapon from a known law enforcement official. A person accused of this crime may defend himself by proving that the law enforcement official was using an excessive amount of force. This crime is a third-degree felony if the accused took the weapon, and a state jail felony if he merely attempted to take it.

Interference with law enforcement

Section 38.15 of the Penal Code states that it is illegal for a criminally negligent person to interrupt, disrupt, or interfere in any way with a law enforcement officer, firefighter, or emergency medical technician. This is a Class B misdemeanor.

Obstruction of civil process

Section 38.16 of the Penal Code declares that it is a Class C misdemeanor to intentionally or knowingly prevent the execution of any process in a civil case.

Failure to stop or report aggravated sexual abuse against a child

Section 38.17 of the Penal Code declares that it is illegal to fail to stop or report aggregated sexual assault against a child. Specifically, it is a Class A misdemeanor to fail to take reasonable steps to assist the child and immediately report the commission of the offense to law enforcement.

Failure to give notice of death

Section 38.19 of the Penal Code states that it is illegal for the superintendent or general manager of an institution to fail to provide notice of the death of any person in custody or residing there. The superintendent or general manager is required to submit a report that includes all the material facts about the death. Failure to do so is a Class B misdemeanor.

Disorderly conduct

Section 42.01 of the Penal Code describes the offenses that, when performed intentionally or knowingly, constitute disorderly conduct. A person is guilty of disorderly conduct if he uses abusive or profane language or makes an obscene gesture in a public place. A person is guilty of disorderly contact if he abuses or threatens another person in a public place, or creates a noxious odor or unreasonable noise there. Fighting constitutes disorderly conduct, as does displaying or discharging a firearm in a public place. Exposing the anus or genitals in a public place with reckless disregard constitutes disorderly conduct, as does spying through a window or door for a lewd or unlawful purpose. Disorderly conduct is a Class C misdemeanor unless it involves a firearm, in which case it is a Class B misdemeanor.

Rioting

Section 42.02 of the Penal Code declares that it is illegal to knowingly participate in a riot. A person may defend himself from this charge by proving that the assembly was lawful at first, and that he departed it when it became unlawful. In most cases, participating in a riot is a Class B misdemeanor.

Obstructing a highway

Section 42.03 of the Penal Code states that it is illegal to intentionally, knowingly, or recklessly obstruct a highway or other passageway. This is a Class B misdemeanor.

Disrupting a meeting

Section 42.05 of the Penal Code states that it is a Class B misdemeanor to obstruct or interfere with a meeting or procession by actions or words, and with the intent to disrupt.

Picketing close to a funeral service

Section 42.055 of the Penal Code states that it is illegal to picket within 10,000 feet of a funeral service for a period beginning one hour before the service and ending one hour after. This is a Class B misdemeanor.

False emergency report

Section 42.06 of the Penal Code states that it is a Class A misdemeanor to knowingly initiate or communicate a false report of a bombing, fire, or other emergency, when this report would place people in fear of imminent serious bodily injury or motivate action by official or volunteer emergency services. If this false alarm involves a public school, public transportation, or utility, it is a state jail felony.

Harassment of 9-1-1 operators

Section 42.061 of the Penal Code declares that it is illegal to knowingly or intentionally call 9-1-1 when there is no emergency and then either remain silent or make abusive statements to the operator. Allowing another person to use a telephone for this purpose is also an offense. These offenses are designated as Class B misdemeanors.

General harassment

Section 42.07 of the Penal Code states that it is illegal to communicate with another person in any manner with the intention of harassing, annoying, abusing, or embarrassing that person. Harassment is a Class B misdemeanor unless the accused has been convicted previously, in which case it is a Class A misdemeanor.

Stalking

Section 42.072 of the Penal Code declares that it is a third-degree felony to engage knowingly in conduct, such as following, that another person will regard as threatening. These actions are collectively known as stalking.

Defacing a corpse or gravesite

Section 42.08 of the Penal Code states that it is a Class A misdemeanor to damage, transport, sell, buy, or treat in any offensive manner a corpse or gravesite.

Cruelty to animals

Section 42.092 of the Penal Code declares that it is a crime to torture, cruelly kill, unreasonably abandon, or seriously overwork an animal. If the actions result in the death of the animal, this offense may be a state jail felony. In most cases, however, cruelty to animals is a Class A misdemeanor.

Dog fighting

Section 42.10 of the Penal Code states that it is illegal to participate in or promote dog fighting. It is also illegal to attend a dog fight as a spectator. Possessing dog fighting equipment, training a dog for fights, and attending a dog fight are all Class A misdemeanors. Fighting dogs, allowing dog fighting to occur on one's property, and earning money from dog fighting are all state jail felonies.

Desecration of the flag

Section 42.11 of the Penal Code states that it is a Class A misdemeanor to intentionally or knowingly damage or destroy the flag of the United States or the State of Texas.

Reckless discharge of a firearm

Section 42.12 of the Penal Code declares that it is a Class A misdemeanor to recklessly discharge a firearm inside the limits of a municipality with a population of 100,000 or more.

Directing a laser pointer at a law enforcement officer

Section 42.13 of the Penal Code states that it is a Class B misdemeanor to knowingly direct a laser pointer at a law enforcement officer.

Illuminating an aircraft

Section 42.14 of the Penal Code declares that it is a Class C misdemeanor to intentionally direct a laser pointer or other light source at an aircraft if the light has sufficient intensity to impair the pilot's control. If the illumination does affect the pilot's ability to control the aircraft, this offense is upgraded to a Class A misdemeanor.

Prostitution

Section 43.02 of the Penal Code states that it is a Class B misdemeanor to engage in or offer to engage in sexual conduct for a fee, or to solicit another person to engage in sexual conduct for hire. Prostitution is illegal for both the person providing payment and the person receiving payment. People who have been previously convicted once or twice of prostitution may be charged with a Class A misdemeanor. People who have been convicted three or more times may be charged with a state jail felony.

Profiting from prostitution

Section 43.03 of the Penal Code declares that it is a Class A misdemeanor to receive money based on prostitution or to solicit another person to engage in sexual conduct with another person in exchange for compensation.

Promoting a prostitution enterprise

Section 43.04 of the Penal Code states that it is illegal to own, finance, control, or manage a prostitution enterprise that employs more than one prostitute. Aggravated promotion of prostitution is a third-degree felony.

Compelling another person into prostitution

Section 43.05 of the Penal Code states that it is illegal to compel another person by force or threat to commit prostitution, or to compel a person younger than 18 years to commit prostitution. Compelling prostitution is a second-degree felony.

Mandatory evidence and testimony in prostitution cases

Section 43.06 of the Penal Code states that any person involved in a prosecution related to prostitution may be forced to provide evidence or testify. However, people who are required to provide evidence or testify may not be prosecuted and may not have their evidence or testimony used against them, except in cases of aggravated perjury. It is possible to convict somebody of a prostitution-related offense simply with the uncorroborated testimony of one party.

Obscene display

Section 43.22 of the Penal Code declares that it is illegal to intentionally or knowingly present or disseminate an obscene visual representation, like a photograph or drawing, or to be recklessly negligent about displaying such materials in the presence of a person who would be alarmed or offended. Obscene display or distribution is a Class C misdemeanor.

Obscenity

Section 43.23 of the Penal Code states that it is illegal to promote or intend to promote wholesale an obscene material or device. These forms of obscenity are state jail felonies. It is also illegal to promote any obscene material or device or to help present an obscene performance. These forms of obscenity are Class A misdemeanors. If the obscene material contains a depiction of a child younger than 18 years of age, the charge is raised to a state jail felony.

Harmful material to a minor

Section 43.24 of the Penal Code states that it is illegal to sell, distribute, or present harmful material to a minor. It is also illegal to display harmful material while being recklessly negligent about the presence of minors. These offenses are Class A misdemeanors unless they involve the employment or use of a minor to accomplish the unlawful presentation, in which case they are upgraded to third-degree felonies.

Illegal inducement of a minor into sexual performance

Section 43.25 of the Penal Code states that it is illegal to employ, authorize, or induce a person younger than 18 to engage in sexual conduct or sexual performance. Parents and guardians may be found guilty of this charge if they consent to the participation of their child in a sexual performance. These are second-degree felonies, unless the child is younger than 14, in which case they are first-degree felonies.

Possession of child pornography

Section 43.26 of the Penal Code declares that it is illegal to knowingly or intentionally possess an image of a child younger than 18 years of age engaging in sexual conduct. Possession or promotion of child pornography is a third-degree felony.

Duty to report child pornography

Section 43.27 of the Penal Code states that any business that handles visual material and identifies some content as being possible child pornography should report it to a local law enforcement agency.

Unlawful carrying of a weapon

Section 46.02 of the Penal Code states that it is illegal to intentionally, knowingly, or recklessly carry a handgun, club, or illegal knife when not on one's own property or inside or en route to one's motor vehicle. Unlawfully carrying a weapon is a Class A misdemeanor, unless it is perpetrated on premises licensed to sell alcohol, in which case it is a third-degree felony.

Places where weapons are prohibited

Section 46.03 of the Penal Code lists some of the places in which weapons are prohibited. Weapons are prohibited at schools, educational institutions, polling places, racetracks, airports, sites of authorized

- 63 -

execution, and government buildings. Carrying an unauthorized weapon in a prohibited location is a third-degree felony.

Unlawful possession of firearms by a convicted felon

Section 46.04 of the Penal Code states that it is illegal for a felon to possess a firearm within five years of being released from confinement, parole, or mandatory supervision. It is also illegal for a convicted felon to possess a firearm at any place other than his home. The unlawful possession of a firearm by a convicted felon is a third-degree felony.

Prohibited weapons

Section 46.05 of the Penal Code lists some prohibited weapons. It is illegal to intentionally or knowingly possess, manufacture, transport, repair, or sell a machine gun, brass knuckles, armor-piercing bullets, a switchblade knife, an explosive weapon, a zip gun, a chemical dispensing device, a silencer, or a short-barrel firearm. A person may defend himself against a prohibited weapons charge if acting in his capacity as a member of the military or law enforcement, if the possession was pursuant to a lawful registration, or if the weapon was being treated solely as an antique. Otherwise, dealing with prohibited weapons is a third-degree felony.

Unlawful transfer of certain weapons

Section 46.06 of the Penal Code states that it is illegal to sell, lease, or give a handgun with the knowledge that the recipient intends to use it unlawfully. It is also illegal to intentionally or knowingly provide any weapon to a child younger than 18 years. It is illegal to intentionally, knowingly, or recklessly sell a firearm or ammunition to an intoxicated person. It is illegal to knowingly sell a firearm or ammunition to a convicted felon within five years of his release from confinement or parole. It is illegal to provide a handgun to a person at whom an active protective order is directed, and it is illegal for a person with an active protective order directed at him to receive a handgun. All of these offenses, collectively known as unlawful transfer of certain weapons, are Class A misdemeanors, unless the offense involves providing a handgun to a minor, which is a state jail felony.

Interstate purchase of firearms and related products

Section 46.07 of the Penal Code authorizes residents of Texas to purchase firearms, ammunition, and related products in other states.

Hoax bombs

Section 46.08 of the Penal Code states that it is illegal to make, sell, purchase, or possess a hoax bomb for the purpose of fooling other people or alarming emergency agencies. These offenses are Class A misdemeanors.

Knowingly possess components of an explosive weapon

Section 46.09 of the Penal Code states that it is illegal to knowingly possess the components of an explosive weapon with the intent to combine them for use in any criminal acts. Possession of the components of explosives is a third-degree felony.

Possession of deadly weapons during confinement

Section 46.10 of the Penal Code states that it is illegal for a person confined in a penal institution to intentionally, knowingly, or recklessly carry or possess a deadly weapon. This is a third-degree felony.

Possession of weapons near a school

Section 46.11 of the Penal Code states that weapons charges are increased to the next-highest category of defense if they are

- 64 -

committed knowingly within 300 feet of a school or in a place where a school function is taking place.

Criminal negligence by allowing a child access to a firearm

Section 46.13 of the Penal Code states that a person may be charged with a crime if his criminal negligence results in a child gaining access to a readily dischargeable firearm. This criminal negligence may include failing to secure the firearm or leaving it in an accessible place. This is a Class C misdemeanor, unless the child discharges the firearm and causes death or serious injury to himself or another person, in which case the offense is a Class A misdemeanor.

Firearms smuggling

Section 46.14 of the Penal Code states that it is illegal to knowingly transport or transfer a firearm known to have been acquired in violation of state or federal laws. A person is considered to have engaged in the business of firearms smuggling if he does so more than once or for remuneration. Firearms smuggling is a third-degree felony, unless it involves three or more firearms in a single episode, in which case it is a second-degree felony.

Gambling and bookmaking

Section 47.02 of the Penal Code declares that it is a Class C misdemeanor to make a bet on the result of a game or contest, to make a bet on the result of a political election, or to make bets for anything of value in a game played with cards, balls, dice, etc. A person may defend against charges of gambling by proving that the actions took place in private, that no economic benefit other than personal winnings was received, and that all participants had the same chances. Section 47.03 of the Penal Code states that it is a Class A misdemeanor to run a gambling operation or engage in bookmaking.

Personal property to be used for gambling

Section 47.04 of the Penal Code declares that it is a Class A misdemeanor to knowingly use or allow another person to use any of one's own property as a gambling place. A person may defend himself against these charges by proving that the gambling occurred in private, that no person received a benefit other than his winnings, and that all participants had the same chances.

Promoting gambling

Section 47.05 of the Penal Code states that it is a Class A misdemeanor to knowingly communicate information that will promote or further gambling.

Possessing gambling equipment or paraphernalia

Section 47.06 of the Penal Code states that it is a Class A misdemeanor to own, manufacture, transfer, or possess gambling equipment or paraphernalia. A person may defend himself against this charge by arguing that the object was to be used in private, that no party would receive any benefit other than personal winnings, and that all the participants would have the same chances of success.

Smoking in forbidden locations

Section 48.01 of the Penal Code states that it is illegal to smoke inside a public school, elevator, enclosed theater, library, museum, hospital, bus, plane, or train. A person accused of this crime may defend himself by stating that there is not a conspicuous sign prohibiting smoking. Also, all of the above named places must be equipped with ashtrays. Smoking in a forbidden location is a Class C misdemeanor.

Trading human organs

Section 48.02 of the Penal Code States that it is illegal to knowingly or intentionally buy or sell any human organ for valuable consideration, unless this is done in the context of medical service. The purchase and sale of human organs is a Class A misdemeanor.

Public intoxication

Section 49.02 of the Penal Code states that it is illegal to appear in a public place while intoxicated to a dangerous degree. Public intoxication is a Class C misdemeanor.

Open container laws

Section 49.031 of the Penal Code states that it is illegal to knowingly possess an open container of an alcoholic beverage in the passenger area of a moving or parked vehicle. This is a Class C misdemeanor.

Section 49.04 of the Penal Code states that it is illegal to operate a motor vehicle in a public place while intoxicated. In most cases this is a Class B misdemeanor with a minimum confinement of 72 hours. If a person is convicted of driving while intoxicated with an open container of alcohol in his immediate possession, the offense is a Class B misdemeanor with a minimum confinement of six days.

Driving intoxicated

Intoxicated with a child passenger
Section 49.045 of the Penal Code states that it is illegal to operate a motor vehicle in public while intoxicated and with a passenger who is younger than 15 years. Driving while intoxicated with a child passenger is a state jail felony. Section 49.05 of the Penal Code states that it is a Class B misdemeanor, with a minimum confinement of 72 hours, to operate aircraft while intoxicated.

Operating a watercraft
Section 49.06 of the Penal Code states that it is a Class B misdemeanor, with a minimum confinement of 72 hours, to operate a watercraft while intoxicated.

Committing assault
Section 49.07 of the Penal Code states that it is illegal to commit assault, either by accident or mistake, while intoxicated and operating an aircraft, watercraft, or motor vehicle. Causing serious bodily injury to another person while intoxicated is a third-degree felony.
Intoxication manslaughter
Section 49.08 of the Penal Code declares that it is a second-degree felony to operate a vehicle while intoxicated and accidentally cause the death of another person. This offense is known as intoxication manslaughter.

Entitlement defense
Section 49.10 of the Penal Code states that a person may not defend himself against charges related to operating a vehicle while intoxicated on the grounds that he has been entitled to use the intoxicating substance.

Culpable mental state
Section 49.11 of the Penal Code states that it is not necessary to prove a culpable mental state in order to convict a person on a charge related to operating a vehicle while intoxicated.

Gang-related crime

Section 71.02 of the Penal Code states that it is illegal to commit any of the following acts in coordination or as a member of a criminal street gang: murder, arson, robbery, kidnapping, assault, forgery, vehicle burglary, gambling, prostitution, weapons violations, drug violations, or obscenity. When these offenses are committed as part of a criminal street gang, they are upgraded one category higher than the most serious offense committed. Conspiring to commit one of these acts is treated the same as if the act was committed.

Required evidence or testimony
Section 71.04 of the Penal Code states that a party to a gang-related offense may be required to furnish evidence or testify, but

this evidence or testimony may not be used to prosecute that person, except for aggravated perjury or contempt of court.

<u>Renunciation defense in a prosecution</u>
Section 71.05 of the Penal Code states that a person may offer an affirmative defense to prosecution for gang-related crimes by demonstrating a voluntary and complete renunciation of the group before the commission of the offense.

Traffic

Driving without a license

Section 521.021 of the Transportation Code forbids people from driving without a driver's license.

License exemptions

Section 521.027 of the Transportation Code names some exemptions to the driver's license requirement: United States or Texas military officers operating a service vehicle; operators of tractors, road machines, or other implements of husbandry; nonresidents on active duty in the United States armed forces; and spouses and dependent children of nonresidents serving in the armed forces who have a license in their home state.

New resident license restrictions

Section 521.029 of the Transportation Code declares that a person who enters Texas as a new resident may only use an out-of-state license for 90 days.

Class A and B licenses

Section 521.201 of the Transportation Code asserts that the department may not issue a license to anyone who is under 15 years of age or is demonstrably addicted to alcohol, a controlled substance, or another drug that impairs driving. The department also may not issue a driver's license to a person whose current driver's license in Texas or elsewhere has been suspended, revoked, or canceled. Texas will not issue a driver's license to any person who has been declared by a court to be incapable of driving, who has a mental or physical disability that prevents driving, or has been reported by a court for failure to pay a fine for a misdemeanor.

Section 521.203 of the Transportation Code states that Class A and B driver's licenses may not be issued to people who are under 17 years of age, or to people who are under 18 years of age unless they have completed a driver training course.

Section 521.081 of the Transportation Code declares that a Class A driver's license authorizes a person to operate a vehicle with a gross vehicle weight rating of more than 26,000 pounds. Section 521.082 of the Transportation Code declares that a Class B driver's license authorizes the holder to operate a vehicle with a gross weight rating of more than 26,000 pounds or a bus with a seating capacity of 24 or more.

Class C licenses

Section 521.204 of the Transportation Code declares that Class C driver's licenses may only be issued to applicants under 18 years of age if the applicant is 16 or older, has completed a driver education course, and has either earned a high school diploma or is currently studying to earn one. Also, minors need parental or guardian permission and must pass an examination to earn a Class C driver's license.

Section 521.083 of the Transportation Code declares that a Class C driver's license authorizes a person to operate vehicles with a gross weight rating of less than 26,000 pounds.

Class M license

Section 521.084 of the Transportation Code declares that a Class M driver's license authorizes the holder to operate a motorcycle or moped.

Section 521.085 of the Transportation Code declares that a driver's license authorizes the holder to operate any vehicle of the type for which that class of license is issued, as well as any lesser type of vehicle besides a motorcycle or moped.

Provisional driver's licenses

Section 521.123 of the Transportation Code declares that people between the ages of 18 and 21 will be issued provisional driver's licenses that clearly indicate the age of the holder and are distinguishable from other licenses.

Restriction or require an endorsement

Section 521.221 of the Transportation Code declares that the department may impose a restriction or require an endorsement related to the type of vehicle a holder may operate, or the special equipment a holder is required to use. A license may also indicate when the holder is allowed to operate a vehicle.

Instruction permits and hardship licenses

Section 521.222 of the Transportation Code declares that people from the ages of 15 to 17 who satisfactorily complete an approved driver education course and pass the examination may be issued a Class A or B driver's license instruction permit. People over the age of 18 may receive an instruction permit after passing all parts of driver education except for the test. An instruction permit entitles the holder to operate a motor vehicle when accompanied by a person who has a driver's license, has at least one year of driving experience, and is at least 21 years old. Section 521.223 of the Transportation Code declares that the department may issue a hardship license to an applicant who is 15 years of age or older in special circumstances, so long as the applicant has passed a driver education course. Hardship licenses may be granted if they are necessary because of economic circumstances or illness.

Restricted Class M licenses

Section 521.224 of the Transportation Code declares that the department may issue a restricted Class M license that only authorizes the operation of a motorcycle with a piston displacement of less than 250 cubic centimeters. A person from the ages of 15 to 17 may obtain a restricted motorcycle license if they pass a motorcycle operator training course.

Moped licenses

Section 521.225 of the Transportation Code declares that a driver's license is required to operate a moped. Also, a person must be at least 15 years old to apply for a moped license. To earn a moped license, applicants must pass an exam.

License and driving without a valid license

Section 521.025 of the Transportation Code declares that vehicle operators are required to carry the appropriate license and to display it on the demand of a law enforcement official. Failure to carry or display a license is a misdemeanor.

Licenses suspended because of racing violations

Section 521.350 of the Transportation Code declares that a person whose license is suspended for racing a motor vehicle will lose their license for one year, and will be required to perform at least 10 hours of community service.

Cancelled, suspended, revoked, or expired licenses

Section 521.457 of the Transportation Code declares that it is illegal to drive with a canceled, suspended, revoked, or expired driver's license. This offense is typically a Class C misdemeanor.

Driver's license requirements

Section 522 of the Transportation Code discusses driver's license regulations, but does not pertain to certain types of vehicles. Specifically, this chapter does not apply to farm equipment, fire trucks and other emergency vehicles, military vehicles, and recreational vehicles driven for personal use.

Commercial driver's licenses

Section 522.011 of the Transportation Code states that a person may not drive a commercial motor vehicle without the appropriate commercial driver's license or without having a commercial driver learner's permit and being accompanied by a person who holds a license.

Commercial driver's license permits

Section 522.014 of the Transportation Code states that the department is allowed to issue a commercial driver learner's permit to people who have passed the Texas vision and written driver education tests.

Nonresident commercial driver's licenses

Section 522.013 of the Transportation Code declares that the department may issue a nonresident commercial driver's license to a person whose home jurisdiction has been deemed to have insufficient testing standards for drivers. However, a person who applies for one of these licenses must surrender the license he was issued in his home jurisdiction. The license issued in Texas must include the word "nonresident." Nonresident licenses must expire no more than 60 days after being issued. A person may not receive more than one non-resident commercial driver's license.

Driver's license waivers for farm employees

Section 522.012 of the Transportation Code states that departments may waive the knowledge and skill tests related to driver education for employees of farm-related service industries. These people may be issued restricted commercial driver's licenses.

Endorsements for these licenses

Section 522.015 of the Transportation Code states a person may drive a commercial motor vehicle in Texas if he has a commercial driver's license or commercial driver learner's permit issued by another state that is in compliance with the minimum federal standards for driver education or by a foreign jurisdiction approved by the United States Department of Transportation. A person may drive with such an out-of-jurisdiction license so long as he has not had a home in Texas for more than 30 days.

Section 522.042 of the Transportation Code lists some of the endorsements for commercial driver's licenses. The department may issue endorsements that authorize the operation of vehicles transporting hazardous materials or towing a double or triple trailer. An endorsement may authorize the driving of a tank or a vehicle carrying many passengers. An endorsement may authorize the operation of a school bus. It is illegal to operate a special vehicle without receiving the endorsement. This is a Class C misdemeanor.

Restrictions

Section 522.043 of the Transportation Code lists the restrictions a department may place on a commercial driver's license. The department may issue a restriction that prevents the license holder from driving a vehicle with air brakes, or from driving a commercial vehicle engaged in interstate commerce. Violating these restrictions is a Class C misdemeanor.

Driving with a disqualified license

Section 522.071 of the Transportation Code states that it is illegal to operate a commercial motor vehicle after being denied a license or after having one's license disqualified. This offense is a misdemeanor.

Compliance with official traffic control devices

Section 522.072 of the Transportation Code states that it is illegal for an employer to knowingly permit a person to drive a commercial motor vehicle when that person has been disqualified from doing so. This is a Class B misdemeanor for the employer.

Section 544.004 of the Transportation Code states that vehicle operators must apply with official traffic control devices unless they are operating an authorized emergency vehicle or are otherwise directed by a law enforcement officer.

Traffic control signals

Section 544.005 of the Transportation Code states that it is illegal to interfere with any part of an official traffic control device or railroad signal.

Prohibited signs and marks on the highway

Section 544.006 of the Transportation Code states that it is illegal to place or display an authorized sign, signal, or device on or in view of a highway if that object attempts to direct traffic flow, looks like an official traffic control device or railroad signal, or diminishes the effectiveness of official traffic devices and signals. This provision of the Code also forbids authorities from putting commercial advertising on traffic signs and signals. There may be no flashing lights within 1000 feet of an intersection unless special authorization is given. Prohibited signs and marks are considered a public nuisance and may be removed without notice.

Approved lights for traffic control signals

Section 544.007 of the Transportation Code states that a traffic control signal with different-colored lights or arrows may only include green, yellow, or red.

Flashing red signals

Section 544.008 of the Transportation Code states that when the driver is faced by a flashing red signal, he must stop at the line indicated. If there is no stop line, the driver should stop before entering the nearest crosswalk at the intersection. If there is no crosswalk, the driver should stop as close to the intersecting roadway as is necessary to obtain a view of traffic.

Lane-direction-control signals

Section 544.009 of the Transportation Code states that when a lane-direction-control signal is placed over a highway lane, drivers may use lanes with green signals but not lanes with red signals.

Driving on the right

Section 545.051 of the Transportation Code states that drivers must stay on the right side of the roadway unless they are passing another vehicle, an obstruction necessitates otherwise, the roadway is divided into three lanes, or the roadway only permits one-way traffic. Slower drivers should drive in the right-hand lane unless passing another vehicle or preparing for a left turn. Section 545.052 of the Transportation Code states that a driver moving in the opposite direction of another driver should remain to the right and should give the other driver at least half of the traveled portion of the road.

Passing other vehicles

Section 545.053 of the Transportation Code declares that when passing another vehicle, drivers should pass on the left at a safe distance. When being passed, a driver should remain to the right and should not accelerate until completely passed by the other vehicle.

Passing

Section 545.054 of the Transportation Code states that a driver may not drive left of center on a roadway to pass another vehicle unless authorized and unless the left side of the road is clearly free of traffic for a sufficient distance. A passing driver should return to the authorized lane of travel as soon as possible and before coming within 200 feet of an approaching vehicle.

Obeying road signs

Section 545.055 of the Transportation Code states that drivers should obey all visible road signs, and should not drive on the left side in a no-passing zone. Section 545.056 of the Transportation Code states that drivers may not be on the left side of the road when they are within 100 feet of an intersection, railroad crossing, bridge, or tunnel.

Passing on the right

Section 545.057 of the Transportation Code states that drivers may only pass on the right if it can be done safely and if the vehicle being passed is about to make a left turn. Drivers may not pass to the right in such a way that requires them to leave the main traveled portion of the road.

Driving on improved shoulders

Section 545.058 of the Transportation Code states that drivers may move onto an improved shoulder on the right of the main portion of the road if it is necessary and may be done safely. This maneuver may only be performed to park, accelerate before entering traffic, decelerate before turning right, pass another vehicle, allow another vehicle to pass, or avoid a collision. Drivers may only drive on the improved shoulder on the left portion of the road if it is safe and is necessary to avoid a collision or stop a disabled vehicle.

Staying within the proper lanes

Section 545.060 of the Transportation Code states that drivers on two-lane roads should stay within a single lane as much as possible. When a road is divided into three lanes and allows two-way movement, drivers should not enter the center lane except to pass another vehicle or to make a left turn.

Three-lane roads

Section 545.061 of the Transportation Code declares that on roads divided into three or more lanes with one-way traffic, drivers entering a lane from the right should yield the right of way to drivers entering the same lane from the left.

Following other vehicles

Section 545.062 of the Transportation Code declares that drivers who are behind other vehicles must maintain a safe distance in order to avoid a collision if the front vehicle suddenly stops.
Section 545.063 of the Transportation Code states that on a highway consisting of two or more roads separated by a space or barrier, drivers should always stay to the right, and should never cross over the space or barrier.

Entering limited- or controlled-access roadways

Section 545.064 of the Transportation Code states that drivers may not enter limited access or controlled access roadways except at authorized entrances or exits.

Stopping for school buses

Section 545.066 of the Transportation Code declares that drivers approaching a school bus from either direction must stop if the bus halts to receive or discharge a student. Drivers may not resume motion until the school bus does so, the driver of the school bus indicates that other drivers may begin, or the visual signal of the bus is no longer active.

On a highway with separate roadways, drivers on the opposite roadway are not required to stop for a school bus. Failing to stop for a school bus is a misdemeanor punishable by a fine of between $200 and $1000.

Making turns in an intersection

Section 545.101 of the Transportation Code states that right turns at intersections should be made as closely as possible to the right-hand curb or edge of the road. Left turns should be approached from the leftmost lane available. On roads designed for two-way traffic, an operator making a left turn should turn in the section of the intersection to the left of center as much as possible.

U-turns

Section 545.102 of the Transportation Code declares that drivers may not make a U-turn when approaching a curve or crest that makes it impossible for their vehicle to be seen from a distance of 500 feet or less.

Turn signals

Section 545.104 of the Transportation Code states that drivers must use the appropriate turn signals to indicate their intention to move right or left. Drivers are required to display the signals for no less than the last 100 feet of movement before the turn. Drivers should not use turn signals to indicate that other drivers should pass.

Stop signals

Section 545.105 of the Transportation Code states that a driver may not stop or suddenly decelerate without giving a stop signal.

Signal lamps

Section 545.106 of the Transportation Code declares that stop signals must be given with the hand or approved lighting signal lamps.

All motor vehicles on the highway must be equipped with signal lamps.

Hand signals

Section 545.107 of the Transportation Code declares that when a driver is authorized to give hand and arm signals, these should be given from the left side of the vehicle. A left turn signal is made by extending the hand and arm horizontally, and a right turn signal is made by extending the hand and arm upward. The intention to stop or decelerate is indicated by extending the hand and arm downward.

Stopping at intersections or paved roads

Section 545.151 of the Transportation Code declares that drivers should stop or yield when approaching an intersection if they are commanded to by a stop sign or light. If a traffic signal is present but not lit, drivers should stop at the intersection. The driver on a single- or two-lane road who approaches an intersection not controlled by a light or sign should yield to any car currently in the intersection. The operator of a vehicle on an unpaved street approaching a paved street should yield to cars on the paved street.

Yielding when making a left turn

Section 545.152 of the Transportation Code states that vehicles making a left turn should yield to vehicles approaching from the opposite direction.

Right of way at intersections

Section 545.153 of the Transportation Code declares that a stop or yield sign may indicate a preferential right of way at an intersection. When a driver approaches an intersection controlled by a yield sign, he should slow to a reasonable speed and yield the right of way to any vehicles already in the intersection.

Entering a highway from a private road

Section 545.155 of the Transportation Code states that vehicles entering a highway from a private road or driveway should yield the right of way to vehicles approaching on the highway.

Yielding to emergency vehicles.

Section 545.156 of the Transportation Code states that when a driver notices the approach of an authorized emergency vehicle using audible and visual signals, he should yield the right of way and immediately drive to a position parallel and as close as possible to the right curb. Drivers should stop and not resume motion until the authorized emergency vehicle has passed.

Passing stationary emergency vehicles

Section 545.157 of the Transportation Code states that when a driver is passing a stationary authorized emergency vehicle, the driver should leave the lane closest to the emergency vehicle if possible, and should slow down to a speed 20 mph less than the posted speed limit if the posted speed limit is 25 mph or more, or 5 mph if the speed limit is less than 25 mph. Failure to do so is a misdemeanor.

Stopping at railroad grade crossings

Section 545.251 of the Transportation Code states that drivers should not stop closer than 15 feet to or farther than 50 feet from the nearest rail when approaching a railroad grade crossing if the crossing gate is lowered, a signal indicates a train is approaching, a train is emitting an audible signal, or a train is plainly visible. Failure to stop is punishable by a fine ranging from $50 to $200.

Protocol for buses
Section 545.253 of the Transportation Code states that buses must stop at all railroad grade crossings. The driver should stop no closer than 15 feet and no farther than 50 feet from the nearest rail. The driver should listen and look in both directions for an approaching train, and should not resume motion until it is safe to do so. Failing to stop a bus at a railroad grade crossing is punishable by a fine ranging from $50 to $200. Section 545.256 of the Transportation Code states that drivers emerging from an alley, driveway, or building must stop before moving onto the sidewalk. Drivers in this situation must yield the right of way to pedestrians, and must yield the right of way to approaching vehicles as they enter the roadway.

Illegal parking

Section 471.007 of the Transportation Code states that it is illegal for a railway company to have a train obstruct a street, railroad crossing, or highway for more than 10 minutes. This offense is punishable by a fine of between $100 and $300. Section 545.301 of the Transportation Code states that drivers may not work or stop on the main traveled part of a highway outside of a business or residence district unless stopping elsewhere is impossible, there is enough unobstructed road to allow passage for other vehicles, and the vehicle is visible for at least 200 feet in both directions. These rules do not apply to disabled vehicles or vehicles involved in the removal or transportation of waste from a location near the highway.

Prohibited parking zones

Section 545.302 of the Transportation Code declares that drivers may not stop alongside another car, on the sidewalk, in an intersection, or on a crosswalk. Drivers may not stop or park alongside roadwork when this obstructs traffic, or where an official sign prohibits stopping. Drivers may not stop on a railroad track, on a bridge, or between a safety zone and the adjacent curb. Also, drivers may not stop for more than a moment in front of a public or private driveway, within 15 feet of a fire hydrant, within 20 feet of an intersection crosswalk, within 30 feet of a road sign, or within 20 feet of the entrance to a fire station.

Proper parking position

Section 545.303 of the Transportation Code states that drivers must park in such a manner that the right-hand wheels of the vehicle are parallel to and within 18 inches of the right-hand curb or road edge. On a one-way road, drivers should stop with the car parked in the direction of authorized traffic movement, and within 18 inches of a curb.

Moving unattended vehicles

Section 545.305 of the Transportation Code states that peace officers may move unattended vehicles that are unlawfully stopped when they are obstructing traffic, are reported stolen, or are believed to have been abandoned. Officers may also move an unattended vehicle if they believe it will interfere with the normal functions of emergency services. In such a case, the officer may have the vehicle impounded or moved to a safer location.

Removing personal property

Section 545.3051 of the Transportation Code states that officers may remove personal property from the road if it is obstructing traffic or endangering personal safety. This may be done without the consent of the property owner. The property owner will in fact be liable for any cost of removal and disposition of the property. Also, the law enforcement officer is not liable for any damage to personal property during such an operation.

General speeding rules

Section 545.351 of the Transportation Code states that drivers may not travel at a speed greater than is reasonable and prudent under the present circumstances. Drivers should reduce their speed appropriately when approaching a hill crest, traveling on a narrow winding road, or crossing an intersection or railroad grade crossing.

Speed limits

Section 545.352 of the Transportation Code states that the speed limit on an urban street is 30 mph, and 15 mph in an urban alley. The speed limit is 70 mph on state and federal numbered highways. On highways not numbered by the state or federal government, the speed limit is 60 mph.

Motorcycles speed limits

Section 545.361 of the Transportation Code states that motorcycles may not go faster than 35 mph at night unless they are equipped with a headlight that can reveal a person or vehicle 300 feet ahead. A vehicle with solid rubber or cushion tires may not travel faster than 10 mph.

Slow driving

Section 545.363 of the Transportation Code states that drivers may not travel so slowly that they impede the normal movement of traffic.

Exemptions to speeding rules

Section 545.365 of the Transportation Code states that speed regulations do not apply to authorized emergency vehicles, police patrols, or doctors or ambulances responding to an emergency. However, municipal ordinances may regulate the speed of ambulances and emergency medical services vehicles.

Reckless driving

Section 545.401 of the Transportation Code defines reckless driving as operating a vehicle in willful or wanton disregard for the safety of persons or property. Reckless driving is a misdemeanor punishable by a $200 fine, a maximum confinement in county jail of 30 days, or both.

Setting a vehicle in motion

Section 545.402 of the Transportation Code states that drivers may not initiate motion from a standstill until they can do so safely.

Safety zones

Section 545.403 of the Transportation Code states that drivers may not travel through or in safety zones.

Protocol for stopping a car

Section 545.404 of the Transportation Code states that drivers may not leave their vehicles unattended without stopping the engine, removing the key from the ignition, setting the parking brake, and turning the front wheels towards the curb or side of the road when on a grade.

Following a fire truck

Section 545.407 of the Transportation Code states that drivers may not follow a fire truck from less than 500 feet when the truck is performing its duties. Drivers also may not enter or park their vehicles in a block where a fire truck is stopped to answer an alarm.

Passing over a fire hose

Section 545.408 of the Transportation Code states that drivers may not travel over an unprotected fire hose unless given permission by firemen.

Child safety seats

Section 545.412 of the Transportation Code states that it is illegal to drive with a child who is younger than 8 years and is not secured in a child passenger safety seat system, unless the child is taller than 4 feet 9 inches. This is a misdemeanor punishable by a fine of no more than $25 the first time and no more than $250 each subsequent time.

Safety belts

Section 545.413 of the Transportation Code states that it is illegal for a person at least 15 years old to be riding in the seat of a vehicle equipped with a safety belt and not be using the safety belt. This is a misdemeanor punishable by fine of between $25 and $50.

Riding in the bed of a truck or trailer

Section 545.414 of the Transportation Code states that it is illegal to drive with a person younger than 18 years in the bed of a truck or trailer. This is a misdemeanor punishable by a fine of between $25 and $200. Section 545.415 of the Transportation Code states that vehicles should not be moved in reverse unless this can be done safely and without obstructing traffic. Vehicles may not be backed up on the shoulder of a highway.

Motorcycle operators and passengers

Section 545.416 of the Transportation Code states that motorcycle operators must ride on the appropriate seat, and may not carry passengers unless the motorcycle is designed to accommodate more than one person. Motorcycle passengers must be at least 5 years old, or else the operator is guilty of a misdemeanor punishable by a fine of between $100 and $200. However, children under the ages of 5 may ride in motorcycle sidecars.

Obstructed view or control compromised

Section 545.417 of the Transportation Code states that drivers may not load their vehicles such that their view to the front or side is obstructed or their control over the driving mechanism is compromised. Also, passengers may not ride in any position that interferes with the driver's view or control of the vehicle.

Opening a door on the side of traffic

Section 545.418 of the Transportation Code states that drivers may not open their door on the side of moving traffic unless it can be done safely and without obstruction. A door on the side of traffic should not be left open longer than is necessary to load or unload passengers.

Occupying house trailers in motion

Section 545.419 of the Transportation Code states that people may not occupy house trailers in motion.

Operating a vehicle that is being towed

Section 545.4191 of the Transportation Code states that it is a Class B misdemeanor to operate a truck or tractor while another person operates a vehicle being towed by that truck or tractor.

Racing

Section 545.420 of the Transportation Code states that it is illegal for drivers to participate in races, acceleration contests, or tests of driving endurance. Racing is a Class B misdemeanor unless the driver is intoxicated or has been convicted previously, in which case the charges become more severe.

Failing to stop for a police officer

Section 545.421 of the Transportation Code states that it is illegal for a driver to willfully fail to stop or to attempt to flee a pursuing police vehicle that is issuing a visible or audible signal. This is a Class B misdemeanor, though it becomes a Class A misdemeanor if the offense includes reckless conduct that places other people in imminent danger of serious bodily injury.

Driving is prohibited

Section 545.422 of the Transportation Code states that vehicles may not be driven on sidewalks, hiking trails, or biking trails. Section 545.423 of the Transportation Code states that drivers may not travel across sidewalks or through driveways, business or residential entrances, or parking lots without stopping.

Restrictions on new drivers

Section 545.424 of the Transportation Code declares that in the year following the issuance of an original class A, B, or C driver's license, a person under 18 may not drive after midnight and before 5 a.m. or while carrying more than one non-family member under the age of 21. Those under the age of 17 who hold a restricted motorcycle or moped license may not drive after midnight and before 5 a.m. in the year after receiving this license unless in an emergency situation or within sight of their parent or guardian.

Driving while using a wireless device

Section 545.425 of the Transportation Code states that drivers may not use a wireless communication device within a school crossing zone unless the device does not require the use of hands or the vehicle is stopped.

School bus

Section 545.426 of the Transportation Code states that a person may not operate a school bus while the door is open or while the bus has more than the recommended number of passengers. School bus drivers should prohibit their passengers from standing or sitting anywhere besides seats.

Operators of emergency vehicles

Section 546.001 of the Transportation Code states that the operator of an authorized emergency vehicle may park anywhere, even when doing so violates other provisions of the Code. Emergency vehicles may also drive through red lights or stop signs, though they must slow down as much as is necessary to ensure safe passage. Emergency vehicles may also exceed the speed limit and ignore traffic rules, so long as they do not endanger life or property.

Emergency vehicle signal requirements

Section 546.003 of the Transportation Code states that emergency vehicles performing their duties must use audible and visual signals.

Exemptions to these requirements

Section 546.004 of the Transportation Code lists some exceptions to the required audible and visual signals. Officers are not required to use audible and visible signals when these signals may alert an offender and allow him to get away. Also, officers are not required to use audible and visual signals in rare cases when their use could reasonably be assumed to increase the chances of an accident.

Emergency vehicle operators

Section 546.005 of the Transportation Code states that, despite exigent circumstances, the operators of authorized emergency vehicles still have the duty to operate with appropriate regard for safety, and are still subject to liability for reckless disregard.

Chapter 547's applicability

Section 547.002 of the Transportation Code declares that the rules of this chapter do not apply to the following vehicles: implements of husbandry, road machinery, farm tractors, bicycles, and golf carts.

Violations

Section 547.004 of the Transportation Code declares that it is illegal to use a vehicle or permit a person to use a vehicle in such a way as to endanger a person or violate vehicle equipment standards or the provisions of Chapter 547. Improper equipment is a misdemeanor but may be dismissed for a small administrative fee or remediation.

Slow-moving-vehicle emblems

Section 547.005 of the Transportation Code declares that slow-moving-vehicle emblems may not be placed on stationary objects or non-slow-moving vehicles. Also, the words "school bus" may not be printed on any vehicle that is not used to transport people to or from school.

Required lighting

Section 547.302 of the Transportation Code declares that vehicles must use the required lighted lamps and illuminating devices at night and when light is so bad that a vehicle on the highway cannot be seen from a distance of 1000 feet. Also, vehicles must choose signaling devices prescribed by this chapter, and must have at least one illuminated lamp on each side of their front. However, no more than four headlights or bright lights may be illuminated on the front of a motor vehicle at the same time.

Signaling devices

Section 547.303 of the Transportation Code declares that with the exception of signaling devices, all the lights on the rear of a vehicle must be or reflect red. Signaling devices may be red, amber, or yellow. Section 547.304 of the Transportation Code declares that lighting requirements do not always apply to farm trailers, boat trailers, and mobile homes.

Vehicle light direction

Section 547.305 of the Transportation Code declares that any motor vehicle lamp that projects a beam of 300 candlepower or brighter and is not a headlamp, spot lamp, emergency lamp, or turn lamp must be directed so that no part of the beam encounters the road at a distance of more than 75 feet. Also, vehicles may only be equipped with alternately flashing lights if they are school buses, authorized emergency vehicles, tow trucks, or church buses. Except in rare cases, a person may not operate a vehicle that has a red light in the center front. Finally, people without authorization may not operate a vehicle equipped with a red, white, or blue blinking or flashing light.

Accordance with federal standards

Section 547.3215 of the Transportation Code declares that all lighting, reflective devices, and related equipment must comply with federal standards, unless specifically prohibited by chapter 547.

Headlamps

Section 547.321 of the Transportation Code declares that a motor vehicle must have at least two headlamps, each of which must be mounted at a height of between 24 and 54 inches, and at least one of which must be mounted on each side of the vehicle's front.

Tail lamps

Section 547.322 of the Transportation Code declares that trailers and vehicles being towed must be equipped with at least two tail lamps. Cars and trucks that were made before 1960 must have at least one tail lamp. Tail lamps should be as wide apart as possible, and should be at a height of between 15 and 72 inches. A tail light should be plainly visible 1000 feet from the rear of the vehicle. Also, vehicles should be equipped with a separate lamp that illuminates the rear license plate in such a manner that it can be read at a distance of 50 feet.

Stop lamp and turn signal requirements for motor vehicles

Section 547.323 of the Transportation Code declares that vehicles and trailers must have at least two stop lamps unless they were manufactured before 1960, in which case they are only required to have one stop lamp. Stop lamps should be mounted on the vehicle's rear, and should emit a red or amber light visible at a distance of 300 feet when the vehicle service brake is applied. It is permissible to include a stop lamp as part of another rear lamp.

Section 547.324 of the Transportation Code declares that vehicles and trailers manufactured after 1960 must have flashing electric turn signal lamps. These lamps should be mounted at the same level and as far apart as possible on the front and rear of the vehicle. They should emit a white or amber light if they are in the front and a red or amber light if they are in the rear. Turn signals should be visible from a distance of 500 feet if the vehicle is at least 80 inches wide, and at least 300 feet from the front and rear of the vehicle if it is less than 80 inches wide.

Reflector requirements

Section 547.325 of the Transportation Code declares that motor vehicles and trailers must have at least two red reflectors on their rear. This may be part of the tail lamp. Each reflector must be mounted at a height of between 15 and 60 inches, and must be visible at night from 100 to 600 feet when directly in front of low headlights, or from 100 to 350 feet when directly in front of upper headlights.

Section 547.326 of the Transportation Code declares that vehicles that are not required to have other lamps must have at least one lamp that emits a white light visible from a distance of at least 1000 feet from the front of the vehicle, as well as either two lamps that emits a red light visible 1000 feet behind the vehicle or one lamp visible from 1000 feet behind and two red reflectors visible from 150 feet behind.

Spot lamps

Section 547.327 of the Transportation Code declares that it is illegal for a motor vehicle to have more than two spot lamps. Also, spot lamps must not shine into the windshield, windows, mirrors, or cabin of other vehicles in use.

Fog lamps

Section 547.328 of the Transportation Code declares that motor vehicles may not have more than two fog lamps. A fog lamp must be mounted on the front of the vehicle between 12 and 30 inches high, and aimed so that no part of its beam projects higher than 4 inches below the level of the center of the lamp at a distance of 25 feet.

Auxiliary passing lamps

Section 547.329 of the Transportation Code states that motor vehicles may be equipped with no more than two auxiliary passing lamps, which must be mounted on the front of the vehicle at a height of between 24 and 42 inches.

Auxiliary driving lamps

Section 547.330 of the Transportation Code states that motor vehicles may have no more than two auxiliary driving lamps, which must be mounted on the front of the vehicle at a height of between 16 and 42 inches.

Hazard lights

Section 547.331 of the Transportation Code states that vehicles may be equipped with hazard lights, but that these lights must be mounted at the same level and spaced as far apart as possible on the front and rear of the vehicle. Hazard lights must be visible from a distance of at least 500 feet in normal light. Hazard lights should flash simultaneously, and should be either white or amber in front and either red or amber in the rear.

Extra lamps

Section 547.332 of the Transportation Code states that vehicles may also be equipped with no more than two side cowl or fender lamps and two or fewer running board courtesy lamps. All of these lamps must be amber or white without glare.

Lighting controls

Section 547.333 of the Transportation Code declares that headlamps should be arranged so that the driver can select different lighting, and may be arranged so that the vehicle adjusts the lighting automatically. Headlamps should be aimed so that they reveal a person or vehicle at a distance of at least 450 feet ahead at all times. The lowermost distribution of light in the headlight should reveal people or vehicles at a distance of 150 feet.

Farm equipment lighting requirements

Section 547.371 of the Transportation Code declares that farm tractors and other implements of husbandry must be equipped with two headlamps, at least one red lamp visible at least 1000 feet from the rear, and at least two red reflectors visible from 100 to 600 feet from the rear. Farmer equipment must also be equipped with hazard lamps that are visible in normal daylight from a distance of at least 1000 feet in front and behind. The lighting requirements are less strict for vehicles manufactured before 1972.

Farm equipment towing and combination vehicles

Section 547.372 of the Transportation Code declares that farm equipment being towed by a tractor must be equipped with at least two rear red reflectors mounted far enough apart to indicate the width of the vehicle and are visible from under 600 feet behind. It is possible to use reflective tape instead of reflectors, so long as the tape meets the visibility requirements.

Section 547.381 of the Transportation Code declares that motor vehicles operated in combination with other vehicles do not have to display any lamp besides a tail lamp in cases where the other lamps are hidden by other vehicles in the combination.

Towed vehicles

Section 547.382 of the Transportation Code declares that when a vehicle is towing something that extends at least 4 feet beyond the back of the vehicle, the thing being towed must display two red lamps visible from at least 500 feet behind, two red reflectors indicating width that are visible at night from 600 feet behind, and two red lamps indicating the maximum overhang that are visible from a distance of at least 500 feet from each side. In some cases, such a vehicle may be required to display red flags at least 12 inches square that mark the extremities of the load.

Section 547.383 of the Transportation Code states that vehicles must be equipped with at least one white or amber lamp that is visible 1000 feet from the front and a red light that is visible 1000 feet from the rear. These lamps must be mounted with at least one of them close to the side of the vehicle on which traffic passes. When these vehicles are parked on the side of a road, they must display one of these lamps.

Brake requirements

Section 547.401 of the Transportation Code declares that vehicles must be equipped with sufficient brakes. The only exceptions are for trailers with a gross weight of 4500 pounds or less, or with a gross weight of 15,000 pounds or less and a top speed of 30 mph.

Section 547.402 of the Transportation Code states that the brakes of a vehicle must operate on each wheel, except in the case of special mobile equipment or trailers being towed at a speed of no more than 30 mph. Trucks and tractors with at least three axles do not have to have brakes on the front wheels, though they must have brakes that operate on the wheels of at least one steerable axle. Breaks must be maintained in good working order.

Horns

Section 547.501 of the Transportation Code states that motor vehicles must be equipped with a horn audible under normal conditions at a distance of at least 200 feet. Only authorized commercial vehicles and emergency vehicles may be equipped with a siren, whistle, or bell. Warnings should only be used when necessary, and should not emit unreasonably loud or harsh sounds.

Parked large vehicles

Section 547.503 of the Transportation Code states that the operators of trucks, buses, or trailers that are at least 80 inches wide or 30 feet long must immediately display hazard lamps unless they are parked lawfully in an urban district, stopped to receive or discharge a passenger, or stopped at the direction of a police officer.

Safety belts

Section 547.601 of the Transportation Code declares that motor vehicles must be equipped with safety belts if these belts were part of the vehicle's original equipment.

Rear-view mirrors

Section 547.602 of the Transportation Code states that all motor vehicles must be equipped with a mirror that provides a view of the road at least 200 feet behind the rear of the vehicle.

Clean moisture from windshield

Section 547.603 of the Transportation Code states that motor vehicles must include equipment to clean moisture from the windshield.

Muffler

Section 547.604 of the Transportation Code states that motor vehicles must be equipped with a working muffler to prevent excess noise.

Exhaust systems, and smoking vehicles

Section 547.605 of the Transportation Code states that the engine and power system of a motor vehicle must prevent the escape of excessive smoke or fumes. Also, motor vehicles manufactured after 1967 must prevent the discharge of crank case emissions into the atmosphere. It is illegal for a person to operate or allow another person to operate a vehicle that emits visible smoke for 10 or more seconds or smoke that remains suspended in the air for 10 seconds or more. This offense is a misdemeanor punishable by a fine of between $1 and $350.

Safety flaps

Section 547.606 of the Transportation Code states that tractors, trailers, and trucks that have at least four tires on the rearmost axle must be equipped with safety guards or flaps that are approved by the department and are suspended by the rearmost wheels within 4 inches of the ground.

Sun screening devices

Section 547.609 of the Transportation Code states that sun screening devices must have a legible label that includes the necessary information regarding light transmission and luminous reflectance. If a sun screening device is placed on a windshield or a side or rear window, it must include a permanent label indicating its compliance with Section 547.613(b)(1) or (2).

Video equipment

Section 547.611 of the Transportation Code states that motor vehicles may be equipped with televisions, DVD players, and similar equipment only if it is located so that the driver cannot see it unless the vehicle is in park or the parking brake is applied. Licensed television station vehicles may have display screens visible from the side of the operator, but may only be used when the vehicle is stopped.

Section 547.613 of the Transportation Code declares that it is a misdemeanor to operate a vehicle in which some object or material on the windshield or side or rear window obstructs the view. It is also illegal to attach a transparent material that reduces light transmission through a windshield or other window. It is permissible to have a sun screening device on the windshield that allows light transmission of 25 percent or more and has a luminous reflectance of 25 percent or less.

School bus mirrors and colors

Section 547.701 of the Transportation Code states that a school bus must be equipped with a mirror that provides the operator with a view of the area immediately in front of the vehicle. A school bus must also have signal lamps that are mounted as high and as far apart as possible, display four alternately flashing red lights, and are visible from a distance of 500 feet in normal daylight. When a school bus is stopped so that students may enter or exit, the driver should activate all flashing warning signal lights. It is illegal to place advertising or other paid announcements on the side of a school bus if these distract from safe driving.

Section 547.7012 of the Transportation Code declares that activity buses may not be painted national school bus glossy yellow.

Sirens, whistles, and bells

Section 547.702 of the Transportation Code declares that authorized emergency vehicles may be equipped with sirens, whistles, or bells, provided these are approved by the department and are audible under normal conditions at least 500 feet away. These alarms should be used to alert other vehicle operators or pedestrians to the emergency vehicle's approach. Authorized emergency vehicles should also be equipped with signal lamps that are mounted as high and as far apart as possible, that display four alternately red flashing lights, and are visible from 500 feet away in normal light.

Slow-moving-vehicle emblem requirements

Section 547.703 of the Transportation Code states that slow-moving vehicles should display a slow-moving-vehicle emblem with a reflective surface visible at a distance of at least 500 feet. This emblem should be clean and should be mounted on the rear of the vehicle between 3 and 5 feet above the road surface.

Motorcycle lighting restrictions

Section 547.801 of the Transportation Code states that motorcycles should be equipped with no more than two headlamps between 24 and 54 inches above the ground. Motorcycles must also have at least one tail lamp between 20 and 72 inches above the ground, as well as a lamp that illuminates the rear license plate. Motorcycles must have at least one stop lamp and at least one red reflector on the rear. Motorcycles must also have multiple beam lighting equipment in which the uppermost distribution reveals a person or vehicle at least 300 feet ahead, the lowermost distribution illuminates a person or vehicle at least 150 feet away, and does not project into the eyes of approaching vehicle operators. Motorcycles may not be operated unless at least one headlamp is lit.

Vehicle inspection

Section 548.051 of the Transportation Code describes the vehicles and equipment that are subject to inspection in Texas. Motor vehicles, trailers, and mobile homes that are registered in Texas must have the following items inspected at an inspection station: tires, wheel assembly, safety guards or flaps (if required), brakes, steering, lights, horns, mirrors, windshield wipers, sun screening devices, front seatbelts, exhaust system, emission system, and fuel tank cap.

Bicycles

Section 551.001 of the Transportation Code states that the provisions of this chapter apply to bicycle riders on highways or paths set aside exclusively for bikes.

Section 551.002 of the Transportation Code states that in most cases the provisions of this chapter apply to mopeds and electric bicycles.

Section 551.101 of the Transportation Code states that except where indicated otherwise, a bicycle rider has the same rights and duties as a vehicle operator.

Bicycle rules

Section 551.102 of the Transportation Code states that bicycle riders must only ride on a permanent seat attached to the bicycle, and may not use the bicycle to carry more people than it is designed to carry. A person may not ride a bicycle carrying an object that prevents him from having at least one hand on the handlebars. Bicycles may not be attached to motor vehicles.

Section 551.103 of the Transportation Code states that a bicycle moving slower than other traffic should ride as far to the right of the road as possible, unless passing a slower vehicle or preparing to turn left. However, a person operating a bicycle on a one-way road with two or more marked lanes may ride as close to the left side as possible. Bicycle riders may ride two abreast, but may not ride more than two abreast unless they are on a road meant exclusively for bicycles.

Bicycle equipment requirements

Section 551.104 of the Transportation Code states that a person may not operate a bicycle that does not have a brake capable of making the wheels skid on dry, flat, clean pavement. A person may not operate a bicycle at night unless the bicycle has a lamp on the front that emits a white light visible from at least 500 feet, and has both a red reflector and a red light on the back, with the light visible from at least 500 feet.

Bicycle races

Section 551.105 of the Transportation Code states that competitive bicycle races may only be held on public roads with the approval of local law enforcement.

Electric personal assistive mobility devices

Section 551.202 of the Transportation Code states that a person may only operate an electric personal assistive mobility device on a public road with a speed limit of 30 mph or less if there is no sidewalk, if he is directed to do so by a traffic device or officer, or while crossing at a designated crosswalk. Electric personal assistive mobility devices may be used on bicycle paths. People using this sort of device should stay as close to the right side of the road as possible.

Sidewalk
Section 551.203 of the Transportation Code states that a person is allowed to operate an electric personal assistive mobility device on the sidewalk.

Speed restrictions
Section 551.303 of the Transportation Code states that neighborhood electric vehicles may only be operated on streets with a posted speed limit of 45 miles per hour or less. They may, however cross roads with a higher speed limit. People may not operate neighborhood electric vehicles at speeds greater than 35 mph or the posted speed limit, whichever is less.

Pocket bikes or minimotor bikes
Section 551.304 of the Transportation Code states that the rules of this chapter may not be interpreted to authorize the operation of minimotor bikes or pocket bikes on sidewalks, bicycle paths, or roads.

Motor-assisted scooters
Section 551.352 of the Transportation Code states that motor-assisted scooters may only be operated on roads with a posted speed limit of 35 mph or less. However, these scooters may cross roads with a higher speed limit. Governments and agencies may prohibit the operation of motor-assisted scooters in areas where it has been determined to be too dangerous.

Pedestrians

Section 552.001 of the Transportation Code states that traffic control signals apply to pedestrians unless the pedestrian is otherwise directed. When a pedestrian is facing a green signal (besides an arrow), he may the cross the road within a crosswalk. When a pedestrian is facing a steady red or yellow signal, he may not cross the road.

Section 552.002 of the Transportation Code states that pedestrian control signals that display the words "walk," "don't walk," or "wait" apply to pedestrians. Pedestrians should not begin crossing a roadway in the direction of a "don't walk" or "wait" signal. If the pedestrian has partially crossed a road when a "don't walk" or "wait" signal begins, he should proceed to the nearest sidewalk or safety island.

Right of way
Section 552.003 of the Transportation Code states that drivers must yield the right of way to pedestrians in crosswalks when there is no operating traffic control signal and the pedestrian is on the vehicle's half of the roadway. However, pedestrians are responsible for not leaving the curb in such a way that a vehicle does not have the opportunity to yield. Drivers may not pass other vehicles that have stopped to let pedestrians pass. When a person fails to honor these rules and causes serious bodily injury or death to a visually impaired or disabled person, this is a misdemeanor punishable by a maximum fine of $500 and 30 hours of community service.

Passage in crosswalks

Section 552.004 of the Transportation Code states that pedestrians should, if possible, walk on the right side of a crosswalk.

Where pedestrians should yield

Section 552.005 of the Transportation Code states that pedestrians should yield the right-of-way to vehicles when crossing in places other than a crosswalk. In the space between adjacent intersections at which traffic control signals are working, pedestrians should only cross at marked crosswalks. Pedestrians should only cross intersections diagonally if they are authorized to do so by a traffic control device.

Where pedestrians should walk

Section 552.006 of the Transportation Code states that pedestrians should not walk on the road if an adjacent sidewalk is provided. When a pedestrian must walk along the road, he should do so on the left side or the shoulder of the highway facing approaching traffic.

Drivers should yield to pedestrians

Drivers emerging from or entering alleys, buildings, or private roads should yield the right-of-way to pedestrians on the sidewalk.

Hitchhiking and soliciting

Section 552.007 of the Transportation Code states that pedestrians may not stand in the road to solicit bribes, money, or employment from drivers unless they have authorization to solicit charitable donations. People may not stand on or near a highway to solicit money in exchange for guarding vehicles while they are parked.

Driver responsibility regarding pedestrians

Section 552.008 of the Transportation Code states that drivers should exercise due care to avoid collisions with pedestrians. When necessary, drivers should alert pedestrians to their presence by sounding the horn.

Subtitle C's applicability

Section 543.001 of the Transportation Code declares that peace officers do not need a warrant to arrest any person found violating Subtitle C, Rules of the Road.

Taking violators before a magistrate

Section 543.002 of the Transportation Code declares that any person arrested for a violation of Subtitle C should immediately be taken before a magistrate if he requests or if the violation was the failure to stop at an accident. The magistrate should have jurisdiction and be the most accessible to the place of arrest.

Issuing written notices

Section 543.003 of the Transportation Code declares that a violator who is not taken before a magistrate should be given a written notice to appear in court at a particular time and place. The notice should also include the offense charged and the violator's identifying information.

Promises to appear in court

Section 543.004 of the Transportation Code declares that officers should issue written notices to appear for speeding or open container violations if the person makes a written promise to appear.

Section 543.005 of the Transportation Code declares that in order to be released from detention, the arrested person must promise in writing to appear in court.

Notices to appear, failure to deliver proper notice

Section 543.006 of the Transportation Code declares that the notice to appear must be set for a date at least 10 days after the arrest, unless the arrested person requests an earlier hearing. Also, the place specified in the notice should be before a magistrate with jurisdiction.

Section 543.008 of the Transportation Code declares that any failure to deliver a proper notice to appear is a misconduct by the officer that is punishable by firing.

Section 543.009 of the Transportation Code declares that a person who has promised in writing to appear in court may satisfy this requirement with an appearance from counsel, but a person who willfully violates a written promise to appear in court is guilty of a misdemeanor.

Section 543.010 of the Transportation Code declares that the complaint and the notice to appear on a charge of speeding should specify the maximum or minimum speed posted at the location as well as the speed at which the defendant was driving.

Motorcycle helmets

Section 661.003 of the Transportation Code states that it is illegal to drive or ride on a motorcycle on a public street or highway without wearing approved protective headgear. It is also illegal to carry a passenger on a motorcycle who is not wearing authorized protective headgear. However, a person may be exempt from these rules if he was at least 21 years old at the time and had completed a motorcycle operator training and safety course. Also, peace officers are not allowed to detain motorcycle operators or passengers for the sole purpose of determining whether they have passed such a course. Failing to wear a helmet on a motorcycle is a misdemeanor punishable by a fine of between $10 and $50. Section 661.004 of the Transportation Code declares that a peace officer may stop or detain any motorcycle operator or passenger in order to inspect his protective headgear for safety compliance.

All-terrain vehicle

Section 663.031 of the Transportation Code states that people may not operate all-terrain vehicles on public property unless they hold a safety certificate, are taking a safety course, or are under the direct supervision of an ATV-certified adult. Those who have received a safety certificate must carry it while operating an all-terrain vehicle, and must display the certificate when commanded to do so by any law enforcement officer.

Age limits
Section 663.032 of the Transportation Code states that anyone under the age of 14 must be accompanied by a parent or guardian or an adult authorized by their parent or guardian while operating an all-terrain vehicle.

Mandatory equipment
Section 663.033 of the Transportation Code states that all-terrain vehicles operated on public property must have functioning brake and muffler systems, as well as a United States Forest Service-qualified spark arrester. These vehicles must display lighted headlights and taillights when operating on public property in the interval from a half-hour after sunset to a half-hour before sunrise, or when visibility is reduced.

Personal protection for operators
Section 663.034 of the Transportation Code states that a person may not operate or ride on an all-terrain vehicle on public property without an approved safety helmet and eye protection.

Public property
Section 663.035 of the Transportation Code states that people may not operate all-terrain vehicles on public property in a careless or reckless manner such that people or property is endangered or damaged.

Passengers
Section 663.036 of the Transportation Code states that a person may not carry a passenger on an all-terrain vehicle on public

property if the all-terrain vehicle is not designed to hold passengers.

Public roads

Section 663.037 of the Transportation Code states that it is illegal to operate an all-terrain vehicle on a public road except in certain situations. For instance, ATV drivers may cross a public road (not an interstate) if they stop completely before crossing, yield the right of way to oncoming traffic, and cross quickly, directly, and safely. Operators may also drive ATVs on public roads if the transportation is in connection with agricultural work or utility services. This type of transportation must occur during the daytime, with all lights illuminated and with an eight-foot long pole holding a triangular orange flag on the back of the vehicle. Section 663.038 of the Transportation Code states that any offenses related to the use of all-terrain vehicles are Class C misdemeanors unless designated otherwise.

Disabled-parking placards

Section 681.002 of the Transportation Code states that the Department of Transportation must provide for the issuance of disabled-parking placards. These placards must be two-sided and hooked. Each side of the placard must include the international symbol of access, centered and at least 3 inches tall. The standard is for the symbol to be white on a blue shield for people with permanent disabilities, and white on a red shield for people with temporary disabilities. The placard must also include an identification number, an expiration date at least 3 inches high, and a seal or other identification of the department. These placards should also contain a hologram preventing their reproduction.

Disabled drivers

Section 681.006 of the Transportation Code states that a vehicle that is being operated by or transporting a disabled person and has a disabled-parking placard and special license plates may be parked for an unlimited time in a special parking place. Also, the owner of such a vehicle is exempt from fees or penalties related to meters.

Create parking for disabled drivers

Section 681.009 of the Transportation Code states that political subdivisions and property owners may designate one or more parking spaces for the exclusive use of disabled people. Also, political subdivisions may require property owners to designate parking spaces for disabled people.

Enforce disabled parking rules

Section 681.010 of the Transportation Code states that peace officers and security guards responsible for enforcing parking regulations may file charges against people who unlawfully park in a space designated for disabled people.

Violations of the rights of disabled drivers

Section 681.011 of the Transportation Code states that it is illegal to park in a space reserved for disabled people. It is also illegal to park a car such that it blocks architectural improvements, like a ramp, designed to aid the disabled. It is illegal to lend a disabled-parking placard to a person who is not disabled. All of these violations are misdemeanors punishable by fines of between $500 and $750.

Counterfeit disabled parking placards

Section 681.0111 of the Transportation Code states that it is illegal to manufacture, sell, or possess a placard deceptively similar to an authentic disabled-parking placard. This is a Class A misdemeanor. It is also illegal to knowingly display such a placard while parking in a space designated for the disabled. This is a Class C misdemeanor.

Section 683.002 of the Transportation Code defines a motor vehicle as abandoned if it has remained immobile on public property for more than two days or is inoperable, more than five years old, and then left unattended on public property for more than two days. A

- 86 -

vehicle is considered abandoned if it has remained on private property without the owner's consent for more than two days, or if it has been left unattended on the side of a highway for more than two days.

Abandoned vehicles

Section 683.003 of the Transportation Code states that the laws regarding abandoned vehicles do not affect laws authorizing the immediate removal of vehicles that are unattended and obstructing traffic.

Taking custody of an abandoned vehicle

Section 683.011 of the Transportation Code states that law enforcement agencies may take into their custody any abandoned vehicles found on public or private property.

Notice of abandonment

Section 683.012 of the Transportation Code states that when a law enforcement agency takes custody of an abandoned vehicle, it must send a notice of abandonment to the last known registered owner of the vehicle, as well as to any lien holder for the vehicle. This notice must be sent by certified mail no more than 10 days after the agency took custody of the vehicle. It should specify the year, make, model, and identification number of the vehicle, as well as the location where the vehicle is being held. It should also inform the owner that he has a right to claim the vehicle within the next 20 days.

Storage fees for abandoned vehicles

Section 683.013 of the Transportation Code states that when an agency takes an abandoned vehicle into custody, it is allowed to charge mobile storage fees for the maximum 10-day interval after the vehicle is taken into custody and before notice is sent, and for the interval after notice has been sent and before the vehicle is moved.

Unclaimed abandoned vehicles

Section 683.016 of the Transportation Code states that when a law enforcement agency takes an abandoned motor vehicle into custody and the vehicle is not claimed, the agency may use the vehicle for its own purposes, transfer it to another government agency, or auction the vehicle off.

All-terrain vehicles on the highway

Section 502.006 of the Transportation Code declares that all-terrain vehicles may not be registered for operation on a public highway. However, governments may license all-terrain vehicles to operate on the driveway to promote public safety. People may operate recreational off-highway vehicles on public or private beaches.

Unregistered motor vehicle

Section 502.402 of the Transportation Code declares that it is a misdemeanor punishable by a maximum fine of $200 to operate an unregistered motor vehicle.

Vehicle registered for the wrong class

Section 502.403 of the Transportation Code declares that it is a misdemeanor punishable by a maximum fine of $200 to operate on a public highway a vehicle registered for a class other than the true class of the vehicle.

Driving without license plates

Section 502.404 of the Transportation Code declares that it is illegal to drive a vehicle without license plates on the front and rear of the vehicle. These license plates must be currently validated by the department. Failure to carry these plates is a misdemeanor punishable by a fine of not more than $200.

Operating an unregistered motorcycle

Section 502.405 of the Transportation Code declares that it is illegal to operate a motorcycle without a registration seal. This is a misdemeanor punishable by a maximum fine of $200.

Expired license tag

Section 502.407 of the Transportation Code declares that it is illegal to operate a vehicle with an expired license plate or a license plate that has not been validated with a current registration insignia. This is a misdemeanor punishable by a fine of no more than $200.

Wrong license tag

Section 502.408 of the Transportation Code declares that it is illegal to operate a motor vehicle with the wrong license plate number or registration insignia attached. This is a misdemeanor punishable by a fine of no more than $200.

Incorrect and obscured license plates

Section 502.409 of the Transportation Code declares that it is illegal to display on a motor vehicle an incorrect, fictitious, altered, or obscure license plate. This is punishable by a fine of no more than $200, unless the alteration of the license plate was performed knowingly, in which case the offense is a Class B misdemeanor.

Changing plates after a transaction

Section 502.451 of the Transportation Code states that when a dealer purchases or receives a motor vehicle, he should remove each license plate and registration insignia issued for the motor vehicle. When a person purchases or receives a motor vehicle and does not have a general distinguishing number, the previous owner should remove each license plate and the registration insignia. The section of the registration period that remains when the car is transferred or sold continues despite the transaction, though the person receiving the vehicle must file documents in order to continue the registration period.

Temporary dealer's tags

Section 503.062 of the Transportation Code states that a dealer may issue a temporary tag so that he or his employees may use an unregistered vehicle to demonstrate its performance to a prospective buyer or to transport the vehicle from one business location to another. A dealer may also issue temporary tags so that the vehicle can be used by a charitable organization.

Dealer's tag database

Section 503.0626 of the Transportation Code states that the department should maintain a current database of vehicles with temporary tags. This database should include information about who owns each tagged vehicle. Dealers must input this information into the database before affixing tags.

Temporary buyer's tags

Section 503.063 of the Transportation Code states that dealers may issue a temporary buyer's tag to the purchaser of a vehicle. This buyer's tag is only valid for either 60 days after purchase or the date on which the vehicle is registered, whichever comes first. The buyer's tag must indicate the actual date of sale. Dealers are responsible for the distribution of these tags, and are not allowed to charge the buyer more than $5 for them.

Database
Section 503.0631 of the Transportation Code States that the department must maintain a current database of temporary buyer's tags. This database must allow law enforcement officers to identify the owner of the tag based on the tag number. Dealers are responsible for entering information about issued tags into the database. Dealers may charge up to $20 for the service. Section 503.068 of the

- 88 -

Transportation Code states that dealers and their employees may not use temporary tags on vehicles for their own personal use. Also, dealer's tags and license plates may not be used on load-bearing commercial vehicles or service vehicles.

Restrictions on temporary tags and the punishment for violations

Section 503.094 of the Transportation Code states that all violations of the rules related to temporary dealer's tags and buyer's tags are misdemeanors punishable by a fine of between $50 and $5000. The fine may be tripled if it is proven that the violation was committed willfully or with conscious indifference to law.

Vehicle insurance requirements

Section 601.051 of the Transportation Code states that a vehicle may not be driven without motor vehicle liability insurance, an approved surety bond, an approved deposit, or approved self-insurance.

Exemptions to these requirements: Section 601.052 of the Transportation Code states that these insurance requirements do not apply to cars that are at least 25 years old or are former military vehicles, vehicles not used for regular transportation, and collector's items. Also, golf carts are not subject to these insurance requirements.

Proof of insurance

Section 601.053 of the Transportation Code declares that motor vehicle operators must be able to provide evidence of financial responsibility, as for instance a motor vehicle liability insurance policy, standard proof of insurance, surety bond certificate, certificate of deposit, or certificate of self-insurance.

Exemptions to these requirements: Section 601.054 of the Transportation Code declares that a person may provide evidence of financial responsibility for another person if the other person is an employee or immediate family member.

Proof of insurance

Section 601.081 of the Transportation Code asserts that the standard proof of motor vehicle liability insurance must include the name of the insurer, the insurance policy number, the policy period, the name and address of the insurer, the policy limits, and the make and model of each covered vehicle.

Penalty for driving without insurance

Section 601.191 of the Transportation Code declares that a person who drives without insurance is guilty of a misdemeanor punishable by a fine of between $175 and $350, unless he or she is a prior offender, in which case the fine is from $350 to $1000.

Charge of driving without insurance

Section 601.193 of the Transportation Code declares that a person may defend himself against a charge of driving without insurance by producing one of the approved documents valid at the time the offense was alleged to have occurred.

Driving someone else's car

Section 601.194 of the Transportation Code states that a person may defend himself against the charge of driving without insurance by proving that the vehicle was only in his possession for maintenance or repair, or that the vehicle is not owned by him.

Failure to maintain evidence of financial responsibility

Section 601.195 of the Transportation Code declares that drivers who fail to maintain evidence of financial responsibility are guilty of a misdemeanor punishable by a fine of not more than $500 and/or a six-month prison sentence.

Driving with suspended registration

Section 601.371 of the Transportation Code declares that it is illegal to knowingly operate a motor vehicle with suspended registration. This is a misdemeanor punishable by a fine of between $100 and $500 and/or confinement in county jail for between 72 hours and six months.

Tampering with warning signals

Section 472.021 of the Transportation Code states that it is illegal to tamper with or remove a barricade, sign, signal, or other device that indicates imminent construction, repair, or detour. This conduct is illegal regardless of whether the warning device has been placed by the state, a political subdivision, a contractor, or a public utility. Tampering with a warning device is a misdemeanor punishable by a fine of between $25 and $1000, a maximum jail sentence of two years, or both.

Obeying warning signs and barricades

Section 472.022 of the Transportation Code states that it is illegal to disobey the instructions of a warning device. This is a misdemeanor punishable by fine of between $1 and $200.

Removing material from a highway

Section 600.001 of the Transportation Code states that any person who drops destructive or injurious material onto a highway must immediately remove it. Those who remove wrecked vehicles from the highway should remove any glass or other injurious substances as well.

Remaining at the scene of a vehicle accident

Section 550.021 of the Transportation Code states that when a driver is involved in an accident that causes the injury or death of a person, the driver must immediately stop the vehicle as close to the scene as possible, and immediately return to the scene and remain there. Failing to stop at the scene of an accident is a third-degree felony, punishable by a jail sentence of one to five years and/or a maximum fine of $5000.

Section 550.022 of the Transportation Code states that when a person is involved in an accident that causes damage to another vehicle, he should immediately stop as close as possible to the scene of the accident without obstructing traffic. Failing to do so is a Class B misdemeanor if the damage to all vehicles is $200 or more, and a Class C misdemeanor if the damages are less.

Providing information at scene of an accident

Section 550.023 of the Transportation Code declares that a driver who is involved in an accident that causes injury or death to another person or damage to another vehicle must give his or her information to the injured party and must provide reasonable assistance, including arrangements for medical treatment.

Unattended vehicle

Section 550.024 of the Transportation Code declares that if a driver runs into an unattended vehicle, the driver must immediately stop and either find the owner of the unattended vehicle or leave a written notice in a conspicuous place. The driver who caused the accident must give the owner of the damaged vehicle his or her name and address. Failing to fulfill these duties is a Class B misdemeanor if the damage to all vehicles exceeds $200, and a Class C misdemeanor if the damages do not.

Highway fixtures or landscaping

Section 550.025 of the Transportation Code declares that a driver who gets in an accident that causes damage to a fixture or landscaping on the highway should take all reasonable measures to find and alert the person in charge of the property. Failing to do so is a Class C misdemeanor if the damages are less than $200 and a Class B misdemeanor if they are not.

Driver responsibilities after accident

Section 550.026 of the Transportation Code declares that when a driver is involved in an accident that results in the injury or death of another person or severe damage to another vehicle, he is required to contact the local police department or the sheriff's office immediately.

Peace officers responsibilities

Section 550.041 of the Transportation Code declares that when a peace officer is notified of a vehicle accident that caused injury or death or estimated property damage of at least $1000, he should investigate and file all justifiable charges regardless of where the accident occurs.

Written accident reports

Section 550.061 of the Transportation Code declares that the driver of a vehicle involved in an accident should prepare a written report if the accident resulted in injury, death, or estimated property damage of at least $1000, provided that the accident has not been investigated by a law-enforcement officer. The operator's accident report should be filed no more than 10 days after the date of the accident.

Section 550.062 of the Transportation Code states that law enforcement officers who investigate a vehicle accident must file a written report when the accident results in injury, death, or estimated property damage of $1000 or more. This report must be filed within 10 days of the accident.

Approval for written accident reports

Section 550.063 of the Transportation Code declares that the police department and the Department of Public Safety must approve the form for all written accident reports.

Accident report forms

Section 550.064 of the Transportation Code declares that the department is in charge of preparing and disseminating the appropriate accident report forms. These forms must require enough information to disclose the causes and conditions of the accident, and should identify the officers or emergency medical services employees who were involved in the aftermath.

Requisite measurements and physical evidence

An officer who arrives at the scene of an accident should, if appropriate, measure the skid marks, vehicles, road grade, and road widths. The officer should determine the point of collision, and should identify the final resting places of the vehicles involved. If the collision scene is complex or the accident has been severe, the officer may want to supplement a sketch with some photography. While taking these measurements, the officer should collect physical evidence such as scuff marks, paint chips, and vehicle fluids. Sometimes, the trail of fluid leaking from the bottom of a car gives the best indication of the car's path. The officer should also collect the vehicle identification numbers and compare these with registration certificates.

Street motorcycle

Motorcycles have become increasingly popular, and police officers must be able to identify the three common types of motorcycles found on the street: sport bikes, street bikes, and cruiser class bikes. Sport bikes are small racing motorcycles typically driven by young men. Street bikes have engines between 250 and 1100 cubic centimeters. Cruiser class bicycles are expensive machines with engines sized between 1100 and 1800 cubic centimeters. These motorcycles are typically driven by older men and women. Many police officers assume that motorcycle operators are more likely to be involved in drugs and crime. Statistics do not support this presumption. Officers should only stop a motorcycle when a violation is suspected or observed. The officer should follow the seven-step violator contact protocol, with the kickstand up and the operator astride the bike.

Scene of a traffic accident

Responding to the scene of a traffic accident can be dangerous for peace officers, so it is important to know the recommended protocol. To begin with, a peace officer should have the following equipment: tape measure; flares or cones; flashlight; sketch paper; chalk, crayon, or paint; and a rolo-tape or laser measuring device. Upon learning of an accident, the peace officer should devise the safest route, and should park his or her car in such a way as to minimize the danger to the accident scene. The peace officer should immediately assess the scene and determine the number of vehicles and people involved. Traffic accidents sometimes damage utilities, like power lines, that can create a hazard. Peace officers should contact the appropriate supplementary personnel, like firefighters, EMTs, and other police officers. Once all the injured parties have been assisted and the scene has been documented fully, the peace officer should coordinate towing and vehicle recovery services.

Interviewing people involved
Upon arriving at the scene of a traffic accident, a peace officer should identify all of the operators, passengers, witnesses, and property owners. Each person involved in the accident should be interviewed separately. To begin with, the peace officer should determine each person's location at the time of the accident. The peace officer should ask each person to describe the accident from his or her perspective. The officer should determine who was operating each of the cars at the time of the accident, and should obtain the driver's license numbers of these people. While conducting these interviews, the officer

should make careful observations. For instance, the officer should be alert to the smell of alcohol or marijuana. In some cases, a person injured in an accident will be in a state of shock and will continue to act somewhat normal. A peace officer should be able to identify this scenario and provide physical assistance.

Intoxicated Driver and Standardized Field Sobriety Testing

Specimen samples and the right to refuse

Section 724.011 of the Transportation Code states that if a person is arrested for an offense related to operating a motor vehicle while intoxicated, then that person is considered to have consented to give one or more specimens of breath or blood to determine the level of alcohol or other illegal substances.

Section 724.012 of the Transportation Code declares that one or more specimens of a person's breath or blood may be taken if the person is arrested and the officer believes he was operating a motor vehicle while intoxicated. A peace officer may force a person who is arrested for any offense in Chapter 49 of the Penal Code (which relates to the operation of motor vehicles and watercrafts) to give a specimen if the person appears intoxicated. The peace officer is entitled to select the method of testing.

Section 724.013 of the Transportation Code declares that if a person has not been arrested for a motor vehicle offense, and there is no indication that he or she is intoxicated, then he or she may refuse to submit a specimen.

Section 724.014 of the Transportation Code declares that licensed morticians or county medical examiners may take a specimen from a dead person or a person who is alive but incapable of refusal.

Section 724.015 of the Transportation Code states that before requesting a person to submit a specimen, the officer must tell him that refusing to submit may be admissible in a subsequent prosecution. The officer must also say that refusing to submit a specimen results in an automatic license suspension of no less than 180 days.

When a specimen is taken from a person 21 years or older and the analysis indicates intoxication, the driver's license is suspended for at least 90 days under any circumstances.

A person who is younger than 21 and has any detectable amount of alcohol in his system will have his license automatically suspended for at least 60 days without exception, though the penalties may be less severe for people who have an alcohol concentration less than the definition of intoxication.

Specimen analysis

Section 724.016 of the Transportation Code declares that the breath specimens taken by peace officers must be analyzed by a certified employee.

Section 724.017 of the Transportation Code states that blood specimens may only be taken by physicians, nurses, chemists, or other qualified technicians. Also, blood specimens must be taken under sanitary conditions.

Section 724.018 of the Transportation Code declares that people who give specimens have a right to see the full test results.

Section 724.019 of the Transportation Code declares that people who submit breath, blood, urine, or other specimens at the request of a peace officer may submit another specimen within two hours.

Refusal to submit

Section 724.031 of the Transportation Code declares that when a person refuses to submit a specimen, he should sign a statement indicating that a specimen was requested, that the consequences of refusal were discussed, and that he nevertheless refused.

Section 724.032 of the Transportation Code declares that when a person refuses to submit a specimen, the attending peace officers should immediately serve notice of license suspension, should take possession of the person's current license, and should make a written report of the refusal to the director. This report should contain the reasons for suspicion of intoxication, the refusal statement, and any other pertinent information.

Section 85.021 of the Local Government Code states that a sheriff must execute all process and precepts directed to him within the appropriate time frame. A sheriff who fails to do so may be punished by the court for contempt with a fine of no more than $100.

Section 86.024 of the Local Government Code states that a constable may be fined for contempt for failing to execute a process, warrant, or precept. This fine will be between $10 and $100, and will be for the benefit of the injured person.

Intoxicated driver stop

There are numerous signs that justify reasonable suspicion that a driver may be intoxicated. If the car is weaving between lanes and scraping against curbs, this indicates that the driver may be intoxicated. Other signs that create reasonable suspicion include erratically speeding up or slowing down, leaving the headlights' high beams on, stopping either far short or beyond a stop sign or traffic signal, and driving on the wrong side of the road. Remember that, although only reasonable suspicion is required to pull a car over, probable cause is needed to arrest. Having stopped the car, the officer should observe the driver for signs of intoxication. Disheveled hair, bloodshot eyes, and ragged clothing all suggest possible drunkenness. If the driver is unable to speak clearly or walk in a straight line, then he or she is most likely impaired. The presence of open or empty alcoholic beverage containers in the car also creates probable cause.

Sobriety testing methods

Perhaps the most common field sobriety test requires the driver to look straight ahead, extend his arms to either side, and then touch his nose by bending his elbow. If the driver is intoxicated, he will most likely not be able to find the tip of his nose. Another common test requires the driver to walk a straight line by placing his feet directly in front of one another, heel to toe. Sometimes an officer will ask the driver to stand on only one foot. Officers should exercise caution when administering a field sobriety test to an extremely drunk individual. These tests should not endanger the driver. In rare cases, a person who appears intoxicated will actually be suffering from diabetic shock or an epileptic seizure. The driver should have an opportunity to provide this information.

Intoxicated driver forms

In Texas, the following intoxicated driver forms are used: DIC-23, DIC-24, DIC-25, DWI case report, and TLE-51. Officers should know how to detect intoxicated drivers when a vehicle is moving, when they have personal contact with the driver, and when they are screening the driver prior to arrest. Officers should understand how to conduct the psychological and preliminary breath tests. Officers must understand nystagmus and divided attention as they relate to intoxication. The different types of nystagmus will have divergent impact on the horizontal gaze nystagmus test. Officers should be familiar with the three standardized field sobriety tests, and should know how to record the results in a field arrest log. Officers should also know how to prepare for trial and deliver effective testimony in court.

Civil Process and Liability

Contempt of court

Most of the time, when a person is described as being held in contempt of court, it refers to a *general contempt of court*. The Government Code in Texas gives courts the right to set standards that ensure respect and dignity for court proceedings. In the county courts and higher, a person may be fined $500 or placed in jail for six months for a general contempt of court. In the justice and municipal courts, contempt may be punished by a fine of $100, three days in jail, or both.

Constructive contempt of court, on the other hand, is a more targeted strategy for encouraging compliance with civil court orders. The target of a constructive contempt of court citation may be placed in jail until he complies with the court order. An example of a violation that would merit a constructive contempt citation is the failure to pay child support.

Civil suit

A civil suit is initiated after a civil wrong occurs and the respective parties cannot reach a settlement. The plaintiffs and defendants are identified, and the plaintiff files a case in a court that has jurisdiction. At this point, the court issues a citation, which is a document that verifies the jurisdiction of the court and directs the defendant as to his rights. The document also includes the plaintiff's petition, in which the grounds for the suit and the relief being sought are detailed. Civil suits may include subpoenas, which call witnesses to court, or prejudgment writs. It is important to note that there may be multiple plaintiffs and defendants in a civil suit.

Service of process

The following officials are authorized to serve process in Texas: sheriff, constable, deputies, those certified by the Supreme Court, and anyone over 18 who is enjoined to do so by a court order. However, any documents that involve the seizure of property or person or evictions must be served by sheriffs, constables, or deputies.

Citations

Citations may not be served on Sunday, and the officer who serves the citation must return a description of the service to the court. This description should include how and when the process was served. Citations may be delivered in person, by mail, or by publication.

Prejudgment writs

Prejudgment writs may be issued after the filing of a suit but before judgment. The point of these documents is to give the court control of property so that its value may be protected during the proceedings. The court will enjoin an officer to seize the property and then serve process to the defendant. Peace officers are not required to accompany the certified server in this situation, in part because it tends to lead to property damage. Prejudgment writs may be served in person, by fax, or through certified or registered mail.

Landlord tenant relations

According to the Texas Property Code, a residential lien may only be enforced if there is a written lease. However, the property of a tenant may not be taken. Before filing an eviction, landlords must give notice to the tenant. Eviction citations may be served directly to the tenant or to anyone over the age of 16 at that address. A hearing related to the service of the citation will be held between six and 10 days from the date of service. Both parties will have five days to appeal the judgment. If the eviction is upheld by the court and the defendant fails to move out within five days, the court may issue a writ of possession authorizing the sheriff or constable to remove the tenant. In this case, the tenant's property may be either placed on the curb or stored. A landlord may lock out the tenant if there is a provision for this in the lease and the tenant is behind in the rent. The landlord must give written notice, and the tenant must be given an opportunity to access his belongings. The tenant may obtain a writ of reentry to resume residence.

Texas Alcoholic Beverage Code

Alcoholic beverage

According to the Texas Alcoholic Beverage Code (TABC), an alcoholic beverage refers to any drink that contains more than one-half of 1 percent alcohol by volume. A liquid with more than this amount of alcohol is not considered an alcoholic beverage if it is not intended for drinking.

Illicit beverage

An illicit beverage is any alcoholic beverage that violates the TABC, whether by being untaxed or handled in a manner contrary to the terms of the Code.

Permittee, and licensee

The permittee is the person who holds a permit referred to in the code, as well as any person employed by that permit-holder. Finally, a licensee is a person who is allowed to manufacture or brew beer. In the Texas Alcoholic Beverage Code, a licensee may live inside or outside of the state boundaries.

Warrantless arrests

Section 101.02 of the Alcoholic Beverage Code asserts that a peace officer may arrest without a warrant any person who is seen violating any provision of the Code. During such an arrest, the officer may take possession of all the illicit beverages in use or possession.

Seizures of illicit beverages

Section 103.03 of the Alcoholic Beverage Code declares that a police officer may seize the following items without a warrant: illicit beverages, containers, and packaging; vehicles used to transport illicit beverages; equipment designed for manufacturing illicit beverages; and materials used to manufacture illicit beverages.

Warrantless seizure of illicit beverages report

Section 103.05 of the Alcoholic Beverage Code declares that when a peace officer makes a seizure, he must report in triplicate the items seized, as well as the place and name of the owner. One copy of this report must be verified by oath, and this copy should be kept in the permanent files of the commission or seizing agency. The verified copy may be inspected by law enforcement agents and members of the legislature. Another copy of the report is delivered to the person from whom the seizure was made. Falsification of such a report is a felony punishable by confinement for between two and five years. A failure to file the reports is a misdemeanor punishable by a fine of between $50 and $100 and/or imprisonment for between 10 and 90 days.

Consumption of alcoholic beverages

Section 101.75 of the Alcoholic Beverage Code states that it is illegal to consume alcohol on a public street, alley, or sidewalk within 1000 feet of the property line of a public or private school. This offense is a Class C misdemeanor.

Alcohol purchase by a minor

Section 106.02 of the Alcoholic Beverage Code declares that it is illegal for a minor to purchase an alcoholic beverage.

Sale of alcohol to a minor

Section 106.03 of the Alcoholic Beverage Code states that it is illegal to sell alcoholic beverages with criminal negligence to a minor. If the minor presents false identification identifying himself as old enough to purchase alcohol, then the vendor has not violated the law. However, this false identification must include a physical description and accurate photograph of the bearer. Negligently selling alcohol to a minor is a Class A misdemeanor.

Carrying a weapon on the premises

Section 11.041 of the Alcoholic Beverage Code declares that permit holders must prominently display a sign indicating that it is unlawful for people to carry weapons on the premises. The only exception is for people who are licensed to carry a concealed handgun. The sign must be at least 6 inches high and 14 inches wide, and must be conspicuous to the public. In some cases, businesses may be required to have to sign in a language besides English. Section 11.61 (b)(21) of the Alcoholic Beverage Code states that a permit may be suspended or canceled if it is determined that the permittee failed to report promptly to the commission a breach of peace that occurred on the licensed premises of the permittee.

Legal hours of consumption

Section 105.06 of the Alcoholic Beverage Code states that, within an extended-hours area, citizens may not consume alcoholic beverages in a public place at any time on Sunday between 2:15 a.m. and 12 p.m., and on any other day between 2:15 a.m. and 7 a.m. In a standard-hours area, a person may not consume alcohol in a public place on

Sunday between 1:15 a.m. and 12 p.m., or on any other day between 12:15 a.m. and 7 a.m.

Section 105.01 of the Alcoholic Beverage Code declares that, except on certain occasions, no person may sell or deliver liquor on Sunday, or before 10 a.m. or after 9 p.m. on any other day, or on New Year's Day, Christmas, or Thanksgiving.

Selling mixed beverages and beer

Section 105.03 of the Alcoholic Beverage Code declares that businesses permitted to sell mixed beverages may do so between 7 a.m. and midnight every day except Sunday. On Sunday, these businesses may sell mixed beverages between midnight and 1 a.m. and between 10 a.m. and midnight. However, from 10 a.m. until noon on Sunday, alcohol must be accompanied by food. In cities or counties with populations of 800,000 or more, businesses permitted to sell mixed beverages may do so between midnight and 2 a.m. any day. Section 105.05 of the Alcoholic Beverage Code states that businesses may sell or deliver beer between 7 a.m. and midnight on any day other than Sunday. On Sunday, businesses may sell or deliver beer between midnight and 1 a.m. and between noon and midnight. On Sunday, businesses that sell beer to be consumed on the premises may only offer beer between 10 a.m. and noon if it accompanied by food. In cities or counties with a population of 800,000 or more, those businesses that hold a retail dealer's on-premise late hours license may also sell and deliver beer between midnight and 2 a.m. on any day.

Code for Minors

Illegal to consume alcohol
Section 106.04 of the Alcoholic Beverage Code declares that it is illegal for minors to consume alcohol. If the beverage was consumed in sight of the minor's parent, guardian, or spouse, this is an affirmative defense to prosecution.

Operation of motor vehicle or watercraft
Section 106.041 of the Alcoholic Beverage Code declares that it is illegal for minors to operate a motor vehicle or watercraft with any amount of alcohol in their system. This offense is typically a Class C misdemeanor, unless the minor has a history of violations.

Purchase of alcohol
Section 106.025 of the Alcoholic Beverage Code states that it is illegal for a minor to try and purchase alcohol. According to the law, a minor has committed a violation if he acts with the specific intent to purchase alcohol, even if his actions fail to yield any alcoholic beverages.

Possession of alcoholic beverage
Section 106.05 of the Alcoholic Beverage Code declares that it is illegal for a minor to possess an alcoholic beverage unless it is within the scope of his or her employment. Also, it is not a violation for a minor to possess an alcoholic beverage if he or she is in sight of his or her parent, guardian, or spouse.

Purchase of alcohol
Section 106.06 of the Alcoholic Beverage Code declares that it is illegal to purchase alcohol for a minor, or to provide alcohol to a minor in any way. However, parents and guardians may provide alcohol to a minor, so long as they are present when the alcohol is consumed. The legal provision of alcohol for a minor is a Class A misdemeanor.

Misrepresent age
Section 106.07 of the Alcoholic Beverage Code declares that it is illegal for a minor to misrepresent his age, either verbally or with a document, in order to obtain alcohol. This offense is typically a Class C misdemeanor.

Health and Safety Code— Controlled Substances Act

Health Code

Mental illness

Mental illness is defined as any condition, physical or emotional, that impairs thought, behavior, or perception of reality. Mental illness must be diagnosed by a trained professional (i.e., psychologist, social worker, or psychiatrist) in accordance with the Diagnostic and Statistical Manual of Mental Disorders, Fourth Edition, Text Revision (DSM-IV-TR). There are five main categories of mental illness: personality disorders, mood disorders, anxiety disorders, psychosis, and developmental disorders.

Insanity

Insanity is a legal rather than a psychological term. It is defined as a decreased ability to distinguish right from wrong, although it should be noted that the precise definition varies across the United States. The definition of insanity is especially important in trials, where a judge or jury must determine whether the accused was capable of knowing his or her actions were criminal.

Paranoid personality disorder

Personality disorders often go undiagnosed. A person with paranoid personality disorder has an unnatural and irrational habit of believing the worst about other people. In particular, a person with a paranoid personality disorder perceives him or herself as being in a position of weakness and susceptible to exploitation by others.

Antisocial personality disorder

Antisocial personality disorder is more often found in males, in whom it manifests as a pattern of irrational or destructive behavior. Antisocial personality disorders are associated with stealing, fighting, destroying property, running away, and many other illegal behaviors. People with antisocial personality disorder often are nonconformists who are aware of the immorality of their own behavior, but persist in it regardless.

Borderline personality disorder

Borderline personality disorder is more typical of females. It manifests in a series of unstable personal relationships, impulsive sexual behavior, and wild mood swings. A person with borderline personality disorder may frequently threaten suicide, may suffer from chronic boredom, or may spend money recklessly.

Depression

Depression is an extremely common mood disorder. Indeed, many experts believe that depression has a definite role in human evolution. People who have experienced recent loss or trauma are understandably prone to depression. Of course, severe or prolonged depression may be a cause for concern. A depressed person may experience rapid changes in weight accompanied by a lack of interest in life. Depressed people have a hard time concentrating, and are unable to act with decisiveness. People with depression sleep more, but may have a harder time getting to sleep at night. Depression is a primary risk factor for suicide, and depressives are also more likely to abuse alcohol. A depressed person usually has very low energy and appetite, and the resulting lack of exercise and nutrition perpetuates the depressive state.

Bipolar disorder

Bipolar disorder is a mood disorder with two components: mania and depression.

During a manic state, the bipolar person will feel extremely enthusiastic and powerful. A manic person overestimates his own abilities, and is prone to risky behavior. Manic individuals sleep less and talk more. At times, a person in a manic state will feel as if his thoughts are moving almost too quickly.

In a depressive state, however, the bipolar individual will feel profoundly hopeless and despondent. He will underestimate his own abilities, and experience difficulty concentrating or making decisions. A bipolar person in a depressive state will have low energy and interest. The transition from mania to depression can occur very quickly. Many bipolar individuals will resist treatment at first because they have become addicted to the highs they experience while in a manic phase.

Anxiety disorders

Anxiety disorders manifest in all sorts of ways: panic attacks, obsession, and compulsion, to name a few. Normal anxiety progresses into a disorder when it leads to self-destructive behavior, is persistent and unyielding, and encourages emotional withdrawal. Anxiety disorders are associated with confusion, irritability, avoidance, dread, and restlessness. In the grips of anxiety, people have a raised heartbeat and higher level of perspiration. Of course, these responses only signify a disorder when they occur at inappropriate times or at extreme levels. The risk factors for anxiety disorders include poverty, family strife, pessimism, chemical imbalances, family history of disorder, and recent trauma. The three most common anxiety disorders are generalized anxiety disorder, post-traumatic stress disorder, and obsessive-compulsive disorder.

OCD

Obsessive-compulsive disorder (OCD)is a pattern of recurring and unwanted thoughts and behaviors. People with this disorder develop behavior rituals that they feel compelled to perform despite their seeming irrationality. This condition usually manifests in people around age 10, though many adults do not develop it until age 21. A family history of OCD, a recent pregnancy, or a stressful situation may trigger OCD. For those with the disorder, obsessions typically revolve around cleanliness and contamination. People with OCD are usually paranoid about germs, and will perform elaborate hygienic rituals. People with OCD may also pick at their skin and pull out their own hair. Often, these obsessions are tied to a fear of causing pain to loved ones: the person may feel that unless he or she performs certain rituals, his or her family and friends will be in danger. The compulsive rituals frequently center on "lucky" numbers. For instance, a person with OCD may feel the need to touch a door knob three times before turning it. The causes of OCD are not fully understood, but there are arguments for neurochemical, environmental, and biological origins.

PTSD

Posttraumatic disorder is caused by a particular traumatic event. An individual suffering from this condition suffers from symptoms for a period of months and even years. This condition often will not improve without treatment. According to the DSM-IV-TR, posttraumatic stress disorder, or PTSD, is a common response to a situation that is perceived to be threatening to one's life. In effect, the brain is unable to explain or organize the experience, and so it continues to relive it through flashbacks until it can be integrated into the psyche. Until this condition was identified as PTSD, it was often referred to as shell shock or combat fatigue. PTSD typically manifests as nightmares, flashbacks, and recurrent episodes of extreme psychological duress. A person suffering from this condition will often try to avoid stimuli that trigger his or her memory. At the same time, the person will become cut off from his or her friends and family, who he or she perceives as being unable to understand. PTSD usually is accompanied by symptoms like difficulty sleeping, irritability, and poor concentration. Some people are physiologically predisposed to the development of this condition.

Psychosis

Psychosis is a set of mental disorders characterized by delusions, hallucinations, and diminished reasoning. A person suffering from a psychosis may hear voices or develop irrational convictions. A delusion is a false belief, while a hallucination is a faulty perception. A psychotic person may dress inappropriately, injure him or herself intentionally, or have a flat or inexpressive affect. He or she may perform a series of repetitive and pointless body movements. Also, psychotic people often develop strange attachments to the totems of childhood, like toys and stuffed animals. A person with a psychosis may demonstrate inappropriate emotions, as for instance the expression of profound grief over a sad movie. At other times, the psychotic will have a very low emotional response to events that seem to warrant more feeling.

Influence of Alzheimer's disease and substance abuse on psychosis: A person suffering from Alzheimer's disease may demonstrate many of the behaviors associated with psychosis. Alzheimer's is categorically distinct from mental illness, however, and the treatment protocol for an Alzheimer's patient is quite different than that for a psychotic. Alzheimer's victims may suffer extreme short-term memory loss while retaining a remarkable amount of long-term recall.

Substance abuse can also generate the same symptoms as psychosis. A person with severe substance abuse issues can develop delusions and hallucinations, and may lose the ability to control his or her mood. A person who severely abuses drugs and alcohol will have impaired memory, cognition, and language skills. Any drug can create dependency if it is used often and in large doses. Also, some drugs create such extreme dependency that withdrawal can produce more severe symptoms than use. Heroin is the classic example of a drug that can produce the symptoms of psychosis when it is used for a long time and then quit.

Schizophrenia

Schizophrenia is a set of psychotic disorders that manifest as impaired perception, hallucinations, and irrational cognition. One of the most troubling facts about schizophrenia is that it tends to emerge in late adolescence and early adulthood, when Americans are moving out of the family home and hence are more vulnerable. Schizophrenia is highly correlated with suicide, with about 10 percent of schizophrenics eventually taking their own lives. A schizophrenic will have an exaggerated response to seemingly minor episodes, and will often demonstrate a poor ability to understand simple ideas and situations. Schizophrenics often display a flat affect and report anhedonia, or the inability to derive pleasure from formerly enjoyed activities. Schizophrenics tend to isolate themselves, and may even begin talking to themselves.

Developmental disabilities

A developmental disability is a severe and chronic impairment of mental and/or physical ability. A developmental disability is likely to persist throughout the person's life. Developmentally disabled people typically have problems in one or more of the following areas: social skills, communication, gross motor skills, and fine motor skills. Autism and intellectual disability are the two most common forms of developmental disability. When dealing with the developmentally disabled, officers should be aware that the encounter will likely alarm the suspect. A developmentally disabled person is likely to lie or give a false confession if he or she believes it will resolve the situation. People with developmental disabilities may only understand basic language, so officers need to speak slowly and simply. Also, many people with developmental disabilities are extremely sensitive to touch, so officers should avoid making physical contact unless absolutely necessary.

Autism and intellectual disability

Autism affects nonverbal communication, social skills, personal interest, and empathy. This condition is typically identified before age 3. There is no cure for autism. Autistic people may engage in repetitive movements.

Intellectual disability is characterized by low intelligence and deficiencies in social skills, communication, and memory. There are four gradations of intellectual disability: profound, severe, moderate, and mild. It may be difficult at first for an officer to identify a suspect with mild intellectual disability. Some signs of possible retardation are being considerably older than other suspects, willingness to confess, and a history of criminal activity. Intellectually disabled people usually move awkwardly and slowly. They often have speech defects and may appear to be inattentive. It is important to avoid humiliating the intellectually disabled, both because it demeans them and because it will aggravate the situation.

Suicide

Many people are surprised to learn that suicide is more common than homicide. Most suicides happen either between the ages of 45 and 54 or after the age of 75. Contrary to popular belief, suicide is not limited to the mentally ill or depressed. However, people with schizophrenia or bipolar disorder are considerably more likely to take their own lives. People are also more likely to commit suicide when they have a family history of suicide, when they have a specific plan for killing themselves, and when they have announced the intention to do so.

"Suicide by cop"
The phrase "suicide by cop" refers to a common scenario in which a suicidal person intentionally engages in criminal behavior

that forces police officers to use deadly force. For instance, a man might wave a gun at police officers in the hopes that they will shoot him.

Mental illness treatment

Mental illness is treated with four categories of drugs:
1. anti-anxiety medications
2. mood stabilizers
3. antidepressants
4. antipsychotics/tranquilizers

Anti-anxiety medications like Xanax and Valium help reduce stimulation of the central nervous system.

Mood stabilizers like Lithium and Depakote counteract the wild shifts in temperament typical of bipolar disorder.

Antidepressants like Prozac and Zoloft adjust brain chemistry to improve mood and reduce feelings of hopelessness.

Antipsychotic medications, also known as tranquilizers, prevent the appearance of hallucinations. Haldol and Thorazine are two common antipsychotics.

All four categories of medication have proven effective at treating mental illness, though not without some negative side effects. Many people report feeling uncomfortable or emotionless when they are on these medications. Some of the side effects of these medications are permanent, so people should be very careful before initiating their use. Older medications, which have more severe side effects, are often still used in prisons and mental institutions.

Crisis

Crisis intervention programs teach officers how to handle, gently but effectively, encounters with mentally disturbed or ill people. A crisis is any situation that disorients a person or makes him or her unstable.

Sometimes, a person's reaction to circumstances is more generative of a crisis than the circumstances themselves. A person who has mistaken beliefs or poor coping mechanisms is more likely to find him or herself in crisis. When dealing with people in crisis, an officer should avoid trying to solve the problem immediately, and should rather allow the person to explore his or her emotions. Officers should control the situation as much as possible, and ensure the safety of all involved. When speaking with a person in crisis, officers should use a soft voice and frequently address the person by name. The officer should avoid confrontation. Officers should give the person physical space, but should also remain alert for movements that could indicate danger.

Communication

Upon initiating contact with a person in crisis, an officer should immediately identify him or herself as law enforcement. The officer should indicate why he or she is there, and that he or she wants to help the person. The officer should give the person a chance to state the nature of the crisis. Talking can be therapeutic, so the officer should always give the person plenty of opportunity to discuss what is on his or her mind. Officers may do nothing more than repeat what the person says, so as to maintain conversation without wandering onto any problematic topics. It is important for the officer to gain the person's trust. If the officer can help prolong the encounter, this is also more likely to produce a positive outcome. The officer should avoid giving sharp directions, and should never give more than one instruction at a time.

Basic evaluation

As police officers work to calm down a person in crisis, they should also evaluate the person's physical and mental status. To begin with, the officer should note the person's clothing and level of personal hygiene. The officer should observe the person's manner of speech, as well. If the person speaks rapidly but incoherently, this is a sign of a disordered mind. If the person speaks hardly at all, it is possible that he or she is profoundly depressed. If the person has difficulty understanding instructions, the officer should determine whether this is because of some native deficiency or because of the stress associated with the current crisis. Officers should be alert to abrupt changes in tone or affect, as these indicate volatility. Also, officers should know the signs of delusion or hallucination.

LEAPS, modeling, and active listening

Many crisis intervention programs help officers remember the fundamental aspects of crisis communication with the initials LEAPS, which stands for listen, empathize, ask, paraphrase, and summarize. Another approach to crisis communication is modeling, in which the officer embodies the behavior (calm and rational) he wishes to see adopted by the person in crisis. In many cases, an anxious person will unconsciously adopt the emotional affect of his or her interlocutor. Active listening is one of the most important approaches to crisis intervention. An active listener pays attention to what the speaker is saying, and uses his responses to elicit more information and to draw the speaker out. An active listener will often just repeat or paraphrase what the speaker has said. Many people find that the simple act of stating their problem and having another person listen is extremely therapeutic.

Emergency detention protocol

Officers may detain a person without a warrant if the person is mentally ill and at risk of harming himself or others. An emergency detention is appropriate when there is not enough time to obtain a formal warrant. The officer's judgment may be informed by his or her own observation or the account of a credible bystander. A person who has been detained in this way should be taken to the nearest appropriate inpatient medical facility. Such a person should not be taken to jail except in an emergency. It is important to keep emergency detainees separate from other suspects. The emergency detention order is a civil court order issued by a magistrate. It provides the basis for an urgent apprehension and transportation to a mental health facility.

Intensity levels of behavior

The necessity of performing an emergency detention depends on the severity of the individual's behavior.

An agitated person is still capable of restraining him or herself, but may show signs of extreme frustration, such as hand-wringing or muttering.

A disruptive person openly refuses to obey the commands of officers, and may also engage in yelling and swearing.

A destructive person causes damage to items in the area, and will most likely need to be restrained with physical force.

A person's behavior is characterized as out of control when he or she is making threats and can be reasonably defined as dangerous. Officers may need to request assistance even when dealing with a person of seemingly slight physical strength, because mental illness and stress can often inspire surprising physical performance.

Mode of transport
When deciding on the appropriate mode of transport for a mentally ill detainee, officers should consider the distance to the destination as well as the condition of the detainee.

State of Texas Jail Diversion Ideal

The Jail Diversion Ideal is an approach to law enforcement developed in the State of Texas that seeks to separate the mentally ill from the criminal justice system. This approach requires officers to receive training in crisis intervention and the varieties of mental illness. Each district should have a centralized location where mentally ill detainees can be evaluated without being introduced to the criminal justice system. There should also be holding facilities where mentally ill people can be kept without being placed under arrest but while they are still considered to be a danger to themselves and others. Departments also need to develop a good process for screening detainees.

There are two basic methods of jail diversion:
1. pre-booking diversion, which occurs before formal charges are made
2. post-booking diversion, which occurs after booking

Post-booking diversion is more common.

Jail diversion advantages

Jail diversion programs have proven to be excellent ways of reducing the damage to the mentally ill caused by needless introduction to the criminal justice system. Because of jail diversion, the State of Texas has been able to reduce the number of prison inmates with mental illness. Many new officers are surprised to learn that almost 10 percent of calls for police service pertain to mental illness in some way. One of the benefits of jail diversion programs is a reduction in criminal justice costs and administrative waste. Jail diversion programs avoid placing the stigma of criminality on the mentally ill. They also increase public safety and reduce the jail population. In general, these programs reduce the amount of violence committed by the mentally ill, as well as the amount of violence committed against the mentally ill in prison. At the very least, these programs give the general public an honest and accurate sense of the relative costs of treating the mentally ill and imprisoning the criminal.

Penalty Group 1

Section 481.112 of the Health and Safety Code states that it is illegal to manufacture or deliver any of the substances in Penalty

Group 1 without a license. If the amount in question is less than one gram, the crime is a state jail felony. If the amount is between 1 and 4 grams, the crime is a second-degree felony. If the amount is between 4 and 200 grams, the crime is a first-degree felony. If the amount is between 200 and 400 grams, the crime is punishable by life in prison and a fine of no more than $100,000. If the amount is 400 grams or more, the crime is punishable by life in prison and a fine of no more than $250,000.

Penalties for possession

Section 481.115 of the Health and Safety Code asserts that it is illegal to possess a Penalty Group 1 controlled substance unless it is accompanied by a valid prescription or the order of a practitioner. If the amount is less than 1 gram, this crime is a state jail felony. If the amount is between 1 and 4 grams, the crime is a third-degree felony. If the amount is between 4 and 200 grams, the crime is a second-degree felony. If the amount is between 200 and 400 grams, the crime is a first-degree felony. If the amount is more than 400 grams, the crime is punishable by life imprisonment or a sentence from 10 to 99 years accompanied by a fine of no more than $100,000.

Penalty Group 1-A

Section 481.1121 of the Health and Safety Code outlines the penalties for manufacture or delivery of a controlled substance from Penalty Group 1-A. If the number of abuse units is less than 20, the crime is a state jail felony. If the number of abuse units is between 20 and 80, the crime is a second-degree felony. If the number of abuse units is between 80 and 4000, the crime is a first-degree felony. If the number of abuse units is more than 4000, the crime is punishable by life in prison or a term of between 15 and 99 years and a fine of no more than $250,000.

Penalties for possession

Section 481.1151 of the Health and Safety Code outlines the punishments for possession

of a substance from Penalty Group 1-A. The severity of the crime depends on the number of abuse units possessed: state jail felony if less than 20, third-degree felony if from 20 to 80, second-degree felony if from 80 to 4000, first degree felony if from 4000 to 8000, and either life imprisonment or a sentence of between 15 and 99 years accompanied by a fine of $250,000 or less if the convicted person has 8000 or more abuse units of the controlled substance.

Penalty Groups 2, 3, and 4

Section 481.113 of the Health and Safety Code outlines the penalties for manufacture or delivery of a substance in Penalty Group 2. If the amount is less than 1 gram, the crime is a state jail felony. If the amount is between 1 and 4 grams, the crime is a second-degree felony. If the amount is between 4 and 400 grams, the crime is a first-degree felony. If the amount is more than 400 grams, the crime is punishable by life imprisonment or a sentence from 10 to 99 years accompanied by a fine of no more than $100,000. Section 481.114 of the Health and Safety Code outlines the penalties for manufacture or delivery of substances from Penalty Groups 3 and 4. If the amount is less than 28 grams, the crime is a state jail felony. If the amount is between 28 and 200 grams, the crime is a second-degree felony. If the amount is between 200 and 400 grams, the crime is a first-degree felony. If the amounted is more than 400 grams, the crime is punishable by life imprisonment or a term of between 10 and 99 years accompanied by a fine no more than $100,000.

Penalty for possession Penalty Group 2
Section 481.116 of the Health and Safety Code outlines the penalties for illegal possession of a substance in Penalty Group 2. If the amount possessed is less than 1 gram, the crime is a state jail felony. If the amount is 1 to 4 grams, the crime is a third-degree felony. If the amount possessed is between 4 and 400 grams, the crime is a second-degree felony. If the amount possessed is more than 400

grams, the crime is punishable by life imprisonment or a prison term of between five and 99 years accompanied by a fine of no more than $50,000.

Penalty for possession Penalty Groups 3 and 4

Section 481.117 of the Health and Safety Code describes the severity of offenses related to possession of a substance from Penalty Group 3. If the amount possessed is less than 28 grams, possession is a Class A misdemeanor. If the amount ranges from 28 to 100 grams, the crime is a third-degree felony. If the amount possessed is from 200 to 400 grams, the crime is a second-degree felony. If the amount assessed is 400 grams or more, the crime is punishable by life imprisonment or a prison term of five to 99 years accompanied by a fine of no more than $50,000. Section 481.118 of the Health and Safety Code describes the penalties for possession of a substance in Penalty Group 4. If the amount is less than 28 grams, the crime is a Class B misdemeanor. If the amount ranges from 28 to 200 grams, the crime is a third-degree felony. If the amount is 200 to 400 grams, the crime is a second-degree felony. If the amount is 400 grams or more, the punishment is life imprisonment or a term of between five and 99 years, accompanied by a fine of no more than $50,000.

Penalties

Section 481.119

Section 481.119 of the Health and Safety Code asserts that it is illegal to manufacture, deliver, or intentionally possess any substance that has been listed on a schedule by the Commissioner but is not listed in a Penalty Group. Manufacture and delivery of such substances are Class A misdemeanors, while possession is a Class B misdemeanor.

Delivery of marijuana

Section 481.120 of the Health and Safety Code describes the penalties for delivery of marijuana. If the amount is less than a quarter-ounce and the person who commits the offense has not been paid remuneration for the marijuana, then the crime is a Class B misdemeanor. If the amount is less than a quarter-ounce and the offender is paid for the marijuana, then the crime is a Class A misdemeanor. If the amount of marijuana is between a quarter-ounce and 5 pounds, it is a state jail felony. If the amount is between 5 and 50 pounds, it is a second-degree felony. If the amount is between 50 and 2000 pounds, it is a first-degree felony. If the amount is more than 2000 pounds, the crime is punishable by life imprisonment or a term of between 10 and 99 years, accompanied by a fine of no more than $100,000.

Section 481.121

Section 481.121 of the Health and Safety Code outlines the penalties for possession of marijuana. If the amount is 2 ounces or less, possession is a Class B misdemeanor. If the amount is between 2 and 4 ounces, it is a Class A misdemeanor. If the amount is between 4 ounces and 5 pounds, it is a state jail felony. If the amount is between 5 and 50 pounds, it is a third-degree felony. If the amount is between 50 and 2000 pounds, it is a second-degree felony. If the amount is more than 2000 pounds, it is punishable by life imprisonment or a term of between 5 and 99 years, accompanied by a fine of no more than $50,000.

Controlled substance to a child

Section 481.122 of the Health and Safety Code outlines the punishments for the delivery of a controlled substance or marijuana to a child, a person who is currently enrolled in a primary or secondary school, or who the offender knows is going to deliver the substance to a child or student. This crime is a second-degree felony.

Manufacture illegal controlled substance

Section 481.124 of the Health and Safety Code asserts that it is illegal to possess or move the following substances with the intent to manufacture illegal controlled substances: anhydrous ammonia, an immediate precursor, or a chemical precursor.

Possession or delivery of these substances is a second-degree felony, if the substance is in Penalty Group 1 or 1-A. The crime is a third-degree felony if the controlled substance is listed in Penalty Group 2. The crime is a state jail felony if the substance is listed in either Penalty Group 3 or 4. Finally, the crime is a Class A misdemeanor if the controlled substance is listed in a schedule issued by the Commissioner.

Use or possession of drug paraphernalia
Section 481.125 of the Health and Safety Code asserts that it is illegal to intentionally use or possess drug paraphernalia. This is a Class C misdemeanor. It is also illegal to deliver or manufacturer drug paraphernalia. These offenses are Class A misdemeanors.

Money obtained through drug violations
Section 481.126 of the Health and Safety Code describes a group of offenses related to illegal bartering, expenditure, or investment. Essentially, it is illegal to barter, spend, or invest money or goods knowingly obtained through drug violations. Depending on the severity of the violation, this may be either a first- or second-degree felony.

Jail felony
Section 481.127 of the Health and Safety Code asserts that it is a state jail felony to intentionally give or obtain information submitted to the director.

Violation of controlled substances
Section 481.128 of the Health and Safety Code states that it is illegal for registrants or dispensers to illegally distribute or manufacture controlled substances, as well as to perform any activity that leads to a violation of controlled substances policies. These crimes are state jail felonies and may be subject to civil penalties as well.

Commit fraud
Section 481.129 of the Health and Safety Code asserts that it is illegal to commit fraud as a dispenser for the purpose of manufacturing or distributing controlled substances.

Depending on the severity of the crime, this may be classified from Class B misdemeanor to second-degree felony.

Fake a drug test
Section 481.133 of the Health and Safety Code asserts that it is illegal to fake or intend to fake a drug test. It is also illegal to contribute to the falsification of drug test results. Faking a test is a Class B misdemeanor, and promoting the falsification of drug test results is a Class A misdemeanor. Sections 481.136 and 137 of the Health and Safety Code deal with the handling of illegal chemical precursors by people who do not have licensure. Possession of these precursors is a state jail felony, while transfer of them is a third-degree felony. Sections 481.138 and 139 of the Health and Safety Code deal with the illegal transfer and receipt of chemical laboratory apparatuses. This crime is a state jail felony, unless the apparatus is knowingly to be used for unlawful manufacture, in which case the crime is a third-degree felony.

Death or serious bodily harm
Section 481.141 of the Health and Safety Code declares that the manufacture or delivery of a controlled substance that causes death or serious bodily injury is a state jail felony, third-degree felony, or second-degree felony, depending on the severity of the offense.

Offer to deliver controlled substances
Section 481.182 of the Health and Safety Code declares that in order to prove an offer to deliver controlled substances, there must be corroboration from a person other than the person to whom the offer was made, or some evidence besides the statement of the person to whom the offer was made.

Possess a dangerous drug
Section 483.041 of the Health and Safety Code asserts that it is a Class A misdemeanor to possess a dangerous drug.

Selling dangerous drugs

Section 483.042 of the Health and Safety Code declares that it is a state jail felony to deliver or sell a dangerous drug.

Manufacture dangerous drugs

Section 483.043 of the Health and Safety Code declares that it is a state jail felony to manufacture dangerous drugs without state authorization.

Forge a prescription

Section 483.045 of the Health and Safety Code declares that it is a Class B misdemeanor to forge a prescription, issue a forged prescription, or attempt to use a forged prescription.

Under a prescription

Section 483.046 of the Health and Safety Code asserts that it is a Class B misdemeanor to deliver a dangerous drug under a prescription and fail to retain the prescription.

Unauthorized prescription refill

Section 483.047 of the Health and Safety Code asserts that it is a Class B misdemeanor to refill a prescription without authorization. There are some extreme circumstances in which a pharmacist may use his or her professional judgment to refill a prescription without authorization.

Refuse an inspection

Section 483.050 of the Health and Safety Code asserts that it is a Class B misdemeanor to refuse an inspection authorized by the Texas Health and Safety Code.

Crimes involving dangergous drugs

Section 483.072 of the Health and Safety Code asserts that it is possible to win a conviction for crimes involving dangerous drugs based on the uncorroborated testimony of a party to the offense.

Conviction

Article 38.14 of the Code of Criminal Procedure States that a conviction may not be based on the testimony of an accomplice unless it is corroborated by other evidence. Also, the other evidence must not only show the commission of the offense, but must also link the defendant with the offense.

Testimony of undercover person

Article 38.141 of the Code of Criminal Procedure states that a person may not be convicted of a drug violation on the testimony of an undercover person who is not a peace officer or special investigator.

Dangerous drugs seized

Section 483.074 of the Health and Safety Code asserts that dangerous drugs may be seized as contraband. Peace officers may then be directed to destroy the controlled substance according to department protocol. However, a full inventory and report must be completed before the substance is destroyed.

Evidentiary rules

Section 481.183 of the Health and Safety Code asserts that in order to prove possession of drug paraphernalia, there must be additional evidence such as statements, the residue of controlled substances, circumstantial evidence, descriptive material, or behavior that indicates the intention to use in the consumption of controlled substances. Section 482.003 of the Health and Safety Code describes the evidentiary rules related to simulated controlled substances. The courts are asked to consider whether the simulated controlled substances were packaged to look like controlled substances, whether the price paid for the substance was aligned with the value of an equivalent amount of the controlled substance, and whether the simulated substance looks like the controlled substance. An offer to sell a simulated controlled substance requires corroboration by some person other than the offeree in order to be proven.

Permits and signage required

Abusable volatile chemicals
Section 485.011 of the Health and Safety Code asserts that it is illegal to sell abusable volatile chemicals without a permit.

Copy of the permit
Section 485.014 of the Health and Safety Code asserts that those who possess a permit for selling abusable volatile chemicals must have a copy of the permit available for inspection by the public wherever that chemical is sold.

Volatile chemical sales
Section 485.017 of the Health and Safety Code declares that businesses that sell abusable volatile chemicals must conspicuously post a sign declaring that it is illegal to sell these chemicals to people less than 18 years of age, and that it is illegal to use these chemicals as controlled substances. The sign should also indicate that illegal use of these substances is a Class B misdemeanor.

Restricted access

Aerosol paint
Section 485.019 of the Health and Safety Code deals with the display of aerosol paint in a commercial setting. Aerosol paints must be placed in the line of sight of an employee, and should only be accessible to customers with the assistance of the employees.

Possession and use
Section 485.031 of the Health and Safety Code discusses the possession and use of abusable volatile chemicals. These crimes are Class B misdemeanors.

Delivery

Section 485.032 of the Health and Safety Code declares that it is illegal to knowingly deliver abusable volatile chemicals to children under the age of 18. This crime is a Class B misdemeanor if the chemical is delivered by a licensed vendor and a Class A misdemeanor if it is delivered by an unlicensed vendor or a prior offender.

Inhalant paraphernalia
Section 485.033 of the Health and Safety Code declares that it is illegal to use or possess inhalant paraphernalia. This is a Class B misdemeanor. It is also illegal to deliver or manufacture inhalant paraphernalia. This is a Class A misdemeanor.

Abusable volatile chemicals

Section 485.034 of the Health and Safety Code asserts that it is a Class C misdemeanor to sell abusable volatile chemicals without posting a conspicuous sign.

Section 485.035 of the Health and Safety Code declares that it is a Class B misdemeanor to sell abusable volatile chemicals without a permit.

Section 485.036 of the Health and Safety Code states that in order to prove an offer to sell an abusable volatile chemical, the accusation must be corroborated by a person other than the offeree's or by some piece of evidence besides the offeree's statement.

Section 485.037 of the Health and Safety Code asserts that abusable volatile chemicals and inhalant paraphernalia are subject to summary forfeiture when they are used as part of an offense.

Informants

Peace officers must work carefully when cultivating informants during investigations of controlled substances and dangerous drug violations. To begin with, officers should interview and thoroughly vet would-be informants. It is important to identify the aspiring informant's motivation. Next, the peace officer should consult with any officers whose work would be impacted by the contribution of the prospective informant. If the informant is approved by all those affected, he should be given an administrative code number so that his actions can be documented and monitored. Peace officers must establish a protocol and a record-keeping apparatus for informants, so that their superiors may perform cost-benefit analysis. Cultivating informants is a tricky proposition, and should only be done with extreme caution, both for the safety of the officer and informant and for the integrity of the investigation.

Surveillance and investigatory equipment

Peace officers must understand the protocols for moving and stationary surveillance of a vehicle, person, or thing. They must be able to discuss the positioning and appearance of the law enforcement vehicle. Officers should also be able to describe the use of TIVEC disposable clothing, industrial-grade rubber gloves, and self-contained breathing apparatuses during the investigation of clandestine drug operations. There is a great deal of danger associated with these raids, so officers must be prepared to deal with hazardous conditions.

Lab investigations

With regard to the investigation of clandestine drug laboratories, officers must be familiar with the hazards of bombs and booby traps. An officer must be able to articulate the proper technique for collecting evidence from a clandestine drug laboratory. Finally, officers must know or know how to find companies that can dispose of hazardous and illicit chemicals safely.

Concealing controlled substances

People often conceal controlled substances in their clothing, in their shoes, or under their belts. It is also common to find substances hidden in body cavities, in thick hair, or under the arms. Some people even tape drugs to their bodies. In a house, the most common places of concealment are toilet tanks, cabinets, freezers, and closets. People also hide drugs in furniture upholstery and waste baskets. When searching a vehicle, officers should be aware that controlled substances are most often hidden in glove compartments,

gas tanks, air conditioning ducts, and ash trays. More sophisticated criminals may stash illicit goods under the hub caps, inside the door panels, under the floor, or behind the dash board.

Drug smuggling and interdiction in Texas

In Texas, the most drug smuggling takes place in and around Houston, Corpus Christi, Brownsville, and the lower Rio Grande Valley. In most cases, drugs are being smuggled from Mexico and Central and South American countries. There is also a great deal of drug activity in the rural areas of Texas, where small and private airports and isolated roads make smuggling safer for criminals. The most smuggling directly from Mexico occurs in the following areas: El Paso, Alpine, Eagle Pass, the Rio Grande Valley, Del Rio, and Presidio. Officers can increase the likelihood of drug interdiction by staying alert and informed. Drug smugglers coming across the border often have suspiciously little luggage, or have their luggage placed on the back seat because the trunk is full of contraband. Also, vehicles used in smuggling are likely to be large and dependable. It is common for the lug nuts or screws on the body of a smuggler's vehicle to appear worn. Finally, officers should be suspicious if the car is not registered to the driver or if the driver cannot identify the owner of the car.

Probable cause in a drug investigation

When interviewing suspects in a drug investigation, officers should be sure to first establish the identity of the interviewee. Officers should determine the origin and destination of the driver's trip, and should inquire as to the purpose of the journey. The officer should see the registration and insurance information, and should find out about the ownership of the vehicle. If there are multiple suspects, they should be separated so that their stories may be compared. An officer has probable cause for a search if the suspect is nervous, or if he has no identification, registration, or insurance.

The appearance of the vehicle may create probable cause, for instance if it appears suspiciously heavy. If the multiple suspects give conflicting stories, this creates probable cause. If the odor of controlled substances is present in the car, or if the driver claims to not have a trunk key, then probable cause exists.

Consent to a search, and protocols

A driver may consent to a search, but his consent must be voluntary and may be withdrawn at any time. The person who gives consent must have the authority to take this action. If possible, officers should obtain written consent, though oral consent may also suffice. When officers discover what they believe to be dangerous drugs or controlled substances, they may positively identify them in a few different ways. Prescription drugs may be identified with a Physician's Desk Reference. Officers should look for the product information, manufacturer's name, trade name, generic name, or drawing of the substance in the reference book. Officers may also use the Scots reagent, Marquis reagent, and Wintergreen field tests to identify suspicious materials. Finally, tests may also be performed by the laboratories associated with the local medical examiner, FBI, or Texas Department of Public Safety.

Family Code and Juvenile Issues

Adolescent's encounter with the police

When an adolescent is confronted by the police, there are some basic factors that may influence the encounter. To begin with, adolescents often begin criminal activity as an expression of their need for independence. Adolescents are becoming intellectually mature but are still dependent on their parents, and they may strain against the restrictions placed on their behavior. Adolescents also may be engaged in rebellion against authority as a mode of identity expression. In other words, adolescents may be defining themselves by measuring their strength against the institutions of society. For many adolescents, breaking the law is a transgression in the name of exploration and learning. Finally, many adolescents will become involved in criminal activity because of peer pressure. Young people are especially susceptible to the influence of their peers, and so police officers should be especially attentive to the relationships between adolescent suspects.

Juvenile gang activities

Juvenile gangs typically come into conflict because of the same set of issues: competition in the gang hierarchy, battles for turf, business conflicts, and cooperation with law enforcement. There are a number of reasons why adolescents become involved with gangs. Many young men have unsupportive home lives, and so they find the connection and sense of belonging they need in a gang. Also, gangs offer economic opportunities to many people who feel themselves excluded from other fields. A young person in the inner city may see gang life as his only path to success. A gang also gives the adolescent an identity and a role within a group. Finally, many young people join gangs out of simple thrill-seeking. Gangs provide excitement and drama to lives that may otherwise be full of impoverished drudgery.

Social context of gangs

Gangs are more prevalent in communities with high unemployment, where membership can seem like the only path to economic prosperity. There are also more likely to be gangs in areas that have few other popular institutions. For instance, places that have strong athletic, religious, and community organizations tend to also have fewer gangs. Gangs thrive in communities that feel marginalized and discriminated against by the larger community.

Finally, gangs are more prevalent in areas where it is clear that illicit activities (such as money laundering and drug dealing) can be profitable. There are three typical stages in gang membership.

1. At first, aspiring members engage in small acts of violence and property destruction. This activity proves the sincerity of the gang aspirant
2. Next, the would-be gang member will make over his image to align with the protocols of the gang. This usually involves special clothing, tattoos, jewelry, and colors
3. Finally, the new gang member will solidify his membership by performing some serious criminal offense, whether violent or drug-related. This bonds the new gang member to the whole group

Delinquent conduct

Section 51.03 of the Family Code defines the delinquent conduct that indicates a need for supervision. Delinquent conduct violates a penal law, a lawful court order, or the Alcoholic Beverage Code. Such conduct indicates a need for supervision, as does running away from home or absence from school for 10 or more days in a six-month period in the same school year.

Waive rights by child or his attorney

Section 51.09 of the Family Code states that any rights granted to a child by this title or by the federal or state constitution or laws may be waived by a child and his attorney, so long as the waiver is voluntary, made in writing, and is made after giving assurance that the consequences of waiving the right are understood.

Child statements

Section 51.095 of the Family Code declares that statements made by children are admissible as evidence in any related future proceedings so long as the child has been advised of his rights and given the opportunity to obtain counsel. Also, the statement must be made in the presence of a magistrate who can confirm the child's comprehension of his or her rights.

Child detained

Section 51.12 of the Family Code lists the places where a child may be detained. A child may be detained in a juvenile processing office, county jail, secure detention facility, certified juvenile detention facility, or place of non-secure custody.

Transport of child

Section 52.026 of the Family Code states that the law enforcement officer who takes custody of the child is responsible for either transporting him or her to the appropriate facility, or releasing the child to a parent, guardian, or custodian.

Child fingerprinted or photographed

Section 58.002 of the Family Code states that children may not be photographed or fingerprinted without the juvenile court's consent unless the child has been taken into custody for conduct that amounts to a felony or misdemeanor punishable by confinement. However, children who are not in custody may be photographed or fingerprinted by law enforcement officers if they receive the voluntary consent of the child's parent or guardian. Law-enforcement departments are required to destroy the identifying information of children regularly.

Officer takes temporary custody of child

Section 58.0021 of the Family Code states that a law-enforcement officer may take temporary custody of a child in order to fingerprint or photograph him or her if the officer has probable cause that the child engaged in delinquent conduct and is reasonably certain that fingerprinting will aid the investigation.

Runaways

Section 58.0022 of the Family Code states that law enforcement officers may use fingerprints or photographs to identify children who are believed to be runaways. Once this task has been accomplished, however, the officer must immediately destroy all copies of the fingerprint records or photographs.

Child taken into custody

Section 52.01 of the Family Code states that a child may be taken into custody pursuant to an order of the court; the child may be taken into custody by a peace officer if there is probable cause that the child has violated a law or condition of probation, or acted in any way that indicates a need for supervision.

Directive to apprehend a child

Section 52.015 of the Family Code states that law enforcement and probation officers may request that a juvenile court issue a directive to apprehend a child when there is probable cause supporting this decision. When this occurs, any officer may take the child into custody.

Child fines

Article 45.050 of the Code of Criminal Procedure states that a judge or court may not confine a child for a court order or for failure to pay a fine. Instead, the court may refer the child to the appropriate juvenile court for delinquent conduct or may levy a fine of no more than $500 and suspend the child's driver's license.

Child convicted of an offense

Article 45.057 of the Code of Criminal Procedure states that when a child is convicted of an offense, the court may refer the child or his parents for services, may require the child to attend a special program, or may place behavioral restrictions on the child's parents. If the child is asked to attend a program, the court may request a maximum of $100 to pay for the costs of the program. The failure by a parent to attend a court-ordered program is a Class C misdemeanor.

Child placed in non-secure custody

Article 45.058 of the Code of Criminal Procedure states that when a child is placed in non-secure custody it should be in an unlocked area such as a lobby or office. When a child is placed in custody in such an area, he or she should not be handcuffed to a stationary object, and should only be there long enough to be identified and processed. Children should be under constant visual supervision while in non-secure custody. Children may not be placed in non-secure custody for more than six hours.

Violation of juvenile curfew or order

Article 45.059 of the Code of Criminal Procedure states that when a child is taken into custody for a violation of juvenile curfew or order, the peace officers should release him or her to his parent or guardian as soon as possible, or should escort the child before a justice, municipal court, or juvenile curfew processing office.

Law enforcement authorized to take children into custody

Section 52.03 of the Family Code states that law enforcement officers who are authorized to take children into custody may dispose of the case without referring it to juvenile court, so long as the officer makes a written report for his agency.

Parent notification

Section 52.04 of the Family Code states that when a child is referred to juvenile court, the law enforcement agency must issue notice to his parents as quickly as possible. This notice should include a complete statement of the child's alleged delinquent conduct, as well as a full description of the circumstances under which the child was taken into custody.

Rights and duties of parents

Section 151.001 of the Family Code outlines the rights and duties of parents. Parents have the right to designate the residence and guide the moral and religious training of their child. Parents have the duty to care for, discipline, and support the child. This support includes providing clothing, food, shelter, medical care, and education. Parents also have the duty to manage the child's estate, and they have the right to the services and earnings of the child. Parents have the right to consent to the child's marriage, military enlistment, and medical treatment. Parents have the right to represent their child in legal actions and to make decisions regarding their child's education. Parents have the right to inherit from and through the child, and to receive and give receipt for payments related to the support of the child.

Rights and duties of conservators

Section 153.074 of the Family Code lists the rights and duties of a person who has possession as the conservator of a child. During the interval in which the person has control of the child, he or she has the duties of care, control, protection, and reasonable discipline. He also has the duty to support the child, including providing the child with clothing, food, shelter, and medical care. He has the right to consent for the child to receive medical care, and the right to direct the child's moral and religious training.

Reporting child abuse and neglect

Section 261.101 of the Family Code states that anyone who has reason to believe the physical or mental health or welfare of a child has been negatively impacted by abuse or neglect is required to make a report. Professionals are required to make such a report within 48 hours of the observation.

The identity of the person who makes such a report will remain confidential.

Report of child abuse

Section 261.102 of the Family Code states that a report of child abuse or neglect should indicate the reporter's suspicions and rationale.

Who to report abuse to

Section 261.103 of the Family Code states that a person who suspects child abuse or neglect should report to local or state law enforcement agencies or to an agency designated by the court as responsible for the protection of children.

Report to include

Section 261.104 of the Family Code states that a report of child abuse or neglect should include the name and address of the child, the name and address of the child's guardian, and any other relevant information.

Neglect reports

Section 261.105 of the Family Code states that when a law enforcement agency receives a report of child abuse or neglect, they should refer it immediately to the proper department or designated agency. Also, departments and designated agencies should notify law enforcement of the reports that they receive.

Immunity

Section 261.106 of the Family Code states that a person who in good faith reports or assists a report of child abuse or neglect is immune from civil or criminal liability.

False report

Section 261.107 of the Family Code states that it is illegal to knowingly make a false report of child abuse or neglect. This is a state jail felony, and the offender may be required to pay the attorney's fees of the falsely accused party as well as a civil penalty of $1000.

Failure to report

Section 261.109 of the Family Code states that it is a Class A misdemeanor to fail to report child abuse or neglect.

Privileged communication

Section 261.202 of the Family Code states that evidence in a proceeding related to child abuse or neglect may not be excluded on the grounds of privileged communication, except with regard to communication between an attorney and client.

Child abuse and neglect

Section 261.301 of the Family Code states that upon receiving a report of child abuse or neglect, the department or designated agency shall make a complete and prompt investigation. If the alleged abuse or neglect is committed by persons other than the child's caregiver, the investigation may be handled by law enforcement.

Investigation

Section 261.302 of the Family Code states that an investigation of child abuse or neglect may include a visit to the home of the child, as well as an interview and full examination of the child.

Missing children and missing person clearinghouse

Article 63.002 of the Code of Criminal Procedure states that the missing children and missing person information clearinghouse is established and administered by the Department of Public Safety, and is available for use by all Texas law enforcement agencies.

Article 63.003 of the Code of Criminal Procedure states that the missing children and missing person clearinghouse is intended to be the central store of information on the subject. It should include a system for exchanging information about missing children, missing persons, and unidentified dead bodies. It should include a means for communicating with the National Crime Information Center. It should also feature a statewide toll-free telephone number so that citizens may report information. Finally, it should have an apparatus for disseminating information to the Texas Education Agency and law enforcement agencies.

Missing person report forms

Article 63.004 of the Code of Criminal Procedure states that the Department of Public Safety is responsible for distributing missing children and missing person report forms. These reports may be given to authorized law enforcement officers.

Law enforcement response

Article 63.009 of the Code of Criminal Procedure states that when a law enforcement agency receives a report of a missing child or missing person, that agency should immediately initiate an investigation. The agency should also enter the name of the person into the clearinghouse and the National Crime Information Center missing person file. The law enforcement agency should tell whoever filed the report that this information has been entered into the clearinghouse and missing person file.

Article 63.011 of the Code of Criminal Procedure states that law enforcement agencies may honor a written request from a parent or guardian for information from the missing children and missing person information clearinghouse that could aid the identification or location of the child.

Amber alert system

Section 411.352 of the Government Code states that the Department of Public Safety is responsible for developing and administrating a statewide alert system to be activated on behalf of the abducted children. This program, known as the Amber alert system, is coordinated with the Texas Department of Transportation, the office of the governor, and other law enforcement agencies.

Terminate activation of the Amber Alert System

Section 411.358 of the Government Code states that the director of the department will terminate the activation of the Amber alert system when a child is recovered, the abduction is otherwise resolved, or the director determines that the system is no longer effective in this case.

Amber Alert System activation

Section 411.355 of the Government Code states that the Department of Public Safety will activate the Amber alert system at the request of local law enforcement agencies when a child younger than 14 has been abducted. The department may also activate the alarm if it believes that the abducted child is in immediate danger of injury, death, or sexual assault. The Amber alert system requires sufficient information so that the public can assist in finding a child.

Clearinghouse records

Article 63.017 of the Code of Criminal Procedure states that clearinghouse records related to the investigation of a missing child, missing person, or unidentified body must remain confidential.

Written and Verbal Communications

Major parts of speech

The major parts of speech are nouns, verbs, adjectives, adverbs, prepositions, and pronouns. A noun names a person, place, or thing. Nouns may be used to represent physical objects or abstractions, like concepts or ideas. A verb describes an action or a mode of being. "Walk," "eat," and "be" are all examples of verbs. An adjective modifies another word. This means that it adds descriptive detail to another word. Words like "red" and "rough" are adjectives. Adverbs modify verbs, prepositions, nouns, and other adverbs. Many adverbs end with "-ly." A preposition links with a noun, pronoun, or noun phrase. Prepositional phrases function much like adverbs, adjectives or nouns. A pronoun stands in for a noun or noun phrase. "He" and "she" are two examples of pronouns.

Complete sentences

Officers must be able to write in complete sentences. A complete sentence expresses at least one entire thought. It contains both a subject and a predicate (that is, it has both a noun and a correlating verb). Police officers are not meant to write with too much style or ornament. The priority of a police officer when writing should be clarity. Written sentences must be clear, as it will not always be possible for the author to expand or rephrase for a confused reader. Officers should avoid sentence fragments, which are incomplete because they lack a subject or verb. They must also avoid run-on sentences, which are so long that they may confuse the reader. Officers should also avoid using double negatives or the passive voice in their written messages. Police communications should also not contain slang or overly technical jargon. Communications should avoid repetition, and should strive to convey all of the relevant information with precision but without unnecessary verbiage.

Field notes

Officers should take field notes, or brief records of their observations, for later use in reports and formal records. Field notes are an invaluable source of information because they contain small details that might otherwise be forgotten. Field notes should be the foundation of reports. If an officer takes effective field notes, it is less likely that he or she will have to contact sources again in the future. Finally, field notes have been demonstrated to provide greater detail and accuracy with respect to the time, sequence, and character of important events. This is especially true when the events in question happened very quickly or were very traumatic. Field notes should center around descriptions of the persons, vehicles, and property involved in a possible crime. These notes should be as specific as possible.

Specific information

An officer's field notes should contain information about the suspects, victims, and witnesses (if there are any). With regard to people, the field notes should record race, gender, height, weight, clothing, hair color, eye color, complexion, nose shape, and any other distinguishing characteristics. The essential vehicle information is expressed by the initials CYMBAL, which stands for "Color, Year, Make (or Model), Body style, and License number." It is also useful to record the vehicle identification number, estimated value, and any other distinguishing characteristics. With regard to other property, field notes should record the manufacturer, model, serial number, cost, size, color, style, use, and location. In general, field notes should include a summary of the date, time, location, involved parties, and any other information that will be required for a report or useful for an investigation.

Information that must supplement field notes for a complete report: In order to produce a thorough report, officers must be able to identify the following for all of the involved parties: full name, aliases (if any), gender, race, involvement, occupation, age, date of birth, and driver's license number. Also, officers need to obtain full contact information for each party, including address and phone number. A report must also identify the crime, the property involved, and the nature of the events leading to the investigation. The notes should contain a summary of the location and the relative positions of the parties, vehicles, and property during the events. If the officer obtains any information relating to possible motives for the crime, this should be included in the report as well. Finally, the report should include a discussion of how the offense occurred and how the officer became initially involved.

Introductory Spanish

Spanish

The number of Spanish-speaking people in Texas continues to grow, and in 1990 was reported to be about 25 percent of the total state population. For the most part, Spanish-speaking people in Texas are from Mexico, though most are legal citizens of the United States. Even peace officers who are not fluent in Spanish should become familiar with certain vocabulary. For instance, peace officers should become familiar with words that suggest the speaker is about to become aggressive. Peace officers should also know the Spanish names for common weapons. Peace officers should know basic questions (like "Where?" and "When?"), as well as the names for family relationships, numbers, colors, and clothes. Officers should be able to ask the typical questions of a field interview, like "Who called the police?" and "Who saw what happened?" Officers should also be able to describe what they are doing to a Spanish-speaking audience. Finally, officers should be able to give basic commands in Spanish, as for instance those related to handcuffing and detention.

Communication with Hispanics

Hispanic Americans feel a very strong bond with their families and communities, which at times can be confusing or misleading to peace officers. For instance, a Hispanic person is more apt to use a plural pronoun ("we") to describe his or her own opinions or observations. Also, a Hispanic person may seem reluctant to talk to a peace officer without the presence of peers or family members. Officers should be aware that Hispanics may have a harder time speaking English if they are stressed or nervous. Many Hispanics have a skeptical view of law enforcement, in part because the authorities in their home countries are more corrupt. Hispanics view communication as a very personal activity, so peace officers should be sure to speak warmly and mind their manners. Also, peace officers should always be clear about their intentions and interests in the conversation, and should never mislead.

Hispanic nonverbal communication

The nonverbal communication patterns of Hispanic Americans are somewhat distinct. For instance, Hispanic Americans are much more likely to avoid eye contact, but this is done out of respect rather than feelings of shame or guilt. Hispanic Americans also use a great deal of body language, like shaking an index finger to indicate "no" or pointing by raising an eyebrow. Hispanics are often quite fearful of law enforcement, typically because of negative experiences with the authorities in their home countries. Occasionally, a peace officer will overestimate the emotional intensity of a Hispanic speaker because of passionate gestures and words. Hispanic Americans are often more comfortable with displays of emotion, and may not be as serious as they appear.

Discrimination against Hispanic Americans

Law enforcement officers should always refrain from language that may be perceived as derogatory to the Hispanic community. Personal relationships are very important to Hispanic Americans, and any indication of a lack of respect will be extremely damaging to police service. At present, Hispanic Americans are far less likely to report crime, and are more skeptical about the abilities of peace officers. This is especially true for recent migrants from countries with corrupt law enforcement, as for instance Chile, El Salvador, and Guatemala. Many law enforcement departments have tried to remedy this problem by training bilingual community service officers, or CSOs, as liaisons to the Hispanic community. These officers are charged with building relationships with Hispanic leaders, learning about the needs of the community, and explaining police actions.

Force Options

Penal Code

Defend themselves against prosecution
Section 9.02 of the Penal Code states that people may defend themselves against prosecution by proving that their conduct was justified by Chapter 9 of the Penal Code.

Confinement
Section 9.03 of the Penal Code states that confinement may be justified in cases where force is justified by this chapter, so long as the actor stopped the confinement as soon as he could safely do so.

Threats of force
Section 9.04 of the Penal Code states that in cases justified by Chapter 9, threats of force may be justified.

Procesuted if reckless injuries or kills innocent third party

Section 9.05 of the Penal Code states that even when a person is justified by the law in threatening or using either force or deadly force, he may still be prosecuted if he recklessly injures or kills an innocent third person.

Section 9.06 of the Penal Code states that the justification of behavior by this chapter does not affect the remedies available for that conduct in a civil suit.

Conduct is justified

Section 9.21 of the Penal Code states that conduct is justified if the person who performs it reasonably believes that it is authorized by law, by the judgment of a court, or is necessary for the execution of process. The use of deadly force, however, is not justified unless it occurs in the lawful course of war or is specifically required by statute.

Avoid imminent harm

Section 9.22 of the Penal Code states that conduct may be justified if the actor reasonably believes it is necessary to avoid imminent harm, and if the desirability and necessity of avoiding harm can reasonably be said to outweigh the harm that will be prevented. Also, conduct may be justified if there is no clear reason to exclude its justification.

Self-defense

Section 9.31 of the Penal Code states that a person is justified in using force when he reasonably believes it is immediately necessary for self-defense. The self-defense justification works if the other person unlawfully and with force entered the actor's home, car, or place of business. Self-defense is justified if the actor believes that the other person was attempting to commit aggravated kidnapping, murder, sexual assault, aggravated sexual assault, robbery, or aggravated robbery. Self-defense is justified if it did not provoke the aggression from the other person. Self-defense is not justified if it is a response to mere verbal provocation, or if it is undertaken in resistance to an arrest or search.

Deadly force

Section 9.32 of the Penal Code states that a person may be justified in using deadly force against another person if this force is immediately necessary to protect the actor against the other person's own attempted use of unlawful deadly force or to prevent the commission of aggravated kidnapping, murder, sexual assault, aggravated sexual assault, robbery, or aggravated robbery.

Section 9.33 of the Penal Code dates that a person may use force or deadly force against another person to protect a third person if he reasonably believes that this intervention is immediately necessary to protect that person from unlawful force, or unlawful deadly force.

Section 9.42 of the Penal Code states that a person is justified in using deadly force to protect land or tangible property if it prevents the other person's imminent commission of arson, burglary, robbery, aggravated robbery, nighttime theft, or nighttime criminal mischief. This deadly force may only be justified if the actor reasonably believes that the land or property cannot be protected by any other means, or that using the other means would expose him to death or serious bodily injury.

Section 9.43 of the Penal Code states that a person may use force or deadly force to protect the land or tangible property of a third person if he reasonably believes that the person has attempted or committed theft, if he believes that his aid has been requested by the third person, or if he has a legal duty to protect that person's land or property. Section 9.44 of the Penal Code states that use of force justification may be applied to the operation of devices that protect land or tangible property, so long as these devices do not create a substantial risk of death or serious bodily injury, and so long as the device is only used in reasonable circumstances.

Using force

Section 9.34 of the Penal Code states that a person is justified in using force, but not deadly force, if it is necessary to prevent another person from committing suicide or inflicting serious public injury to himself. If it is necessary to do so to preserve another person's life in an emergency, a person is justified in using force and deadly force.

Section 9.41 of the Penal Code states that a person is justified in using force to the extent necessary to prevent or terminate trespass or unlawful interference with his land or property.

Section 9.51 of the Penal Code states that peace officers are justified in using force when it is reasonably believed to be necessary to make an arrest, conduct a search, or to prevent escape. Force is only justified when the actor reasonably believes the arrest or search is lawful, or that the warrant supporting the action is valid. Also, before using force, the officer must identify himself and his intentions, unless these may reasonably be assumed to be known by the other party. People other than peace officers may use force against other people if they reasonably believe it is necessary to make a lawful arrest or prevent escape and if the other party can be assumed to understand the reasons for the force. Peace officers are justified in using deadly force to the extent the peace officer reasonably believes is necessary to make an arrest or prevent escape after the perpetration of a crime involving deadly force. Peace officers may also use deadly force in situations where they believe the other party will cause death or serious bodily injury to another person if allowed to continue.

Section 9.52 of the Penal Code states that the use of force is justified to prevent the escape of a detainee so long as that level of force would have been appropriate for the offense that caused the person's original arrest. One exception is that the guards at correctional facilities may use deadly force to prevent the escape of a prisoner.

Section 9.53 of the Penal Code states that correctional facility employees may use force against detainees to the extent they reasonably believe necessary to maintain security and safety.

Section 9.61 of the Penal Code states that, short of deadly force, any use of force against a person younger than 18 is justified if it is committed by the child's parent and is necessary to discipline the child or promote his welfare.

Section 9.62 of the Penal Code states that any use of force short of deadly force is justified by educators to the extent necessary to promote discipline in a school group.

Section 9.63 of the Penal Code states that the use of force, but not deadly force, is justified against a mental incompetent if the actor is a parent or guardian and the force is necessary to either maintain discipline or promote the incompetent's welfare.

Strategies of Defense—Mechanics of Arrest

Weaponless strategies of defense

A peace officer will occasionally be required to use weaponless strategies of defense. These require excellent body control and coordination, as well as attention to the details of the situation. The officer must be aware of the suspect's body, whether he or she has any weapons or accomplices, and whether there are any readily available escape routes. Weaponless defense depends on constant verbal communication with the suspect and with fellow officers. An officer engaged in such a procedure must maintain enough distance from the suspect as to be able to observe any furtive movements, such as reaching for a hidden weapon. Some of the most common methods of weaponless defense are joint-locking; pressure points; hand and foot strikes; and blocks involving the hands, arms, or legs.

Deadly force

Officers should only use deadly force when their lives or the lives of others are under direct threat. It may also be acceptable to use deadly force when extreme bodily injury is threatened. Deadly force may be applied with firearms, control weapons, chemical and electrical devices, vehicles, and even the hands.

Peace officers common weapons

Peace officers have access to a number of weapons but, with the exception of handcuffs, they all require special training. For instance, a peace officer may learn to use impact weapons such as straight, expandable, and side handle batons. A peace officer may also receive training with chemical and electrical weapons, such as mace, tasers, and stun guns. It is appropriate to use a baton in any situation which necessitates force but is not severe enough to require the use of deadly weapons. For instance, if a suspect who can be reasonably assumed to have committed a crime fails to comply with verbal commands, the officer may use a baton. When an officer is assaulted by an unarmed suspect or by a suspect with a weapon besides a firearm, he or she may use a baton. Officers may also use a baton for crowd control when part of a tactical squad.

Baton

A peace officer should never use a baton against the head or throat of a suspect on purpose. Instead, the officer should try to aim for the meaty areas of the arms or legs, or at the abdomen. The officer should never aim for the chest, groin, or center of the back. When the baton is used, the officer should try to maintain a defensive posture. It is acceptable to wield the baton with either the right or left hand. The baton should be held between the officer and the suspect in most cases. These rules apply to straight, expandable, and side handle batons. The baton is capable of inflicting serious injury, and even of killing a person, but it should never be used with this intention. The baton may be used whenever force is required, but deadly force is not necessary.

Physical process of arrest

An officer must use his or her own judgment regarding the necessity of arrest and the amount of force required to make an arrest. For instance, an officer will need to judge whether the suspect has a behavioral disorder which could lead to erratic or violent conduct. The time and location of the encounter also have an influence on the necessity of arrest. For instance, suspects are more likely to run or to conceal weapons from an arresting officer at night. If a suspect is intoxicated, it is more likely that he or she should be arrested. Also, when spectators or associates of the suspect are nearby, it may be necessary to perform a quick arrest in order to defuse the situation. In all of these cases, the law grants a great deal of discretion to the arresting officer.

Confronting a suspect

When approaching a suspect directly, the officer will be able to observe all of the suspect's movements. However, the suspect will be fully aware of the officer's presence, and will have time to prepare either an attack or escape attempt.

Approaching the suspect from the rear enables the officer to surprise him or her, though sometimes this surprise will cause the suspect to react violently or unpredictably. This is especially true because the suspect will not know that he or she is being approached by an officer.

When approaching a suspect from the side, an officer should be aware that he or she cannot see all of the suspect's actions. For instance, an officer approaching from the suspect's right would not be able to see what the suspect is doing with his or her left hand.

Two officers confrontation

When two officers approach a suspect together, they should maintain constant communication, both verbal and visual. They should not approach the suspect from the same side, as this will make it easier for the suspect to either attack or attempt escape. It is generally better if one of the officers takes the lead. While this officer directly confronts the subject, through interview or arrest, the other should observe the suspect's movements. When a subject is being interviewed, the non-interviewing officer should stay a short distance from the subject, so as to improve observation and keep movement unrestricted. The suspect should be frisked whenever it is believed that he or she may have weapons or other materials that could be a hazard to the safety of the officer or public. When a subject needs to be physically engaged or arrested, officers should try to communicate the reasons to the suspect.

Handcuffing skill

Handcuffs are a mandatory piece of equipment for peace officers, and an officer must understand how to cuff a suspect who is lying down, kneeling, sitting, or standing. An officer who is cuffing one suspect should bring the suspect's hands behind his or her back, and apply the cuffs with the palms out and the keyhole of the cuffs up. Handcuffs must be double-locked. If it is necessary to restrain two suspects with a single set of cuffs, the officer should either cuff right hand to right hand or left hand to left hand, as this will impede the suspects' ability run quickly. When restraining two suspects with two sets of cuffs, the procedures should be the same as for applying a single set of cuffs to a single subject. In some cases, it may be necessary to use plastic handcuffs, shoelaces, a belt, or a tie to augment the traditional cuffs. Handcuffs should never be applied too tightly, as this can lead to charges of excessive force.

Physical search

When searching a prone (lying down) suspect, an officer should first force him or her to extend his or her arms outward, perpendicular to the body. The legs should be spread as well. When searching a standing suspect in an open area, the officer should perform the search from behind, and should watch the suspect's arms vigilantly. While one of the officer's arms searches the suspect, the other should hold onto the waistband of the suspect's pants. Searching a kneeling suspect is slightly easier. The kneeling suspect should have his or her legs crossed, with the hands behind the head and the fingers intertwined. The back of the kneeling suspect should be arched. At all times, the officer should watch the suspect's arms for sudden movements. Some departments have slightly different recommendations for searching females.

Walking with a suspect

When one officer is escorting a single suspect on foot, the officer should stand behind and somewhat to the side of the suspect, with the gun side of the officer on the opposite side from the suspect. The officer should hold onto the back of the suspect's pants, between the cuffed hands. When leading two cuffed suspects, the officer should stand behind and in between them. When two officers are escorting one suspect, they should both be behind the suspect, with one on either side holding on to one of the suspect's arms. When two officers are escorting two suspects, they should both be standing behind the suspects, with each officer to the left or right side of the suspect and with one hand between the cuffed hands of the suspect and on the suspect's waistband.

Transporting suspects in cars without cages

When an officer is transporting a single suspect in a car with no cage, he should place the suspect in the right front seat, with the seat belt fastened and the car doors locked. The officer's gun should be on the opposite side from the suspect. A single officer should not attempt to move more than one suspect at a time without special equipment. When two officers are transporting one suspect in a car with no cage, they should place the suspect in the right rear seat, with one of the officers in the left rear seat. Each of the officers should have their guns on the left, the doors should be locked, and the suspect's seat belt should be fastened. When two officers are transporting two suspects in a car without a cage, the suspects should be placed in the back right and back center seats, with one of the officers in the back left seat. The doors should be locked and the officers should both have their weapons on their left.

Strategies of Defense—Firearms

Firearms

With regard to shooting at or from a motor vehicle, firing warning shots, destroying an animal, carrying back-up weapons and using off-duty weapons, peace officers are advised to follow departmental policy. Peace officers must be able to demonstrate the safe handling of a handgun and a shotgun. Also, peace officers must be able to demonstrate the process of unloading these weapons. Peace officers must be familiar with the rules of the shooting range, especially with regard to safety. Officers should be adept at shooting in broad daylight, at night, and when the light is low. Officers should know the techniques of quality marksmanship, and should be able to demonstrate holstering and reloading while maintaining eye contact with an interlocutor.

Firearms proficiency standards

Peace officers must be able to shoot a handgun from 3 yards with one hand. They must be able to shoot a handgun with two hands from distances of 7, 15, and 25 yards. A peace officer's work with the handgun must include at least one timed reload. They must be able to shoot a shotgun accurately from a distance of at least 15 yards. In each course, peace officers must fire a minimum of 50 rounds with a handgun and five rounds with a shotgun. The minimum qualification score for these exercises is 70 percent of the total possible score. In addition, peace officers must be able to demonstrate the ability to clean and inspect a weapon. In rare cases, peace officers may be granted an exemption from this requirement.

Emergency Medical Assistance

Patient assessment

A peace officer should know how to assess an injured person quickly. To begin with, the officer must ensure that the location is safe for the injured party and the officer. If not, the officer should take whatever measures are necessary to move the injured person to a safer location. The officer should then conduct a primary survey, beginning by ascertaining whether the airway is open. The officer should then check the injured person's breathing and circulation.

If the person is bleeding, the officer should cover the wound with whatever dressing is available and apply direct pressure. The wounded part of the body should be raised above the heart if possible, and supplementary bandages and dressings should be applied as necessary. In cases where direct pressure to the wound does not stop bleeding, the officer should apply pressure to the relevant artery. The officer should obtain medical care as soon as possible.

Burns, shock, and broken bones/sprains

Treating a burn begins by removing or eliminating the source of the injury. The officer should then attempt to cool the burn with water if available. The burn should be immediately covered with dry, clean bandages.

A person in shock should be forced to lie down. The officer should elevate the person's legs, except in cases where the officer suspects that the head, neck, or spine may be injured. The officer should stay with the victim and provide comfort, but should not administer food or drink.

When dealing with a broken bone or severe sprain, the officer should immediately immobilize the affected area and, if appropriate, apply a splint. Signs of a broken bone or sprain include numbness, restricted mobility, bruising, and swelling. In any of the above scenarios, the officer should solicit medical help as soon as possible.

Poisoning and exposure

If a person has been exposed to poisonous chemicals, the affected area should be immediately flushed with water. If a person has been bit by a snake or spider, the wound should be cleaned and immobilized such that it is lower than the heart. If a person has ingested chemical poison, his or her vital signs should be checked while emergency medical attention is requested. A person who was ingested poison should not be given anything else to eat or drink. A person suffering from cold exposure should be immediately removed to a warmer location. His or her clothing should be removed, and dry blankets should be applied. A person who is suffering from heat exposure should be escorted to a cooler location and given water. Any restrictive clothing should be loosened, and cool, damp cloths should be applied directly to the skin.

Choking victims

An officer who encounters a choking person should immediately perform the Heimlich maneuver. This is done by standing behind the victim and placing one fist just above the victim's navel. The thumb side of the fist should be against the person's skin. With the other hand, the officer should grab his or her fist and deliver a series of quick, upward thrusts. This should be continued until the choking is resolved. If rescue breathing is required, the officer should tilt the victim's head back and lift his or her chin. Pinching the victim's nose shut, the officer should cover his or her mouth with the officer's own and deliver two slow breaths. If the victim's chest rises, this indicates that there is no airway obstruction. Then, the officer should deliver a single slow breath every five seconds for a full minute. So long as the victim has a pulse, the officer should continue this breathing pattern.

Diabetic coma, insulin shock, stroke, or seizure

If an officer encounters a person who has lapsed into a diabetic coma, the victim should be moved to a hospital as soon as possible. A person who has gone into insulin shock should be given sugar in some form (juice, candy, or honey, for example) if he or she is conscious. If he or she is unconscious, a small amount of sugar should be placed under the tongue, and the person should be moved to a hospital as soon as possible. Stroke victims should have their airways checked and should be kept immobilized. The attending officer should provide comfort and should slightly elevate the head, neck, and shoulders. The head should be slightly rotated to one side. The victim's temperature should be monitored, and medical help should be obtained immediately. A person who is having a seizure should be placed on the ground but not forcibly restrained. Any restrictive clothing should be loosened, and the patient should be encouraged to rest even after the seizure is over. The most important thing during a seizure is to prevent the person from injuring him or herself.

CPR

CPR, short for cardiopulmonary resuscitation, is a series of chest compressions meant to restart the heart and continue circulation. In effect, the person delivering CPR is performing the work of the victim's heart. The officer should begin by making sure the patient's airway is clear. The officer should then deliver a few deep breaths into the victim's mouth, followed by a series of several chest compressions. The chest compression should be delivered to the center of the victim's rib cage.

When dealing with a woman who is about to give birth, an officer should support the head of the baby as it emerges. Next, the officer should assist with the exit of the upper shoulder, and should support the body and feet of the baby as they exit the mother. The officer should immediately swipe a finger across the back of the baby's throat to ensure that the airway is clear. If the baby is not breathing, it may be necessary to perform CPR using very slight chest compressions. Obviously, an officer dealing with a situation of this type should obtain medical assistance as soon as possible.

Communicable disease

If they are not careful, officers are at risk of acquiring a communicable disease from an injured or ill person. Communicable diseases are those that can be transferred from one person to another, typically through body fluids like saliva, mucus, and blood. The most common communicable diseases for peace officers and other first responders are influenza, hepatitis B, and HIV/AIDS.

The best way to avoid contracting a communicable disease is to avoid exposure to the fluids of other people. Whenever possible, an attending officer should wear gloves, goggles, and a mask. It is always a good idea to wash thoroughly those areas of the body that have come into contact with the victim. If exposure is suspected, the officer should get tested as soon as possible.

Transporting injured persons

The first step in the transfer of an injured person by any means is stabilization. The injured person should be laid on his or back, if possible, and secured to a stretcher. Any injured limbs should be held in place. If the person is to be transported by air, he or she should be protected from any lurching or swaying that may take place during the trip. If the person is to be transported by water, he or she should also be protected against unexpected motion. There is a certain protocol for approaching a boat that will be used to transport an injured person. When the injured person is to be transported on the ground, he or she should be secured to a stretcher or gurney with appropriate straps.

Emergency Communications

Precise communication

It is essential that communications made during an emergency situation be as precise as possible. To begin with, the communications should be made over broadcasts that are likely to reach a large and appropriate audience. Emergency communications should be limited to the most extreme circumstances, or else the public may cease to pay close attention. It is also important that emergency messages introduce themselves as such in clear language. Emergency communications should be delivered at times that will maximize the audience.

Many emergency messages must deliver information about a suspect or other person. There is a standard order in which this information should be presented: name, gender, race, date of birth, height, weight, hair

- 124 -

color, and eye color. Once this information has been delivered, the message may describe the person's skin tone, physical markings, and clothing. With regard to vehicles, the message should inform in the following order: color, year, make, body-style, and license number. When applicable, emergency messages should describe the types of weapons involved, and should obey local radio traffic standards.

Radio broadcaster

An effective radio broadcaster must be able to project his or her voice and maintain clarity. There is also a prescribed rate of speech that broadcasters are expected to maintain. Broadcasters should remain in control of their tone of voice, and should remain calm regardless of the situation. One component of proper broadcasting is understanding the proper positioning of the microphone. Also, experienced broadcasters will learn to use phrases and pronunciations that make it easier for the audience to comprehend the message.

Officer should not transmit message

There are some situations in which an officer should not transmit a message. For instance, occasionally the base will recommend that the officer stand by until brief interference has come to an end. Also, officers are dissuaded from transmitting long messages unless there is no other option. When an emergency situation is occurring elsewhere, officers are asked not to transmit messages unless absolutely necessary. Finally, police departments ask that officers refrain from any unnecessary radio traffic that is not related to the availability of the given unit.

Professional Police Driving

Liability situations

There are some situations in which police officers may be held liable for their driving. Police officers are liable when they fail to demonstrate appropriate regard for the safety of other people on the road. Also, law enforcement departments are liable when they fail to develop a formal written policy with regard to police pursuits. If a police officer acts with criminal negligence or commits a wrongful act while behind the wheel of a law enforcement vehicle, the department may be held liable. Finally, officers may be held liable for any accidents that occur when not in direct pursuit of an actual or suspected criminal, or when not responding to an authentic emergency. In other words, police officers may only use emergency driving techniques in exigent circumstances.

Law enforcement agency's pursuit policy

For most law enforcement agencies, the pursuit policy discusses the requirements for a pursuit to begin, and the conditions that should cause a pursuit to be stopped. A law enforcement agency's pursuit policy will also typically describe the conditions in which the light and siren may be used. Finally, the document will usually outline the pursuit procedures. Police officers should be aware of the effects of emergency equipment. For instance, the use of regular headlights will decrease the effectiveness of emergency lights. Also, on especially bright days the emergency lights will have decreased visibility. Also, the effectiveness of sirens is diminished as the car gains speed. In heavy traffic, or around loud equipment, sirens will also be less audible. In dense urban environments, where there are many tall buildings and a great deal of concrete, sirens may reverberate, which will make it difficult for other drivers and pedestrians to identify the source of the sound.

Pre-shift vehicle inspections

Before every shift, police officers should inspect their vehicles. There are three main reasons for this inspection: to foster the officer's confidence in the vehicle, to keep the vehicle in good condition, and to prevent faulty equipment from causing traffic accidents. A pre-shift vehicle inspection has four components: interior check, exterior check, mechanical check, and required inventory.

Steering techniques

Police officers must master several different steering techniques, among them shuffle steering, evasive steering, counter steering, and handling unavoidable collisions. In most situations, officers are required to abide by the principles of defensive driving. Defensive driving varies somewhat depending on the road and weather conditions.

Traffic collisions

Traffic collisions often occur because a driver is overconfident or impatient. Drivers are also more likely to get in an accident when they are distracted. This is one reason why many communities have banned the use of cell phones or computers while driving. There are certain driving maneuvers that have proved to be the most hazardous for law enforcement officers. Officers are more likely to be involved in collisions when backing up, making a left turn, or parking. Officers frequently assume that they have the right of way, which can lead to accidents when those assumptions are incorrect. Also, officers are more likely to get in accidents when they operate their vehicles at a speed that is unsafe in the current conditions. Fatigue can lead to accidents as well, because it slows down reaction speed and diminished visual perception.

Vehicle safety

Aggressive pursuit is not always the best option. When deciding whether to pursue, an officer must take into account factors like the density of traffic, the type of vehicles involved, and the presence of pedestrians. Prospective officers should always be able to describe the pros and cons of opting for pursuit in a given situation. Officers should also be able to discuss the conditions that will influence a car's stopping distance. These include the skill of the driver, the make and model of the vehicle, the road conditions, the weather, and the speed at which the car is moving. Speed has a profound effect on the ability to stop or turn a vehicle. When a car's speed increases, it will need more space to complete a turn. Also, the traction limits of the vehicle's tires may be exceeded when the speed increases. Finally, the car's distribution of weight transfers more profoundly when the car is moving at a high speed. This is why cars are more subject to rolling over when turning at high speeds.

Driving skills

A peace officer must demonstrate acceleration, maneuvering, and braking skills during driving exercises. Aspiring officers must demonstrate correct weight transfer control, throttle control, braking accuracy, road position, and steering accuracy. A peace officer must be able to stop on command or displace the vehicle to the right or left side. A peace officer must demonstrate efficient braking skills when stopping completely, before turning, and in the midst of an emergency. A peace officer must be able to reassert control over a vehicle that is in the middle of a front skid. Finally, aspiring peace officers must be able to avoid hazards, as for instance cross traffic, dips in the road, and other obstacles. The precise course layout and driving protocols will vary by department.

Problem Solving and Critical Thinking

Effective communication strategies

Creating a climate of effective communication requires more than choosing the right words. There are also some physical choices that a peace officer can make to improve his or her interactions with colleagues and others. To begin with, peace officers should make the setting of communication as comfortable and peaceful as possible. Also, officers should be mindful of personal space. During a private conversation, officers should be close enough to hear one another easily, but far enough apart for each interlocutor to feel comfortable. A good communicator also maintains consistent but not continuous eye contact to indicate sincere interest. When communicating while standing, an officer should maintain good posture, which conveys confidence and authority. When appropriate, officers may signify particular interest by leaning forward slightly.

Nonverbal cues of facial expressions and timing

Officers improve their communication skills by paying more attention to nonverbal cues. For instance, officers should attend to facial expressions, which often provide a wealth of information about a person's thoughts and feelings. Officers should pay attention to the amount of eye contact they have with their interlocutor. Sometimes, a person may have an unwitting habit of making faces. Officers should consider how to manage other people by using appropriate facial expressions.

Officers should also recognize that there are times to speak and times to be silent. Officers should remember that it is important to take turns in a conversation, and that it is not right for one party to do all of the talking. Officers should also know that the time restrictions on conversation must be eased in certain scenarios. For instance, if a commanding officer says to a subordinate, "I only have five minutes," but the subordinate then introduces an important and complex subject, it may be necessary for the commanding officer to extend the conversation.

Common facial expressions

Facial expressions convey a wealth of information about a person's thoughts and feelings, but too few officers are adept at interpreting them. Facial expressions are especially useful because they are typically not intended by the person who makes them, and therefore they provide information that the person would perhaps rather not have conveyed. For instance, flared nostrils indicate arousal, whether emotional or sexual. Pursed lips suggest disagreement or frustration. A raising of one upper lip, in a sort of snarl gesture, indicates contempt or repulsion. A pouting of the lower lip indicates uncertainty or doubt. Raised brows indicate interest or surprise, while sticking out the tongue suggests distaste. When a person's pupils are dilated, that means he or she is feeling full of emotion. Dilated pupils may also indicate that the person feels a threat is imminent. On the other hand, looking down indicates that the person is feeling sheepish or ashamed.

Proxemics

Proxemics is the study of the relative distance between people during communication. Researchers in this area have identified three general orientations: social distance (from 5 to 10 feet), personal distance (3 to 5 feet), and intimate distance (3 feet or less). The appropriate distance for a given conversation depends on the setting, the relationship between the interlocutors, and the nature of the communication. Many people make a normal conversation feel less comfortable by standing either too close or too far away from the other person. There is also some science related to the posture of the body during communication. When a person likes or admires his interlocutor, he tends to face that person directly (i.e., with his shoulders parallel to the other person). A person who is disliked or distrusted may be approached from an angle. Indeed, some research suggests that the level of distaste for the other person is proportionate to the angle at which a person turns away.

Kinesics

Kinesics is the study of body movement. It can be applied to communication in fruitful ways. To begin with, there are certain physical movements that have acquired a cultural connotation. For instance, pointing at another person typically indicates a threat or a challenge. When a person makes hand gestures with his or her palms up, on the other hand, the appearance is more friendly and welcoming. Crossed arms may indicate defensiveness if they are held tightly against the body, or relaxation if they are held loosely. People even reveal how they are feeling by the way they position their feet during conversation. If a person's toes are pointing out, it is indicative of a feeling of dominance. Toes pointed in, on the other hand, indicate submission. A person tends to point his feet towards people he likes and away from people he dislikes.

Paralinguistic and haptic factors

The paralinguistic factors of a communication are all of the aspects of vocal production besides the content of the message. This may include the volume, tone, or rhythm of speech, to name a few. A person's tone of voice indicates his emotional state. Haptic factors are those related to touch. The presence and quality of physical contact during a communication provides a great deal of information. When a person touches another gently or lightly on an extremity (i.e., arm or leg rather than chest), it is usually meant to convey affection. When a person touches another person more forcefully, however, it may indicate aggression or dominance. There are many situations in which any physical contact between interlocutors is inappropriate.

Observation

Officers constantly have to evaluate a social situation quickly. The ability to do this well relies heavily on intuition, but it can also be improved through learning and taking the right approach. To begin with, officers should be sure to note the relative positions of the people. If people are standing close together, it may mean that they know each other well or are about to get in a fight. If people are standing apart from one another and not speaking, they may be strangers. Experienced officers become skilled at assessing the relationships between people. They can enter a room and quickly understand not only who knows whom, but who is in charge and who is subservient. One of the most important assessments an officer needs to make is the energy level of the situation. Agitated physical movements, loud voices, and dilated pupils all indicate high levels of emotional arousal.

Good listening skills

Officers must be able to listen effectively if they are to handle unfamiliar and new situations with authority and justice. One of the major prerequisites to effective listening is the temporary suspension of judgment. Officers must be able to listen with an open mind, even when they already have some assumptions. An officer should always give other people the chance to provide more information or context to a situation. Officers should not only pay attention to the content of the message, but also to the emotional state of the speaker. When a speaker is aroused and excited, he is more apt to use exaggerated language. An officer may also be able to obtain useful information from the physical carriage of the speaker. In particular, a person's posture indicates his level of confidence. An officer should always try to isolate the most important elements of the person's speech. Some officers find it useful to remember these elements as the "five Ws and an H": who, what, when, where, why, and how. If these questions are resolved, the officer has understood the core of the message.

Active listening

Many officers struggle to listen effectively because they consider listening to be a passive activity. However, the best listening is active listening, meaning that it requires participation and even action by the listener. Active listening begins with close attention to what the other person is saying. An active listener nods or shows in some other way that he is paying attention. Active listeners confirm their understanding by paraphrasing what the speaker has said, or by asking for clarification on key points. An active listener also attends to the emotional state of the speaker, and considers how this state can be improved or managed. Most importantly, an active listener demonstrates comprehension by taking steps in response to the message. If the speaker has a legitimate complaint, for instance, the officer tries to remedy it. If the speaker does not have a legitimate complaint, the officer gives a respectful counterargument.

Requests

Officers must handle requests from colleagues and citizens frequently. It is important to handle these requests in such a way as to minimize conflict. This leads to deeper trust and improved morale. At the same time, an officer must be able to verify the legitimacy of the request and its author. Fulfilling a request is most beneficial when there is some means of verifying compliance. This applies to requests made of and by officers. For instance, if an officer asks a citizen to do something, there should be a nonintrusive way for the officer to confirm compliance. It helps if an officer can provide incentives for compliance. The incentives should be appropriate to the person, and should be positive. For instance, when a person has complied with an officer's request, the officer should be sure to say thank you.

Critical thinking

Critical thinking is the analysis, evaluation, and interpretation of information, followed by the application of this work to future actions. Critical thinking should not be conflated with criticism or even cynicism: it is an honest attempt to understand a problem from all perspectives. Critical thinking begins with a posture of skepticism. All claims must be supported by evidence, and counterarguments must be considered. Officers must be able to evaluate arguments, and must try to find holes even in those arguments for which they feel an automatic sympathy. Critical thinking requires evaluation of one's own prejudices and biases. Critical thinking entails coming up with arguments as well as evaluating them, however. A critical thinker needs to empathize with other people, and as best as possible to see the world from their perspective. A critical thinker must know how to ask the right questions and identify the prejudices and assumptions of others.

Effective problem solving

Problem solving is most effective when an officer maintains a positive attitude and does not become prematurely attached to a particular viewpoint. An officer should avoid guessing at solutions, and should be willing to break a problem down into its constituent parts before proceeding.

SARA model

Some departments recommend the SARA model for problem solving. This model has four components: scanning, analysis, response, and assessment. In the scanning phase, the officer identifies the problem, and lists its most essential components. Analysis entails gathering information from multiple sources and identifying patterns. The response phase focuses on actions that prevent future offenses or crimes, protect the probable victims of crimes, or make the environment less amenable to crime. Finally, the assessment phase involves the officers looking at the impact of their response, and trying to determine how efforts can be improved in the future.

Crime triangle

Some departments recommend the crime triangle as a useful tool for organizing thoughts about a particular problem. The crime triangle has three elements: offender, victim, and location. The officer should attempt to gather as much information as possible about these three subjects. All three of these elements must be present for the commission of a crime. Once the three elements have been identified, an officer may begin considering how they relate to one another. For instance, what effects does the location have on the behavior of the criminal or the victim? If the location is slightly adjusted, will this have an effect on crime? As an example, an officer might note that the criminal encountered the victim on a dark street. Illuminating the street could diminish the likelihood of a similar crime occurring there in the future.

Problem-oriented policing

Many departments are currently espousing problem-oriented policing, meaning that they focus on resolving the most pressing crime problems in their patrol areas. It is important to note that the prioritization of problems should be based on public opinion, not on the preferences of the department. In problem-oriented policing, the effectiveness of implemented solutions is the most important thing. As much as possible, these departments rely on the data they have collected over the years. Also, problem-oriented police departments seek to learn from the experience of their most veteran officers, especially those who are familiar with the community and physical setting around a crime problem. Problem-oriented police departments recognize that the criminal

justice system is not always the best instrument for solving community problems; sometimes, law enforcement is more effective when it simply supports other institutions. Finally, problem-oriented police departments are committed to finding solutions, which means that they are not afraid to take risks and endure temporary failures along the way.

Patrol/Consular Notification

Patrol

In order to patrol effectively, an officer should be familiar with the geographic and socioeconomic characteristics of the area. It is best for officers to patrol the same areas repeatedly, so that they continuously improve their local knowledge. An officer should be familiar with the crimes that are typical of the area, as well as any offenders who are known to reside there. Officers should know all of the streets and traffic patterns in the area, so that he or she will be able to move about with speed when necessary. Before beginning each patrol, officers should be briefed on any special circumstances such as stolen property, outstanding warrants, and planned gatherings. Also, officers should ensure that their equipment is clean and prepared, and that their physical person is clean and organized.

Patrol hazards

Officers often put themselves at risk by failing to avoid problematic scenarios when on patrol. For instance, officers should avoid drawing attention by revving their engines, slamming the car door, or having the radio on too loud. When approaching a possible crime scene, officers may want to avoid parking too close. Officers should also avoid placing themselves in positions where they become easy targets. This error is called silhouetting.

Officers should never stand in the middle of a doorway or hallway, and should never look for an extended period through open or broken windows. Officers should avoid actions that tell a suspect the extent of the patrol force or the path of officers' approach. To this end, officers should never point their flashlights at one another at night. When a suspect has his hands in his pockets, the officer should not let him remove them. If the suspect's hands are out of his pockets, however, the officer should not let him insert them. Whenever possible, suspects should be forced to place their hands out with the palms facing up.

Five common patrol patterns

In some areas, it is best for the patrol to follow an unpredictable pattern, though this can make it more difficult to ensure that the entire area is covered. In a circular patrol pattern, the car proceeds either from the center of the area outward, or from the perimeter of the area inward. In a double-back pattern, the patrol car consistently goes back over each area it has covered. This pattern is recommended for officers who are just becoming familiar with the area. Patrol cars should be in the center-most lane for observation but should move to the lane nearest the curb in situations where a quick stop may be necessary.

Officers should also be familiar with strategic parking. For instance, a visible parked patrol car can improve compliance with traffic laws, while a concealed patrol car can allow an officer to observe without influencing behavior. In a crime-ridden area, officers may employ a preventive patrol with high visibility, or an apprehension patrol, in which the main intention is surveillance and low visibility.

Modes of patrol

The most common mode of patrol is the automobile, which offers speed and visibility while allowing officers to carry essential equipment. Motorcycle patrol also enables officers to respond quickly, but they cannot

transport suspects. Motorcycles are often used in police escorts. Patrolling on foot enables officers to develop personal contacts in the community, which refines police service. Bicycle patrol also encourages officers to mix in the community. Moreover, bicycles are able to go places where cars and motorcycles cannot. In some cases, officers patrol on horseback. This offers excellent visibility and improves relations with the community. Citizens generally feel less hostile to a police officer on horseback. Finally, some special patrols may be conducted via helicopter. A helicopter patrol can cover a large area in a short time.

Patrolling alone and with a partner

When an officer patrols alone, he or she is responsible for all aspects of the work. The result is that these officers tend to be more competent in a wider variety of areas. Also, solo patrols eliminate the possibility of conflicts between officers. For many departments, the best thing about solo patrols is that they divide the number of patrol vehicles required by two. This not only saves money, but increases the amount of preventive enforcement that results from police visibility.

A two-officer patrol has some advantages as well. These patrols are better able to observe the area, and are considered to be safer for officers. It is easier for a two-officer patrol to use the radio and drive at the same time. Also, younger officers learn faster when they patrol in the company of a veteran.

Pedestrian stops

Officers should stop a pedestrian who is behaving erratically, carrying a suspicious object, loitering, or harassing other people. When stopping a pedestrian, officers should take steps to minimize the danger to themselves and others. For instance, a pedestrian stop should take into account all of the possible escape routes, as well as the possibility of a hostage situation. Whenever making a pedestrian stop, the officer should first report his or her location to the dispatcher. During the pedestrian stop, the officer should speak clearly and calmly. Whenever possible, officers should approach from the right side, maintain eye contact, and be alert for sudden movements or attempts to escape. There are a few court cases that have influenced the strategy for making pedestrian stops: *Terry v. Ohio* (1968), *Michigan v. Chesternut* (1988), and *California v. Hodari* (1991).

Strategies for interviewing people

When a single officer is interviewing one person, the officer should stand at least an arm's length away with his or her gun on the opposite side of the interviewee. When interviewing two or more people, the lone officer should stand in a similar position, but in such a way as to observe all of the interviewees. The officer should avoid letting the people circle around. When two officers are interviewing one person, one officer should stand in the above position while the other stands to the right or the left-rear of the interviewee. This position is recommended so that officers will not be in each other's line of fire. When two officers are interviewing two or more people, they should stand with one of them in the normal position, and the other at a slight distance so as to maintain observation of the entire scene.

Violator contact method

The first step of the violator contact method is to greet the person and identify the police agency being represented. An officer should always try to begin the interview on a note of courtesy and professionalism. Then, the officer should explain why the person has been stopped. The suspect should be given an opportunity to justify his or her actions. The officer should then identify the driver and judge the status of driver and vehicle. Then, the officer should describe the action to be taken. It is a good idea for the officer to avoid identifying him or herself as the one taking

the action, as this provides the violator with a chance to argue on personal grounds. The fifth step is to take the action that has been described, such as writing the ticket or arresting the suspect. The officer should then describe what the suspect must do to comply. Finally, once the matter has been satisfactorily resolved, the officer may leave.

High-risk vehicle stops

Although officers should always assume that a vehicle stop may be dangerous, there are certain steps recommended for especially perilous stops. To begin with, the officer should alert the dispatcher of the location, vehicle description, and number of occupants. The officer should ask for NCIC/TCIC to determine whether the vehicle has been stolen. If the vehicle is stolen and stopped, the officer should request backup and move to secure it immediately. When stopping a suspicious or stolen vehicle, the officer should try to park to the left. The suspect vehicle should be lit up with a flashlight or headlights. The officer should direct the suspects to exit the vehicle slowly with their hands in the air. The suspects should open the doors from the outside. Suspects should then lie down in front of the patrol car with their legs and arms spread.

Safe building search

Before searching a building that may have been illegally entered, officers should alert the dispatcher and ask for assistance. Officers should then secure the point of entry and any other exits. If appropriate, the officer should ask the dispatcher to contact the building owner and find out the location of the safe or office. It is always best for at least two officers to enter the building together, with enough officers outside to secure the perimeter. Officers should wear protective gear if it is available. During the search, members of the search team should maintain contact and stay aware of each other's location. Most law enforcement departments recommend the leap frog method of movement, in which officers alternate between moving ahead and covering one another. The search team should proceed through the building systematically, fully exploring each room before moving on to the next. It is better for the intruder to encounter police outside of the building, so officers should always give him or her a chance to exit.

Bomb threat protocol

The protocol for responding to a bomb threat will vary somewhat depending on the population density and arrangement of the surrounding area. In some cases, it may be necessary to evacuate the building first. Whenever possible, the building should be secured and police should bar unauthorized persons from entering. Police officers should immediately request appropriate assistance, whether from the military, fire department, or bomb squad. Police officers may conduct a search of the building if they believe there is time and if they have a reasonable understanding of the bomb's location and set-up. During a search, officers should be alert for any suspicious objects. However, officers should never touch or move any object that could be a bomb. There should be no smoking during a bomb search, and all radios should be disabled within 500 feet of the building. Sometimes, it will be necessary to enlist the aid of people, like janitors or building managers, who are familiar with the location's layout.

Response to an active shooter

An active shooter has the goal of mass murder and must be stopped as soon as possible. Officers participate in Homicide in Progress School to learn how to deal with active shooters. Officers should understand that an active shooter is not interested in evading capture, but rather is concerned with inflicting as much pain as possible. Active shooters typically open fire in crowded public areas, like restaurants or schools. In this scenario, the immediate objective of law enforcement is to save as many lives as possible. This can be done by isolating,

disabling, or killing the shooter. Of course, taking immediate action means that officers will be less organized and informed. There is likely to be great confusion at such a crime scene. Also, it is unlikely that the first responders will have the best equipment for handling an active shooter. Nevertheless, quickly moving to neutralize the suspect is the recommended course of action for police officers.

Homicide in progress

When responding to a homicide in progress, officers should first locate and positively identify the suspect. As quickly as possible, officers should learn the floor plan or layout of the area in which they are operating. Officers will have to balance the desire to help the wounded with the necessity of apprehending the suspect as quickly as possible. The location, relative distance to the suspect, and presence of other officers will affect these difficult decisions. Officers who respond to a homicide in progress will likely experience the symptoms of extreme stress: increased heart and breathing and decreased peripheral vision, fine motor skills, and auditory ability. Afterwards, many officers report feeling intense self-doubt and grief about their actions, even if they behaved admirably.

Contact and rescue teams

To help officers organize their thoughts and actions when responding to a homicide in progress, law enforcement officials recommend an immediate action plan, in which a group of four officers becomes either a contact or rescue team. A contact team focuses on locating and neutralizing the suspect. It may do so by reducing the movements of the suspect, for instance by sealing off exits. The contact team will prioritize apprehension even at the expense of helping victims. A rescue team, on the other hand, focuses on helping the wounded or stranded. If possible, the rescue team will locate and neutralize the suspect, but its predominant mission is to find victims and remove them to a safe location. Research suggests that assigning officers particular objectives during a stressful situation helps eliminate some of the second-guessing and self-criticism later.

Diamond team formation

When responding to a homicide in progress, police officers may need to make use of a diamond formation. This formation requires a minimum of four officers. The team leader, known as the point man, is the first to enter each room. He or she is responsible for responding to immediate threats that arise upon entry. As the team leaves the room, the point man will serve as the rear guard. On the left flank of the group should be the first contact or rescue officer. This person's job is to maintain radio communication with other officers, to look for victims, and to guard the group against attacks from the left side. On the right flank, the second contact or rescue officer is charged with physically removing victims and staying alert for threats from the right side. Finally, at the back of the group will be the rear guard, whose job is to protect the team from attacks from behind and to serve as point man as the team exits a room.

Crowd management

Police officers should be prepared to handle disturbances when large groups of people gather. One way to prepare for these scenarios is to consult with community leaders in advance of the gathering. Even those leaders who are not associated with the assembled people may have useful information for law enforcement. Unruly crowds can emerge during scheduled marches or demonstrations, or they can be a spontaneous result of controversial events (court decisions, acts of violence, etc.). These situations can be very dangerous for officers, so the immediate priority of a first responder should be to ensure his or her own safety. The first officer on the scene should provide a detailed summary to the dispatcher, including

the size and general behavior of the crowd and the best way for other officers to arrive on the scene. The primary objectives of law enforcement officials when confronting an angry crowd are to arrest miscreants and disperse the assembly.

Crowds types

Police officers distinguish crowds by their behavior, composition, and reason for assembling. An aggressive crowd in most cases has been assembled for a particular reason and has at least a somewhat organized leadership. This sort of group moves quickly and directly to accomplish a goal, and is likely to behave with violence and belligerence to police. An expressive crowd is also assembled for a particular purpose, but is less likely to become hostile. Expressive crowds usually have a defined leadership, and are exemplified by political assemblies and meetings of striking workers. A cohesive crowd lacks leadership, but is assembled for a particular purpose. The constituent members of a cohesive crowd are unlikely to behave in a unified manner at the behest of any single leader. A casual crowd lacks common purpose and organized leadership. Indeed, the members of a casual crowd are likely to change over time, as people arrive and leave almost at random. A mob, on the other hand, is a crowd with a single purpose, whether aggression, escape, or looting.

Public service in police work

Police work is improved by public service. Public service improves the perception of police officers, and diminishes the barriers between the public and the department. When police officers fail to provide adequate public service, they risk losing the trust of the public. This can lead to political and professional obstacles. One of the best ways for police officers to promote public service is by talking with the community in a non-professional setting. Many police officers deliver speeches at community organizations, for instance. Police officers should also encourage citizens to provide feedback about police service. Programs like Crime Stoppers encourage citizens to participate in law enforcement. Less formally, police departments may benefit from engaging citizens in polite conversation while out on patrol.

Prevent crime

Police officers should work to prevent crime by identifying and eliminating its causes. Indeed, many departments focus on crime prevention rather than punishing offenders. Officers should consider the types of crime committed in their patrol areas, and how these crimes can be mitigated. It is always a good idea to enlist the aid of citizens in crime prevention. To begin with, citizens should be made aware of the common crimes in their area, and should be given some basic tips for reducing the prevalence of these crimes. In many neighborhoods, residents voluntarily participate in security surveys and neighborhood watches. In a security survey, residents give information about their homes and property, so that law enforcement will be better able to identify suspicious behavior. Neighborhood watches are voluntary programs in which citizens cooperate with law enforcement to identify and eliminate suspicious and illegal behavior.

Arrest of a foreign national

When a foreign national is arrested, the officer should determine whether his or her native country is on the list of mandatory notification. If the arrested person's country is not on this list, the officer should ask whether he or she would like to have his or her consulate notified. This conversation should be recorded. This rule applies even when the arrested person is in the United States illegally.

Consular notification

Notification is required by the terms of the Vienna Convention on Consular Notification treaty, as well as by a number of other bilateral treaties. Once a foreign national has been arrested, consular officials from his or her home country have the right to visit, call, or write to the detainee. Consular officials are also allowed to provide certain services, like helping with legal representation and providing some amenities while the suspect is incarcerated.

Victims of Crime

Crisis reaction

Officers must be sensitive to the thoughts and emotions of crime victims. The crisis reaction is remarkably similar for people of all backgrounds and in all situations. It has both a physical and a mental component. The physical response to trauma is the fight-or-flight instinct: the bloodstream becomes saturated with adrenaline, the person vomits or defecates, the heart and breathing rates increase, and the senses become very sharp. This reaction cannot be maintained for a long time, and the person will eventually experience temporary debilitating effects from adrenaline withdrawal. The mental response to crisis has three stages: shock and disbelief, emotional cataclysm, and the return to equilibrium. At first, the person will not be able to organize his thoughts and will deny that the crisis was as bad as it seems. Then, he or she will enter a whirlwind of emotions, ranging from terror to sorrow to anger. Finally, the person will begin to integrate the experience into his or her consciousness, and will return to a more balanced emotional state.

Recovery from trauma

The extent to which a person is able to recover from trauma depends on both internal and external factors. For most people, however, recovery is improved and accelerated by at least some external intervention. Recovery from trauma depends in part on the severity of the event. An especially vicious crime will be more durably troubling. Also, some crimes have greater resonance in certain cultures. For instance, rape is always an extremely devastating event for the victim, but it can be even more problematic for devout Muslims, who may become ostracized by their communities and families as a result of a rape. Recovery from trauma also depends on the ability to comprehend and articulate the traumatic event. One reason why people continue to have adverse reactions to trauma is that they are unable to organize the events in their mind. Instead, their brain reviews the incident incessantly, trying to make sense of it. The ability to express what has happened is extremely useful in moving forward.

Reaction to crime

The reaction to crime can be broken down into three phases: impact, recoil, and reorganization. The impact is the crime itself, the recoil is the victim's changed emotional trajectory as a result of the crime, and the reorganization is the victim's efforts to restore balance and order in his or her life. The effects of crime are not limited to victims, however.

Crime also has an impact the family and friends of the immediate victim.

These secondary victims, as they are known, can be especially vulnerable to adverse reactions precisely because their own energy and the attention of other caregivers are focused on the immediate victim.

Service providers, like police officers and emergency medical personnel, also pass through a multi-stage response to crime. All of these people need attention in the wake of a traumatic event. In particular, immediate victims, secondary victims, and other affected people should be given the opportunity to articulate their own experience and emotions.

Secondary victimization

Secondary victimization occurs when the victim of a crime is mistreated or neglected, thus aggravating the original trauma. Secondary victimization is not always the result of intentional action, but it can be devastating nonetheless. The criminal justice system is notorious for this phenomenon, in part because the victims of crime must defend themselves and their account of events on the witness stand. However, the media and the medical community have also been guilty of secondary victimization on occasion. Police officers should avoid any behavior or comments that imply guilt on the part of the victim (e.g., "You shouldn't have been walking alone through that part of town."). One of the worst things about secondary victimization is that it discourages the victim from seeking help anywhere else. Also, crime victims may be confused and depressed, and may not realize they are being mistreated until the damage is already done.

Notification of death

When forced to notify friends or family of a person's death, officers should always do so as quickly as possible after the body has been identified. Officers should always notify in person, and never over the phone. It is important for officers to be in uniform when notifying family of a death, as this conveys respect and professionalism. The notification should always be made to an adult, and should be expressed in simple and thoughtful language. Family and friends will often demand more information, and officers should provide it so long as they do not endanger an ongoing investigation. Officers should convey empathy, and remain with the family and friends until they receive permission to leave. They should never leave a grieving person alone, and should always offer to help the bereaved make immediate arrangements. Officers should never talk to

- 136 -

the media unless they have received explicit permission from the family.

Family Violence and Related Assaultive Offenses

Victim's response

In Texas state law, violence that occurs in the home or between family members is referred to as family violence. The term "domestic violence" is not used in Texas. The victims of family violence are likely to display a common set of behaviors. Victims will likely feel guilty, in particular when their children have witnessed a violent episode. The victims of family violence often blame themselves for violence. Victims may feel that they cannot trust anyone, not even law enforcement officials, to provide help. Some victims may deny that violence has occurred, or that it was as severe as it appears. The victims of family violence are under severe stress, which can cause many of them to behave erratically and even to question their own sanity.

Family violence offenders

There are a few common profiles for family violence offenders. Offenders are likely to have a very low self-opinion, which they project onto the objects of their aggression. It is common for an offender to be from a home in which violence was the norm, and in which he or she was frequently beaten or threatened. A family violence offender will often act quite differently in public, and may have an almost complete division of home and public personalities. An offender often abuses drugs and alcohol and engages in aggressive sex. Family violence offenders are often solitary individuals who demonstrate extreme mood swings. These people, who are usually males, take little responsibility for their own behavior and may indeed believe that they have done nothing wrong, and that they are merely acting as the head of the household.

Physical, emotional, and sexual abuse

Physical abuse is the classic form of family violence. It includes any act that causes physical pain to family members.

Emotional abuse, on the other hand, is more subtle. It can be as simple as ignoring a child for long periods, or withholding affection. The destruction of another person's property can be a form of emotional abuse. Humiliating a family member also qualifies as emotional abuse. When a parent prevents his or her child from having contact with other people outside of the home, this may qualify as emotional abuse. Obviously, calling another person names or otherwise belittling them is an example of emotional abuse. Sexual abuse is the third type of family violence. It may be rape, forced performance of repugnant sexual acts, refusal to use birth control, or sex in inappropriate places (e.g., with children present).

Identifying the predominant aggressor

In the initial investigation of family violence, there is a tendency to identify and arrest multiple offenders. However, most episodes of family violence have a predominant aggressor who begins the violent episode. Sometimes, the other participants have acted violently only in order to defend themselves, and should be given comfort and treatment. Therefore, it is important for officers to identify the predominant aggressor as quickly as possible. Officers should consider what witnesses have to say, and should take into account the relative sizes of the parties involved. Officers should gauge the relative severity of the injuries sustained by each party, and should find out whether one of the parties has a history of violence. Some injuries, as for instance scratches on the forearms, are clearly the result of self-defense.

Family violence response

Family violence situations can be volatile, so it is always better for multiple officers to respond. The officers should try to gather as much useful information as possible beforehand, and should minimize their arrival by leaving their lights and sirens off. Officers should approach carefully and watch for escaping suspects. Officers may enter the residence once any resident consents. If the officers believe that circumstances inside the house call for immediate action, they may enter without consent. The immediate priority of the officers should be to stop whatever violence is occurring. Officers should interview the parties involved, and try to get a complete picture of events before making any judgments. If there are any weapons loose in the house, officers should secure them quickly. Officers should document the scene by taking photographs and making notes. Officers should keep the suspects and victims appraised of their thoughts and intentions, and should advise suspects before placing them under arrest.

Protective orders

Section 82.002 of the Family Code states that an application for a protective order related to family violence may be filed by any member of a family to protect the applicant or any other member of the family or household. Also, an application for a protective order may be filed by an adult member of a dating relationship. Protective orders that aim to safeguard children from family violence may be applied for by any adult. Also, a protective order may be filed to protect any person alleged to be a victim of family violence by a prosecuting attorney or the Department of Protective and Regulatory Services.

Where to file protective orders

Section 82.003 of the Family Code states that applications for protective orders related to family violence may be filed in the home county of the applicant or the respondent.

Application for protective order

Section 82.004 of the Family Code states that an application for a protective order related to family violence must include the name and county of residence of each applicant, the name and county of residence of each alleged offender, the relationships between the applicants and the alleged offender, and a request for one or more protective orders.

Court decision

Section 85.001 of the Family Code states that at the end of the hearing regarding a protective order application, the court must decide whether family violence has occurred and is likely to occur in the future. If the court finds in the affirmative, the court must issue a protective order applying to the alleged offender, and may issue a protective order that applies to all parties.

Protective order contents

Section 85.021 of the Family Code states that a protective order may prohibit one party from removing a child from either the possession of a certain named person or the jurisdiction of the court. A protective order may also prohibit one party from transferring or disposing of property mutually owned by the various parties named in the order. A protective order may grant exclusive possession of a residence to one party, and then order another party to leave the residence. A protective order may provide exclusive access to a child for one party. It may also mandate the payment of support for one party or for a child of the party.

Prevention of future violence

Section 85.022 (a) of the Family Code states that a protective order may require one party to perform specific acts that will prevent or reduce the likelihood of family violence in the future. For instance, the party might be required to meet with a counselor or complete a battering intervention and prevention program.

Officer access to protective orders

Section 86.001 of the Family Code states that law enforcement departments must set up procedures so that officers will have access to protective orders when they are performing their duties. It is necessary that officers who are responding to calls be aware of the existence and terms of protective orders related to family violence.

Protective order for family violence

Section 85.025 of the Family Code states that protective orders related to family violence are effective for two years, unless the order indicates otherwise. After one year, the subject of a protective order may file a motion for review. If the subject of the protective order is confined on the date of the order's expiration, the order will remain effective until the first anniversary of the person's release from confinement.

Protective order delivery

Section 85.041 of the Family Code states that protective orders related to family violence must be delivered to the respondent either in the same manner as a writ of injunction or in open court at the end of the hearing.

Treatment for children

Section 32.001 of the Family Code states that the following people may consent to a child receiving medical or psychological treatment if the child's parent or guardian cannot be contacted: grandparents, adult brothers or sisters, adult aunts or uncles, authorized educational institutions, courts with jurisdiction, or peace officers with lawful custody of the child.

Children may give their consent

Section 32.003 of the Family Code states that children may give their consent to medical, dental, psychological, and surgical treatments under certain conditions. For instance, a child may do so if he is on active duty with the United States Armed Forces or if he is 16 years or older, lives by himself, and manages his own affairs. A child who is unmarried and pregnant may consent to ethical care related to pregnancy. Any child may consent to care related to drug or chemical use.

Medical professional

Section 32.005 of the Family Code states that if a licensed medical professional has reasonable grounds to believe that a child's physical or mental condition has been negatively impacted by abuse or neglect, and then he may examine the child without consent. This examination may include x-rays, blood tests, and photographs.

Child's health or safety

Section 262.003 of the Family Code states that a person who takes possession of a child without having a court order is immune from civil liability if it can be proven that there was reasonable cause to suspect immediate danger to the child's health or safety.

Voluntary delivery of a child

Section 262.004 of the Family Code states that law enforcement officers and juvenile probation officers may take possession of a child even without a court order, so long as the child is voluntarily delivered by his or her parent, guardian, or custodian.

Missing children

Section 262.007 of the Family Code states that a law enforcement officer who discovers that a child has been reported missing may take the child into custody if he believes that a person may flee with or conceal the child.

An officer in this situation should immediately deliver the child to his or her parent or to the Department of Family and Protective Services.

Emergency possession of a child

Section 262.104 of the Family Code states that in an emergency, when there is no time to obtain a temporary restraining order, law enforcement officers and other government officials may take possession of a child without a court order. This may be done when there is reasonable suspicion that the child is in danger.

Improper places for placing a child

Section 262.108 of the Family Code states that children who are taken into possession in emergencies by law enforcement officers or other government officials may not be held in isolation or in jails, juvenile detention facilities, or other secure detention facilities.

Temporary possession of a child without a court order

Section 262.110 of the Family Code states that when any law enforcement officer or other government official takes temporary possession of a child without a court order because of concern that the child is in imminent danger, he or she should as soon as possible deliver the child to his or her parent, guardian, or custodian. A law enforcement officer or government official may retain possession of a child without a court order for up to five days.

Crisis Intervention Training (CIT)/Mental Health Code

Origins and intentions of CIT

Crisis intervention training (CIT) was developed after a tragic incident in Memphis, Tenn., in which a mentally disturbed man was killed by police officers. In Texas, crisis intervention programs have existed for a long time, with the primary intention of separating people with mental illness from the general criminal population. One of the hallmarks of crisis intervention training programs is the emphasis on avoiding confrontation: officers are taught to defuse situations that, because of the suspect's mental illness, can easily get out of control. These programs strive to teach officers effective strategies for establishing communication with disturbed people, and for resolving conflicts without violence. In part, these programs are important because law enforcement loses credibility with the public when officers use lethal force against the mentally ill. Moreover, in most cases officers have discovered that using less force actually gives them more control over the situation. This is known as the control paradox.

Texas Education Code

Trespass on school grounds

Section 37.107 of the Texas Education Code states that it is a Class C misdemeanor to trespass on the grounds of a school.

Intentional disruptive behavior

Section 37.123 of the Texas Education Code states that it is illegal to intentionally engage in disruptive behavior on a campus or property of any private or public school. Disruptive activity could be seizing control of the building, preventing a lawful assembly with the threat of violence, or obstructing the passage of people in an exit or hallway. Disruptive activity on school grounds is a Class B misdemeanor.

Disrupt conduct of classes/activities

Section 37.124 of the Texas Education Code declares that it is a Class C misdemeanor to intentionally disrupt the conduct of classes or school activities.

Firearm

Section 37.125 of the Texas Education Code states that it is a third-degree felony to exhibit, use, or threaten to exhibit or use a firearm on any school property or school bus.

Lawful transportation of children

Section 37.126 of the Texas Education Code declares that it is a Class C misdemeanor to intentionally disrupt the lawful transportation of children on a school bus or authorized school vehicle.

Code of Criminal Procedure's

Article 56.02
Article 56.02 of the Code of Criminal Procedure outlines the rights of crime victims. Crime victims, the guardians of victims, and the close relatives of deceased victims have the right to adequate protection from harm during prosecution efforts. They have the right to have their safety considered when fixing bail for the accused. They have the right to be informed of the progress of court proceedings. They have the right to be informed about the bail of the accused. They have the right to provide testimony during sentencing hearings. When their property has been taken into custody by the state, they have the right to get it back as soon as possible. They have the right to counsel and legal representation.

Article 56.04
Article 56.04(c) and (d) of the Code of Criminal Procedure state that local law enforcement agencies must appoint a crime victim liaison who will ensure that the rights of crime victims are upheld.

Article 56.045
Article 56.045 of the Code of Criminal Procedure states that the victims of alleged sexual assault have the right to be joined by a special advocate during a forensic medical examination. This advocate is allowed to provide counseling and information about the rights of crime victims. The cost of the examination will be paid for by the sexual assault program of which the advocate is a representative.

Article 56.09
Article 56.09 of the Code of Criminal Procedure states that the address of a victim should not be included in a court file unless it is necessary to identify the location of the offense. A victim's phone number should never be included in the court file.

Family Code

Article 56.07

Article 56.07 of the Code of Criminal Procedure states that law enforcement agencies are responsible for providing crime victims with written notice about the investigation as soon as possible. This notice should contain information about available emergency and medical services, a full disclosure of the victim's rights, the contact information for a victim assistance liaison, and the contact information for the state attorney.

Article 42.21

Article 42.21 of the Code of Criminal Procedure states that before releasing a person who has been convicted of a family violence offense, there should be a reasonable attempt to notify the victim.

Major court decisions related to the use of force by police

Young v. City of Killeen
In *Young v. City of Killeen*, the Fifth Circuit Court of Appeals ruled that a police officer had acted negligently by forcing a citizen into an action that could be interpreted as endangering the officer. This case arose from an incident in which a peace officer stopped a driver and ordered him to leave the car. When the man reached down to the

- 141 -

floorboard of the car, the officer shot and killed him. The court ruled that the officer should have let the man remain in the car because he was doing so peacefully.

Graham v. Connor (1989)

In *Graham v. Connor* (1989), the US Supreme Court ruled that a citizen's claim that a peace officer used excessive force should be subject to the standard of objective reasonableness. In other words, the court has the liberty to decide whether a citizen who claims to have been brutalized during the course of an arrest or seizure has described a credible series of events. This decision protects law enforcement officers from wild accusations.

Saucier v. Katz (2001)

In *Saucier v. Katz* (2001), the Supreme Court granted qualified immunity to a police officer, meaning that charges against him must establish that the officer's conduct violated a clearly established constitutional right.

Milstead v. Kibler (2001

In *Milstead v. Kibler* (2001), the Fourth Circuit ruled that officers are not liable for damages caused by force unless their actions violate a federal statutory or constitutional right, that such a right was clearly established at the time of the action, and that a reasonable person would have foreseen that the use of force would violate that right.

Saucier v. Katz (2001)

In *Okonkwo v. Fernandez* (2003), the Texas courts ruled that officers may receive qualified immunity from suit or liability for damages resulting from actions that a reasonable person could not have known would infringe statutory or constitutional rights. The officer must explicitly plead for qualified immunity in court, however.

Graham v. Connor (1989)

Finally, in *Graham v. Connor* (1989) the United States Supreme Court asserted that the use of force by police officers should be judged according to the facts available to the officers at the time, not according to the motivations of the officers.

Hazardous Materials Awareness

HAZMAT

Hazardous materials, also known as HAZMAT, are defined by the United States Department of Transportation (DOT) as any substances that could endanger health, safety, or property during transportation. The DOT has divided hazardous materials into nine hazard classes. The three main types of hazardous materials are infectious materials, ionizing radiation, and toxic materials.

Infectious materials are human, animal, and plant pathogens (disease-causing substances). Human pathogens may be either bacteria (e.g., anthrax) or viruses (e.g., small pox or influenza). Some common plant and animal pathogens are foot and mouth disease, classical swine fever, and exotic Newcastle disease.

Ionizing radiation is a hazardous material that emanates from unstable substances. The radiation may take the form of neutron, alpha, beta, gamma, or X-rays.

Finally, toxic materials can be biological toxins, chemical warfare agents, agricultural chemicals, or toxic industrial materials.

Exposure

People can be exposed to hazardous materials by means of injection, ingestion, absorption, and inhalation. Injection may be in the form of a puncture wound, but it can also be delivered by an insect. Hazardous materials may be ingested through direct eating or drinking, or just by placing a contaminated object in the mouth briefly. Hazardous materials may be absorbed through the skin, eyes, or mucous membranes (i.e., nostrils or lips). Finally, tiny and airborne hazardous materials are often inhaled. Obviously, exposure to hazardous materials can result in immediate and grave physical consequences including death, disability, and permanent impairment. Hazardous materials can also diminish the utility of farmlands, destroy food, and preclude the occupation of lands or buildings. Hazardous materials can decrease the availability of natural resources, render roads and public transportation useless, and tax the health care system.

Response to HAZMAT situations

Upon first arriving at the scene of a hazardous materials event, officers should determine what level of personal protection equipment (PPE) is appropriate. There are four PPE levels:

1. Level D includes gloves, mask, and a basic uniform
2. Level C includes chemical resistant clothes, double-layered gloves, and an air-purifying respirator
3. Level B combines Level C with a self-contained breathing apparatus
4. Level-A requires a fully encapsulated suit

Officers should assess the extent of the exposure and the risk of continuing exposure. This assessment should inform requests for additional resources. The officers should limit the contamination while escorting those who have been exposed from the scene. As much as possible, officers should stay away and upwind from the source of the contamination. Law enforcement officers are generally discouraged from making any bold decisions regarding HAZMAT before consulting experts.

Criminal Investigation

Criminal investigation components

The basic elements of a criminal investigation are forensic science; information gathering; and the relevant laws of arrest, search, and seizure. Forensic science continues to develop rapidly, and is most commonly used in fingerprint analysis, DNA analysis, ballistics, and serology. Information gathering is the most important element of an investigation. Information is collected from victims, witnesses, suspects, and other resources. For instance, an investigator might obtain useful information from other police reports or from departmental records. The protocol of the investigation is structured by the laws of arrest, search, and seizure. Unless these laws are followed by investigators, it may be difficult for charges to be successfully prosecuted in court.

Corpus delicti

The Latin phrase "corpus delicti" refers to the body of the criminal act. The presence of a corpus delicti indicates that a crime has indeed been committed. A corpus delicti does not have to be a literal body: it could instead be a piece of damaged property, for instance.

Circumstantial evidence

Circumstantial evidence suggests but does not confirm that a person was involved in a crime. For example, if a person cannot account for their whereabouts at the time of a crime, this could be a piece of circumstantial evidence.

Criminal investigation

In a criminal investigation, the complainant is the person who demands the investigation in the first place. For example, a person whose bike is stolen and who then calls the police would be identified as the complainant.

Modus operandi

The Latin phrase "modus operandi" refers to a criminal's method of operation, or style. For instance, if a carjacker repeatedly victimizes elderly women driving with the windows down, then these details would be part of his modus operandi.

Probable cause

Probable cause is evidence that would convince a reasonable person of the commission of a crime. Criminal investigators must establish probable cause in order to justify continuing their inquiry.

Reasonable doubt

Reasonable doubt is the criteria for a juror to acquit the accused party in a criminal trial. A reasonable doubt is based on information and logic, and takes into account all of the pertinent data in the case. An investigator must keep in mind this concept, because it will be his or her job to amass enough evidence to prove guilt beyond a reasonable doubt.

Thief

A thief is the most basic professional criminal. A thief attempts to stay out of sight, but is perhaps more careless than a burglar. Thieves usually operate according to a plan and specialize in the theft of certain types of property. A thief steals for money.

Burglar

A burglar, on the other hand, operates with a greater degree of stealth and sophistication. A burglar breaks into buildings, which may require specialized skills. A burglar often cooperates with a fence, which is a person who is adept at moving and selling stolen goods.

Robber

A robber, finally, uses violence in order to take the property of others. Robbers may plan their operations carefully, but their crimes tend to be bolder and more brazen. A robber's plan often depends on ambushing the victim. Habitual thieves, burglars, and robbers all develop a modus operandi that helps criminal investigators track and catch them.

Identity theft

Identity theft is the criminal act of impersonating someone else in order to engage in fraudulent financial transactions. An identity theft results in a loss for the person whose identity has been assumed. Identity theft requires the acquisition of the victim's personal data, such as his or her date of birth, address, social security number, credit card, or driver's license. The Internet has enabled many new forms of identity theft, though this crime also takes place in the real world. Check fraud and bank fraud are both forms of identity theft. One common Internet version of this crime is phishing, in which a criminal sets up a phony version of a bank or credit card website in the hopes of inducing people to enter their personal information.

Con artists

A con artist is someone who tricks people into willingly giving away their money by making them false promises. In many cases, a con artist exploits the victim's greed, for instance by getting the victim to invest money in a scheme guaranteed to produce a profit and then disappearing with the investment. Because they prey on the gullible, con artists often focus their attention on the elderly and young. Con artists are generally nonviolent.

Semi-professional thieves

A semi-professional thief, meanwhile, tends to work sporadically and at times of personal need. A thief of this type is less likely to plan his operations in advance, and will often try to steal from whoever happens along. Because a semi-professional thief does little planning, his operations are more likely to go awry, and he is therefore more likely to resort to violence. Semi-professional thieves are often drug addicts who occasionally need money to support a habit.

White-collar criminals

White-collar criminals are people who commit nonviolent financial offenses. The two most common varieties of white-collar crime are business fraud and consumer fraud. Business frauds include embezzlement, advanced fee fraud, securities fraud, and insurance fraud.

One of the most infamous forms of business fraud is the Ponzi (or pyramid) scheme, in which a criminal attracts a series of investors, with the initial contributions of new investors serving as the "dividends" for earlier investors. The continuation of a Ponzi scheme requires a steady supply of new investors, which eventually becomes untenable, leading to the collapse of the system.

The two most common consumer frauds are the bait-and-switch, in which the victim is promised one item but delivered another; and repair fraud, in which the criminal charges the victim for unnecessary or even damaging services. White-collar criminals often intend to return their illegally gotten gains before they are noticed. Indeed, many people begin as white-collar criminals without ever really thinking of their actions as illegal.

Auto theft

Criminal investigators distinguish five types of auto theft: use-in-crime theft, insurance fraud, professional theft, stripping and dismantling, and use of a motor vehicle by an unauthorized offender. In a use-in-crime theft, the car is stolen to be used in the commission of another crime.

Insurance fraud is committed by the owner of a car when he or she abandons or destroys a vehicle in order to claim it has been stolen and collect insurance money. A professional theft is perpetrated by a person who has a means of selling expensive stolen cars. Cars that are professionally stolen are often shipped out of the country. Some parked cars are stripped of valuable parts, and some cars are stolen only to be dismantled and sold for parts later. Finally, some cars are stolen by people, usually juveniles, who are not authorized to drive. These cars are typically left on the side of the road once they have served the purposes of the thief.

Salvage switches

A salvage switch is a crime in which the vehicle identification number (VIN) of a stolen car is replaced with the VIN of a totaled car. In effect, then, the stolen car becomes the totaled car, which itself is destroyed. Perpetrating a salvage switch requires a degree mechanical expertise, as well as the forging of a new MVI certificate.

Gray market vehicles

A gray market vehicle, on the other hand, is a foreign-made vehicle that has been shipped to the United States, but is not usually sold in the country. Most gray market vehicles are made by Mercedes-Benz. Gray market vehicles are not technically illegal, though they must meet the requirements of the Department of Transportation and the Environmental Protection Agency. These vehicles often resemble stolen cars because they have unusual vehicle identification numbers.

Identifing a stolen car

There are some common indications that a car has been stolen. Most obviously, a broken window suggests that the car was entered forcibly. If the license plate does not match the registered VIN, the car may be stolen. If a car is lacking an up-to-date registration sticker or a front license plate, it may be a stolen car. Stolen cars often have dirty license plates or vehicle identification tags. This is especially suspicious if the rest of the car is clean. If a car has license plates from different states on the front and back, it is more likely to be stolen. License plates that are attached to the car by magnets or string suggest a possible car theft, as these plates will be easier to change in a hurry. If the left side of the steering column is broken, this indicates that the car has been hotwired. Sometimes, auto thieves will insert a dummy key after hotwiring a vehicle, so an officer should be suspicious when a driver refuses to turn off his or her car.

Homicide

Criminal investigators distinguish homicides by their motives and methodologies. A felony murder occurs during the commission of some other crime. In a murder-suicide, the perpetrator kills another person and then him or herself. Some murders are committed for profit, while others are committed for revenge. The latter crimes typically involve people who know one another well. An anger killing is not premeditated, and may resemble an exceptionally violent assault. In a triangle killing, the perpetrator murders his or her cheating spouse as well as the person with whom the spouse has been cheating. A sadistic murder involves unusual cruelty and even torture. Many sadistic murders are sexual in nature. Of course, many crimes fall into more than one of these categories.

Sexual assault characteristics

A sexual assault is any violent act of a sexual nature. A nonconsensual sexual activity of any kind is considered sexual assault. It is common for the perpetrator of a sexual assault to drug his or her victim, or to threaten force. The general intention of a sexual assault is to demonstrate the power of the perpetrator over the victim. Sexual assault cases are extremely delicate for law enforcement, because the victims are often highly traumatized and resistant to cooperation with the law. In many cases, the victim will blame him or herself for the assault, or will be too embarrassed to assist in law enforcement. One increasingly prevalent form of sexual assault is date rape, in which the victim knows the perpetrator and has voluntarily joined him or her.

Rapist

A rapist may be motivated by sadism, anger, power, or opportunism. A sadistic rapist finds aggression and violence sexually arousing, and seeks out his victims accordingly. A sadistic rapist often incorporates bondage and other equipment during the act. A sadistic rape is likely to last a long time and involve physical and verbal degradation. Sadistic rapists are typically men in their 30s.

An anger rapist, on the other hand, is less concerned with sex than with the chance to demonstrate virility and to punish the victim. An angry rape usually lasts for only a short time, and is accompanied by violent language and other forms of physical assault.

A power rapist commits the crime in order to create a feeling of personal agency. A power rapist may seem strangely concerned with the victim's feelings, and may even apologize after the act. Power rapists select their victims carefully.

An opportunistic rapist does not plan his crime, but rather takes advantage of a person who has become incapacitated or unable to defend herself. An opportunistic rapist may not commit the crime more than once.

Pedophilia

Pedophilia is a sexual interest in prepubescent children. Pedophilia may manifest as fondling, forced sex acts, or possession of child pornography. Criminal investigators distinguish between situational pedophiles, who only have sexual contact with children when opportunity arises or stress drives them to it, and preferential child molesters, who actively look for children to violate.

Situational pedophiles may be regressed, morally indiscriminate, or naïve. A regressed pedophile is only temporarily involved with children, and is usually stable in every other respect.

- 146 -

A morally indiscriminate pedophile abuses children as well as other people.

A naïve pedophile is unaware that his behavior is wrong, often because of his low IQ.

Preferential child molesters may be either mysoped or fixated. A mysoped hates children and wants to damage them, and his crimes are planned and sadistic. A fixated child molester claims to love children and has no real adult relationships. An offender of this type is often very childlike himself.

Children react to violence

Children respond to violence in diverse ways: aggression, confusion, guilt, fear, and shock, just to name a few. Wetting the bed, throwing temper tantrums, and regressing to an earlier stage of development are all symptomatic of a response to violence.

Children between the ages of 3 and 6 will have an extremely difficult time reacting to violent episodes. A child at this age will not be able to describe the violent episode in full, though he or she will often be able to state the offender and the offense.

A child between the ages of 6 and 11 will be very disoriented by violence, and may even try to mimic the behavior of the offender (especially if the offender is a parent). Children at this age may blame themselves for violent acts committed by others. An adolescent or teenager is more likely to respond to violence with aggression. Children at this age often blame the victim of the violent acts.

Abusive parents

Abusive parents will often perceive their children as evil or sinister, or as a punishment for their own bad deeds. When an officer confronts an abusive parent about his or her child's injury, the parent will be unable to respond, or will have an unconvincing response. It is common for abusive parents to have been abused as children, or to have had parents who placed unreasonably high demands on them. Many parents become abusive because they demand too much of their children, whether in terms of behavior or affection. Abusive parents are more likely to overindulge in alcohol and drugs, and are often immature. Abusive parents may beat their children at random, or may administer wildly inappropriate and severe punishments for minor offenses.

Elder abuse

Elder abuse typically takes the form of neglect, exploitation, or physical/emotional abuse. In most cases of neglect, the victim has not created adequate protective structures for him or herself. For instance, a person who is physically disabled may place all of his or her needs in the hands of a stranger, who then has the opportunity to neglect those needs. People who are mentally ill are more likely to be neglected. Neglect is the most common form of elder abuse. Exploitation is the immoral and unlawful use of the victim's money, means, or body by the perpetrator. Sexual abuse and theft are both forms of exploitation. It can be difficult for law enforcement officials to handle cases of elder abuse, because the victim may be reluctant or unable to provide the necessary information. Also, elder abuse tends to occur behind closed doors, whether in the home or in a nursing facility, where there are fewer witnesses.

Hate crimes

A hate crime is an assault or other criminal act distinguished by its motive: prejudice against those of another race, culture, religion, age, gender, or sexual orientation. Criminal offenses are punished more severely if they are proved to be hate crimes. Officers should exercise special care when responding to a hate crime. Although the general rules of response are the same, the officer must be particularly aware of the victim's feelings and the motives of the perpetrator. The officer should endeavor to obtain as much detail related to the bias of the perpetrator as possible. Hate crimes are often committed in a ritualistic fashion, accompanied by the symbols and totems (e.g. swastikas, heavy boots) of the hate group. Crimes that are committed on special holidays are especially likely to be hate crimes.

Investigating property crime

The first step in the investigation of a property crime is to determine whether a crime has indeed taken place. If possible, the perpetrator of the crime should be placed under arrest. If the perpetrator has fled, the officer should obtain and relay essential information that could lead to apprehension. The officer can then interview the victim and any witnesses. It is important to acquire contact information for all of the people interviewed. The crime scene should be secured, and any possible evidence should be collected. Early areas of interest should include the type and value of property taken, the nature of any personal injuries, and the characteristics of the crime. All information about the crime should be recorded in words and photographs.

Investigating child abuse, sexual assault, or assault

The initial steps in the investigation of a personal crime vary depending on the nature of the offense. When investigating child abuse, the officer should first develop an idea of what has transpired, and whether a crime has been committed. The child in question should be protected, and often will need to be taken into protective custody. When investigating a possible sexual assault, the first step is to help and comfort the victim. Then, the investigating officer should collect all of the important evidence and make a record of the injuries sustained by the victim. The victim and any witnesses should be interviewed as soon as possible.

The procedure for investigating an assault begins in much the same way. The officer should first attend to the victim, and then should collect and record as much evidence and information about the crime scene as possible. The final step in the initial phase of any criminal investigation is the preparation of a preliminary report.

Investigating homicide

As with any crime, the first step in the investigation of a homicide is to help injured people. The attending officer should also make a quick initial survey of the crime scene, attempting to determine the nature of the crime and the important pieces of evidence. It is essential to maintain the arrangement of the crime scene by creating barriers and keeping unrelated people out. The victim and any witnesses should then be identified. From the start, an investigating officer should be trying to work out a general theory of the crime while obtaining as much information as possible from the scene and the witnesses. The officer should get complete contact information (name, address, phone number) from all witnesses. As much as possible, the officer should try to determine the time, place, cause, and means of death. The recent activities of the victim should be investigated. At this point, the officer should create a preliminary report.

Continuing investigation

A continuing investigation repeats some of the steps of the initial investigation, though it is more targeted and refined. The information obtained through the initial interviews and evidence should be used to develop leads, which should be pursued until the perpetrators are apprehended.

Investigating officers usually maintain a general theory of the crime, although this theory is likely to be adjusted over time. During a continuing investigation, officers will pay particular attention to the legal value of evidence: that is, whether it will be admissible in court. Officers often rely on advice from prosecutors in this process. Witnesses may be interviewed again, and physical evidence may be subjected to laboratory analysis. Once a likely suspect has been identified, he or she should be located and arrested.

Autopsies

An autopsy is performed to determine cause of death, though it may also yield the following information: time of death, blood alcohol level of the victim, evidence of sexual assault, contents of stomach, unrelated illnesses or injuries, and physical traces of people besides the victim. Some autopsies involve the removal of objects, like bullets, that can provide essential information about the cause of death.

Rigor mortis is the Latin phrase used to describe the stiffening of body tissues after death. The process begins in the jaw, usually about five hours after death, and proceeds down the body. After approximately 36 hours, the effects of rigor mortis are reversed. Temperature and cause of death may influence the timing of rigor mortis. When a person is extremely anxious before death, rigor mortis may occur almost at once. The decomposition of tissues, a process known as putrefaction, may also provide information about the cause and time of death.

Laboratory procedures

One of the most well known laboratory procedures used in criminal investigations is DNA fingerprinting, in which body fluids and other samples are analyzed to determine identity. Blood, hair, semen, and vaginal fluid all contain DNA. DNA testing has become a major part of criminal investigation in the past decade.

Luminol is a chemical used to detect the presence of faint blood stains. In chromatography, lab technicians isolate and identify the various substances in compounds. This sort of analysis is useful when trying to detect the presence of drugs or poison. In an atomic absorption test, lab technicians convert a substance into a vapor that can then be analyzed to identify its components. A similar technique, called spectrographic analysis, is useful for isolating the components of mineral and inorganic compounds.

Crime scene search

In a strip search, officers organize the crime scene into a grid with stakes and lines, and then search each section of the grid in order. This technique is especially useful for outdoor searches. (This technique is not to be confused with strip searches in which suspects must remove their clothing.)

In a point-to-point search, officers begin with the most obvious piece of evidence, and proceed through the crime scene from object to object. This form of search is a good first step, but it lacks an organizing principle.

In a circular search, officers begin with some central point in mind, and then either move away from it or towards it in concentric circles. This type of search is appropriate when looking for an important but missing object.

In a quadrant search, officers divide the search area into sections. This search is similar to the strip search, though it is used more commonly when the search area contains natural landmarks.

Implementation

In most cases, a crime scene search has a logical starting point. However, in some cases, officers will begin the crime scene search at the perimeter so that they can simultaneously search and seal off the area. As the crime scene search begins, a headquarters should be set up somewhere outside the perimeter so that searching officers can gather and exchange information. All of the participating officers should be briefed on the nature of the alleged crime and the intentions of the search.

Commanding officers often prescribe a certain speed for the search, depending on the relative obscurity of the evidence being sought. While a search is ongoing, officers should maintain regular communication with the commanding officer and with one another. If an area needs to be searched again, it should be done by different officers.

Photography and sketches

Crime scene photography and sketches can be invaluable to an investigation if they are prepared correctly. Before beginning to photograph the crime scene, the officer should take a photo that indicates the photographer, date, location, and case number. The photo set should move from the exterior of the crime scene to the interior, as this will help to orient the viewer.

Photographs of objects should always begin at a distance and proceed to a close up. The roll of film should be identified with the photographer's name, date, location, and case number. There are special rules governing crime scene photography in cases of sexual assault, family violence, and child abuse. Crime scene sketches accompany photography by providing information about the arrangement of the objects and evidence depicted. In some cases, photography may be too detailed, and sketches may be able to provide a better general map of the crime scene.

Crime scene measurement and sketching

When measuring a crime scene, officers may either use the triangulation method, in which the distance from two different points to the object is recorded, or the rectangulation method, in which two perpendicular lines indicate the location of the object. Initial crime scene sketches do not need to be drawn to scale, though they should be composed with attention to the relationships between objects.

Final sketches will need to be drawn according to a scale. In a perspective sketch, objects are drawn as they would be seen by a fixed observer.

A projection sketch is in three dimensions, and usually is seen from above. A schematic sketch attempts to recreate a series of events, like the path of a bullet.

Finally, a detailed sketch is used to depict an important area that, for whatever reason, is not sufficiently displayed in the projection sketch.

Chain of custody

The chain of custody is the protocol for recording the movement of evidence after it has been acquired by law enforcement officers. When an item is presented in court, it must be accompanied by a clear and thorough account of the chain of custody, so that the judge is assured the evidence has not been disturbed or manipulated.

A comprehensive chain of custody report includes the following information: where the item was found, who found it, when it was taken into custody and marked, when it was moved, and where it was stored. Of course, the primary intention with regard to evidence is to preserve its usefulness in court. However, when dealing with an item that will eventually be returned to its owner, law enforcement officials also take steps to preserve the item's value. Chain of custody is typically indicated by marking the item, whether by writing directly on it, tagging it, or placing it in a bag or envelope.

Preserving evidence

When packing evidence, officers should try to place each item in its own container, and fit all of the containers closely together within a larger box. This is done to prevent the items from rattling. Liquid blood that has been

- 150 -

collected as evidence must be refrigerated. Wet items, like stains, should be dried before they are packed. When handling evidence, officers should wear latex gloves and wash their hands before and after. In the investigation of an assault, robbery, or murder, relevant evidence includes weapons, bloodstains, and stolen property. In the investigation of a burglary, the relevant evidence includes the stolen or damaged property, footprints, fingerprints, and any instruments used in the crime.

When collecting firearms as evidence, officers should note the position and state of the weapon before it is packed away. Weapons to be used as evidence should be unloaded, and nothing should be placed inside the barrel. When collecting paint evidence, officers should submit the entire item rather than collect a sample whenever possible.

Interviewing

When interviewing complainants, witnesses, victims, and suspects, officers should first allow the interviewee to tell the story from his or her own perspective. Only after hearing this account should the officer ask targeted questions. The officer's questions should be aimed at acquiring as much detailed information as possible. An officer should never interview complainants and victims in the same area or within sight of suspects.

It is a misconception that all suspects must be given a Miranda warning before an interview; a Miranda warning is only necessary prior to a custodial interrogation. However, it is illegal for an officer or magistrate to obtain a statement from a suspect without first advising the suspect of his or her rights. This rule stems from *Miranda v. Arizona* (1966).

Procedure for search during booking

A search may be conducted during booking for any number of reasons: to protect other inmates, to guard against the possibility of suicide, or to maintain the security of the

facility itself. This search should begin with a shakedown from behind, with the prisoner removing his coat, hat, tie, belt, and shoes. After running a hand or comb through the prisoner's hair, the officer should check the prisoner's shirt collar and then run his hands down the prisoner's sleeves. The officer should then do a systematic pat-down of the prisoner's torso and legs. It is important to check any areas where contraband might be hidden: belt loops, zippers, pockets, and button areas. The prisoner's shoes and belt should be inspected thoroughly. When searching a female, the bra and waistband of the underwear should be assessed. Of course, prisoners should always be searched in private by officers of the same sex.

Vehicle and arrest data

When a prisoner is being booked, officers must record the following personal data: name; date; nickname; alias; race; sex; date of birth; age; place of birth; weight; height; color of hair and eyes; complexion; tattoos, scars, or other marks; address; driver's license number and issuing state; social security number; emergency contact; place of employment; occupation; marital status; spouse's name if applicable; and names of people with whom the prisoner was arrested.

The following vehicle data must be recorded: color, make, year of manufacture, model, license plate number, and location. Finally, the following arrest data must be recorded during booking: charge; place, date, and time of arrest; name of arresting officer; name of booking officer; time of booking; name and address of complainant; general circumstances of arrest; bond amount; names and contact information of witnesses; phone calls granted, if any; whether Miranda warning has been issued; and name of attorney.

Testimony

Officers are often called upon to deliver testimony during trial, so they must become adept at remembering key details. To begin with, the officer should review his or her participation in the case, from beginning to end. The officer should look over any reports, interviews, photographs, or evidence related to his or her actions in regard to the trial. Some officers elect to use notes during testimony. This ensures that the officer will not forget key details, but it raises the possibility that the notes will be admitted as evidence and subject to cross-examination. It is sometimes assumed that jurors will be discouraged by seeing an officer refer to notes, but research suggests that many people are actually reassured by this preparation. In any case, officers should exercise extreme care when preparing notes to be used as reference during the delivery of testimony.

Court procedure

Officers typically deliver testimony at the beginning of a trial, during the presentation of evidence against the defendant. During the direct examination, the prosecuting attorney interviews the officer. This is when the officer gives a general summary of his or her participation in the case. If the defense attorney raises an objection during the direct examination, the officer should remain silent until the judge rules. If the objection is sustained, the officer may not answer; if it is overruled, he or she may. After the direct examination, the officer will be questioned by the defense attorney during what is known as the cross-examination. Then, the prosecutor will have another opportunity to question the officer during the redirect examination. The defense attorney gets a final opportunity to question the officer during the recross-examination. When delivering testimony, officers should strive for clarity, honesty, objectivity, and brevity. Also, officers should never provide answers which they are not qualified to give.

Exclusion of a witness

Article 36.03 of the Code of Criminal Procedure states that a court may order the exclusion of a witness at the request of one party if the witness is a victim, close relative of a deceased victim, or guardian of a victim, and if it can be proven that the witness' testimony would be materially affected by his or her presence during other testimony. The other side may ask the court to require the requesting party to prove the necessity of the exclusion. Of course, the court may also exclude witnesses and other people to maintain decorum. The court will usually give instructions to scheduled witnesses at the beginning of the trial as to whom they may communicate with while the trial is ongoing. Violators of these instructions may be punished for contempt of court.

Witness under rule

Article 36.05 of the Code of Criminal Procedure states that witnesses under rule must be attended by an officer, and should not be allowed to hear any testimony in the case.

Witnesses who are placed under rule

Article 36.06 of the Code of Criminal Procedure states that witnesses who are placed under rule shall be told not to speak with one another or with any other person about the case, except with the explicit permission of the court. Also, witnesses placed under rule should not read any reports or commentary about the case. Officers are required to report any violations of these instructions.

Case management process

Law enforcement departments must develop detailed and comprehensive case folders in order to demonstrate their own professionalism and integrity. Case management helps prosecutors by underscoring the quality of the police work behind the case. A typical case folder includes offense reports, voluntary confessions, fingerprint cards and a comparison report from an expert, witness statements, victim statements, and any other useful information. The case summary should include the basic facts surrounding the case, the legality of the arrest and seizure of evidence, and the names of witnesses. The preparation of the case files gives officers a chance to work directly with prosecutors, and this cooperation often proves fruitful in unexpected ways. At the least, the preparation of the case files gives officers an opportunity to review the facts of the case and to identify any potential areas of weakness.

Practice Test

Practice Questions

1. Which of the following represents the number one cause of death in the United States?
   a. Cancer
   b. Heart disease
   c. Accidents
   d. Strokes

2. Among the FITT guidelines for fitness training thresholds, which two incorporate the exercise principle of Progressive Overload?
   a. Frequency and intensity
   b. Frequency and time
   c. Intensity and time
   d. Time and type

3. To which of the following persons or entities should a peace officer NEVER make a referral?
   a. Bail bondsman or a private attorney
   b. District Attorney or County Attorney
   c. State Department of Health and Human Services
   d. State Department of Mental Health and Mental Retardation

4. Which of the following choices accurately describes a difference between traditional and community-based models of policing?
   a. The community-based model is more simplified.
   b. The community-based model is incident-driven.
   c. The community-based model is based upon CFS.
   d. The community-based model is more pro-active.

5. Which of the following choices represents an example of physical courage?
   a. Refusing to accept gratuities from any citizens
   b. Abstaining from participating in any cover-ups
   c. Confronting an armed and barricaded suspect
   d. Avoiding racial/ethnic/gender humor

6. Which of the following statements regarding unethical conduct by peace officers is TRUE?
   a. Unethical behavior by peace officers is subject to prosecution only by State government.
   b. Specific statutes have been designed to prevent violations of civil rights by peace officers.
   c. If a peace officer is accused of violating civil rights, a special State entity initiates an investigation.
   d. Local authorities regulate investigations of peace officers for civil rights violations.

7. When was the United States Constitution ratified by the first of the 13 States?
   a. 1774
   b. 1776
   c. 1778
   d. 1787

8. Which of the following statements about the U.S. Bill of Rights is correct?
   a. Both the Bill of Rights and the Constitution were ratified at the same time.
   b. The Bill of Rights is a distinct document unrelated to any Amendments.
   c. The Bill of Rights guarantees societal rights but not any personal rights.
   d. The Bill of Rights protects citizen rights but does not limit government.

9. Which of the following is a typical feeling or attitude of most prejudiced individuals?
   a. A feeling of inferiority
   b. A sense of deprivation
   c. A xenophobic attitude
   d. An approach of no fear

10. What statement accurately reflects a basic assumption about impartial enforcement of the law?
   a. In the same situation, one person should not be favored over another.
   b. Impartial enforcement should be specific to the situation and the law.
   c. Impartiality applies only to interactions between officers and citizens.
   d. Enforcing the law impartially can be achieved perfectly in a democracy.

11. Which of the following rights is included in the Texas Code of Criminal Procedure (CCP)?
   a. Freedom of speech
   b. Freedom of the press
   c. Right to a trial by jury
   d. These are all included

12. According to the Texas Code of Criminal Procedure (CCP), which of the following statements describes who is considered a Peace Officer?
   a. Officers from adjoining states are not considered Peace Officers.
   b. The Texas Rangers are Peace Officers.
   c. Railroad Officers are not Peace Officers.
   d. Special Investigators are not included.

13. "In the absence of other effective measures the following procedures to safeguard the Fifth Amendment privilege must be observed: The person in custody must, prior to interrogation, be clearly informed that he has the right to remain silent, and that anything he says will be used against him in court; he must be clearly informed that he has the right to consult with a lawyer and to have the lawyer with him during interrogation, and that, if he is indigent, a lawyer will be appointed to represent him." This provision is popularly known as:
   a. Arizona rights.
   b. Custody rights.
   c. Miranda rights.
   d. Arresting rights.

14. According to the Fourth Amendment, which of the following statements about probable cause is true?
   a. An officer can establish probable cause through a person's behaving abnormally.
   b. Commission of a surreptitious act does not give probable cause for search or arrest.
   c. An occurrence in an area with a high crime rate cannot constitute probable cause.
   d. The officer's subjective good faith can establish probable cause for search or arrest.

15. According to the Texas Penal Code, which of the following statements regarding Intoxication and Alcoholic Beverages Offenses is correct?
   a. Stopping a vehicle on reasonable suspicion of intoxication or for traffic violations is the same.
   b. Evidence that a driver is dangerous to self or others must be provided by an arresting officer.
   c. It is more important to stop a vehicle as soon as possible than to waste time video recording.
   d. Drawing blood is never required, and there is no legal recourse to draw it if a driver refuses.

16. According to the Texas Penal Code and Texas law, what is required to be found guilty of organized crime?
   a. The accused person must have the intention to commit the organized crime.
   b. The person must intend to make/keep/partake of/profit from a crime group.
   c. The accused person has collaborated with others to commit a criminal offense.
   d. Both answers A and B are required, but answer C alone is insufficient reason.

17. Which of the following statements is true about Texas laws on motorcyclists wearing helmets?
   a. Any motorcyclist 20 years of age or younger is not required to wear a helmet.
   b. Motorcyclists 20 years of age or younger are exempt from wearing helmets with proof of completing a training and safety course.
   c. Motorcyclists 21 years of age or older are exempt from wearing helmets with proof of having a medical insurance policy.
   d. Officers may detain motorcyclists only to determine whether they are required to wear a helmet.

18. Which of the following statements is true regarding traffic-related incidents?
   a. Traffic-related incidents are considered the second deadliest activity for police officers behind responding to crimes in progress.
   b. Over 40 percent of officer deaths in the line of duty are traffic-related.
   c. An officer is more likely to be struck by a vehicle and killed than from involvement in an automobile crash.
   d. An officer is more likely to be killed in a motorcycle crash than in an automobile crash.

19. Which of the following statements is most true about characteristics of vehicle operation related to intoxication?
   a. A driver who stares fixedly at one point is concentrating and probably sober.
   b. A driver who maintains a constant, unvarying speed most likely is intoxicated.
   c. A driver who stops short of or beyond a light or stop sign often is intoxicated.
   d. A driver weaving from lane to lane more likely is distracted than intoxicated.

20. Which of the following tests is classified as a chemical test rather than a field sobriety test?
   a. Index finger-to-nose test
   b. Heel-to-toe walking test
   c. Standing on one leg test
   d. Breath specimen test

21. According to the US Code on civil process, if a civil infringement by an officer is alleged, who can be held liable?
    a. only the individual officer
    b. the officer and employing agency
    c. the employing agency and government
    d. the officer, employing agency, and government

22. Which of the following statements correctly states a difference between civil law and criminal law?
    a. In criminal law, the plaintiff bringing the action owns the suit.
    b. In civil law, the officer is directly responsible for filing charges.
    c. In criminal law, the court finds the defendant guilty/not guilty.
    d. In civil law, guilt must be established beyond reasonable doubt.

23. Which of the following statements is true regarding the Texas Alcoholic Beverage Code (TABC)?
    a. Consuming alcoholic beverages near schools is not addressed.
    b. Possessing intoxicants on public school grounds is another code.
    c. Purchase of alcohol by minors is covered, but attempting to purchase alcohol by minors is not.
    d. Selling alcohol to minors is prohibited, but giving alcohol to minors is not prohibited.

24. Which of the following statements is correct regarding information needed for taking administrative action for violations under the Texas Alcoholic Beverage Code (TABC)?
    a. The premise that is licensed to sell alcoholic beverages must be identified.
    b. The premise or person with a permit to sell alcoholic drinks is not needed.
    c. The arresting officer does not need to supply dates, times, and location of arrest.
    d. Stating the reason for being at alcohol-licensed premises is unnecessary.

25. Punishment for violating Texas drug laws can be affected by certain "Enhancements." Which of the following codes governs drug-related offenses committed in Drug-Free Zones?
    a. Texas Penal Code
    b. Texas Government Code
    c. Texas Health and Safety Code
    d. Texas Code of Criminal Procedure

26. Which of the following statements about the Texas Health and Safety Code regarding simulated controlled substances is correct?
    a. Manufacture/delivery is not an offense because these substances are basically placebos.
    b. Manufacture/delivery in the discharge of peace officer duties is defense to prosecution.
    c. Manufacture/delivery if believing it is a controlled substance is a defense to prosecution.
    d. Manufacture/delivery in duties of a licensed pharmacist is not a defense to prosecution.

27. Which statement is most accurate regarding juveniles' interactions with police officers?
    a. Peer pressure motivates teenagers to conform, so they are more compliant.
    b. Teens' more dependent status means they are less likely to take the initiative.
    c. Adolescents idolize authority figures, so they are respectful of police officers.
    d. Normal internal and external factors cause teens to act out and defy authority.

28. Which of the following statements is true about the Uniform Interstate Compact on Juveniles?
    a. Juvenile delinquent parolees or probationers must be supervised by their own states.
    b. Non-delinquent juveniles who run away from home are not covered by this compact.
    c. Juvenile delinquents who escape or abscond are returned by other states in this pact.
    d. It does not allow additional cooperative measures to protect juveniles and the public.

29. What are the only 2 offenses that by themselves are not sufficient grounds for arrest in the State of Texas?
    a. Jaywalking and running a stop sign
    b. Stalking and possession of a controlled substance
    c. Expired license and disturbing the peace
    d. Speeding and open container

30. Which of the following statements is true regarding a peace officer's written communications?
    a. Evaluations of a peace officer's competence do not consider his or her writing.
    b. The written communications of a peace officer are seen by only private readers.
    c. Judicial and administrative proceedings may employ them as source documents.
    d. Police reports are not commonly used for statistical data or reference materials.

31. As a peace officer, if you encounter Spanish-speaking persons in an accident investigation and one of them appears injured and in pain, which of the following statements is the most appropriate question to ask?
    a. "¿Dónde le duele?"
    b. "¿Hay alguien herido?"
    c. "¿En qué puedo servirle?"
    d. "¿Es usted el dueño del carro?"

32. Regarding Hispanic culture and nonverbal communication, if a peace officer perceives Latin American persons as using tones of voice, gestures, and speech that seem overly emotional, which is the most appropriate response?
    a. The officer should try to calm them down because something must be wrong.
    b. The officer should realize that at least two major cultural reasons can account for these characteristics.
    c. The officer should confront such individuals before they progress to violence.
    d. The officer should avoid trying to reassure them that they will not be harmed.

33. According to court rulings as precedents regarding the use of force by police officers, which of the following statements is correct?
    a. Officers performing discretionary functions are always immune from liability for civil damages and from suits.
    b. Officers performing discretionary functions whose conduct violates a constitutional right have qualified immunity.
    c. Officers performing discretionary functions whose conduct violates a federal statutory right will not be immune.
    d. Officers unaware of constitutional or statutory rights or who do not understand that their conduct violates them are immune.

34. Which of the following statements is correct regarding the role of law enforcement in arrest?
    a. With involved in a physical arrest, the police officer plays an essentially offensive role.
    b. When a police officer initiates confrontation of a lawbreaker, it is deemed aggression.
    c. When a lawbreaker is unarmed but combative, a police officer then should use force.
    d. With regard to control, an officer must have complete self-control to control another.

35. Which of the following actions is NOT considered a weaponless defense strategy?
    a. touching
    b. leg blocks
    c. handcuffs
    d. hand strikes

36. Which of the following reasons is justification for a peace officer using deadly force?
    a. to prevent serious bodily injury
    b. to prevent the commission of a Class A misdemeanor
    c. to prevent the commission of a Class C misdemeanor
    d. to prevent the commission of a felony

37. Which of the following correctly states distances and hands of the minimum proficiency requirements for handgun use by a police officer?
    a. 3 yards using two hands
    b. 7 yards using one hand
    c. 15 yards using two hands
    d. 25 yards using one hand

38. How often must a peace officer complete firearm proficiency requirements?
    a. monthly
    b. annually
    c. biennially
    d. triennially

39. When making a patient assessment in emergency medical assistance, which of the following is the first step?
    a. assuring site safety
    b. assuring an airway
    c. rescue breathing
    d. bleeding control

40. Which of the following statements is true about emergency medical assistance for a victim in shock?
    a. The victim should be sitting up, with the feet lower.
    b. Wait for medical help to arrive and control bleeding.
    c. Reassure the victim even if s/he appears to be calm.
    d. Get the victim food and/or drink as soon as possible.

41. In emergency radio communications, which of the following statements is accurate?
    a. The 10-codes used are uniform across all the radio services.
    b. Individual police departments may use different ten-codes.
    c. In general, hearing a code of 10-30 is no reason for concern.
    d. Confusing 10-22 and 10-33 would not cause serious trouble.

42. Which of the following statements is correct about the phonetic alphabets used for spelling names in radio transmissions?

    a. The American Law Enforcement and Military Phonetic Alphabets use identical names for letters.

    b. The Military and American Law Enforcement Phonetic Alphabets' letter names are all different.

    c. Phonetic alphabet words always should be spoken as "A as in ADAM," or "B like in BRAVO," etc.

    d. In both Military and American Law Enforcement's versions, names chosen are most understood.

43. What is the correct sequence for the components of total stopping distance when driving?

    a. perception of danger; decision/reaction; braking

    b. braking; perception of danger; decision/reaction

    c. decision/reaction; braking; perception of danger

    d. all three are simultaneous; there is no sequence

44. In the problem-solving approach to community policing, which of the following is a true statement about the SARA model?

    a. The Scanning step involves identifying relationship, similarities, or recurrence of incidents.

    b. The Analysis step defines what, where, when, and who has occurred, but not why the incident is occurring.

    c. The Response step entails immediate protection action rather than long-term prevention.

    d. The Assessment step measures response impact via one single source after the response.

45. Which of the following is an accurate statement about four of the five patrol patterns?

    a. When on patrol, an officer's lane selection should always be the same.

    b. When using a circular patrol pattern, the circle always should be inward.

    c. A double-back patrol pattern is for re-checks, not for learning the beat.

    d. A random patrol pattern stops criminals from predicting a beat pattern.

46. As a peace officer, you encounter an adult victim of a violent crime curled in a fetal position. The victim is able to walk, but crawls instead. This victim displays a number of other childlike behaviors. Under the circumstances, which of the following choices is the most appropriate and reasonable assumption prior to obtaining more information?

    a. This victim has mental illness.

    b. This victim has intellectual disability.

    c. This is a perpetrator trying to distract you.

    d. This is regression secondary to the trauma.

47. Which of the following choices accurately describes a common characteristic of family violence offenders?

    a. taking personal responsibility for aggressive and/or violent actions

    b. always behaving the same way in public as they do in their homes

    c. having a history of being a victim and/or witness of family violence

    d. confirming and/or exaggerating how serious their violent acts are

48. Which of the following answer choices represents an element of the paradox of Crisis Intervention Training (CIT) for mental health crises in Texas law enforcement?
    a. Law enforcement is using CIT less since it differs from traditional suspect encounter trainings.
    b. Less controlling/authoritative approaches in mental health crises give more control/authority.
    c. Governmental funding allocated for mental health services in Texas is consistently increasing.
    d. Texas is near the national average for the amount of mental health funding it receives.

49. Which of the following choices is NOT classified as a Hazardous Material?
    a. air pollution
    b. toxic materials
    c. ionizing radiation
    d. infectious materials

50. In a homicide investigation, which of the following is most likely to provide evidence that the body was moved after death?
    a. post-mortem lividity
    b. rigor Mortis
    c. body temperature
    d. putrefaction

Answers and Explanations

1. B: According to recent available statistics, heart disease accounts for 39 percent of US deaths. Cancer accounts for 22 percent of US deaths. Accidents cause 5 percent of US deaths. Strokes are the cause of 7 percent of deaths in the US. Other causes are attributed to 27 percent of US deaths.

2. C: Intensity = how hard you exercise. Time = how long you exercise. Both how hard and how long you exercise incorporate the principle of Progressive Overload. Frequency = how many workouts you do per week. Frequency incorporates the exercise principles of Regularity and Recovery. Type = the kind of exercise you do. Type incorporates the exercise principle of Specificity and Balance. Frequency, Intensity, Time, and Type = FITT.

3. A: A peace officer should never make a referral to either a bail bondsman or an attorney in private practice because a lawsuit could be filed against the officer for this action. Officers should refer citizens to the District or County Attorney for filing cases directly, or for applications for family protective orders. They should refer to their State Department of HHS for child or elderly protective services or emergency financial assistance. Referrals to the State Department of MHMR are for obtaining social services related to mental illness and intellectual disability.

4. D: The newer, community-based model of policing is more pro-active, i. e. more preventive and less reactive than traditional models. It is not more simplified; rather, it is more complex as the officer assumes more roles, e. g. planning, solving problems and community organizing as well as enforcing laws. Traditional policing models are more incident-driven, and officer activity is based more upon calls for service (CFS) than in the community-based model.

5. C: Confronting a suspect who has barricaded himself/herself in a building and is armed is an example of physical courage for a peace officer. Refusing gratuities offered by citizens, not partaking in cover-ups, and not making fun of or joking about race, ethnicity, gender, etc. all are examples of moral courage for a peace officer.

6. B: Specific statues in the law have been designed to prevent violations of civil rights by peace officers. Unethical behavior by peace officers is subject to Federal prosecution. If a peace officer is accused of violating civil rights, the FBI rather than a State entity has a specialized role of investigation such accusations. These investigations are not regulated by local authorities but by Federal government in Washington, D. C. in order to avert compromise of the investigation by friendships and/or working relationships between peace officers and locally stationed FBI agents.

7. D: The US Constitution was ratified by the first of the States, Delaware, on September 17, 1787, at the Continental Congress. The first meeting of the Continental Congress was held in September of 1774. The American Declaration of Independence from England was introduced at the Continental Congress in June 1776, and made official on July 4, 1776. The Articles of Confederation, the first attempt at a constitution, were adopted in 1778 but found unsatisfactory, hence the new Constitution.

8. A: The Bill of Rights was attached to the US Constitution, and both were ratified by a majority of the States on December 17, 1791. The Bill of Rights consists of the first ten Amendments to the US Constitution. Societal rights are guaranteed in the Preamble to the Constitution. Personal rights are covered in the first four Amendments and thus included in the Bill of Rights. The Bill of Rights not only protects the rights of American citizens; it also limits the power of the Federal government.

9. C: Xenophobia, i. e. the fear or dislike of the strange, is typical of prejudiced individuals. They regard other social groups as strange, rejecting and excluding them for being different. Most prejudiced persons also possess a feeling of their own superiority over others. They tend to have a sense not of deprivation, but automatic entitlement to certain rights via group membership. Another common characteristic is fear, a foundation of prejudice: prejudiced people feel threatened by others and react against them.

10. A: One of the basic assumptions about impartial enforcement of the law is that the officer should not favor one person over another in the same situation by treating them differently. Impartial enforcement of the law is not restricted to the specific situation or specific law: a basic assumption is that it also applies to the general concept of impartial enforcement and of impartial treatment by the whole criminal justice system. Impartiality does not apply only to interactions between officers and citizens: it also applies to officers' interventions in interactions *between/among citizens.* Another basic assumption asserts that impartial law enforcement cannot be achieved perfectly in the real world; instead, it is an ideal toward which to strive in a democracy.

11. D: These are all basic rights included in the Texas CCP. In the US Constitution, freedom of speech and freedom of the press are included in the First Amendment; right to a trial by jury is in the Sixth Amendment. These Constitutional rights are hence also deemed basic rights in the Texas Code of Criminal Procedure.

12. B: The Texas Rangers have been designated as Peace Officers since the early 1900s. Special Texas Rangers and Special Rangers of the Southwestern Cattle Raisers Association also are considered Peace Officers. According to the Texas CCP, officers from states adjoining Texas are still Peace Officers when in Texas. Railroad Peace Officers also are included under the Texas CCP. Additionally, Special Investigators are considered Peace Officers in Texas.

13. C: The rights named in this provision are popularly referred to as "Miranda rights" after the Supreme Court case *Miranda v. Arizona*, 384 US 486 (1966) establishing this law after the plaintiff in the case had been arrested and interrogated without first being informed of these rights.

14. A: Factors that officers can use to establish probable cause for search or arrest include objective observations regarding a suspect's abnormal conduct; that a suspect commits an act surreptitiously/furtively (as if to hide it, rather than doing it openly); and that the suspected activity is in a high-crime area. However, the subjective opinion of the officer, even in good faith, is not sufficient to establish probable cause for search or arrest.

15. B: According to Texas Penal Code 49. 02, arresting officers must explain facts and circumstances establishing that, at the time of the arrest, the driver arrested was dangerous to self and/or others. Stopping a vehicle on reasonable suspicion of intoxication is NOT the same as stopping a vehicle for traffic violations. Officers stopping vehicles for traffic violations may issue tickets/warrants/arrests for the traffic violations, but not for intoxication if there is no reasonable suspicion of it. If the officer has reasonable suspicion of intoxication and this is borne out upon stopping the vehicle, arrest for intoxication is indicated. It is also important to capture as much of the relevant driving behavior on video before stopping the vehicle. In some circumstances, drawing blood IS mandatory; when a blood draw is NOT mandatory, a search warrant may be obtained if the driver refuses.

16. D: According to the Texas Penal Code and by the precedent of the Texas Criminal Appeals Court case of *Nguyen v. State,* 1 S. W. 3d 694, 697 (1999), to be found guilty of organized crime, the person accused must *both* intend to commit the crime *and* intend to create, sustain, take part in, or

- 163 -

partake of profits from a criminal organization. Having collaborated with others in committing only one offense is judged insufficient grounds for being found guilty of organized crime.

17. C: According to the Texas Traffic Code (TC) and the Insurance Institute for Highway Safety's Highway Loss Data Institute, all motorcyclists age 20 or younger must wear helmets. Motorcycle riders aged 21 or older are exempted from wearing helmets if they can show proof of EITHER having completed a course in motorcycle operator training and safety OR having a medical insurance policy. Another provision of the Texas TC is that peace officers may not stop or detain motorcycle drivers or motorcycle passengers only for the purpose of ascertaining such training completion or insurance coverage.

18. B: Statistics gathered from 1998 to 2007 showed that over 40 percent of officer deaths in the line of duty were traffic related. Traffic-related incidents were by far the deadliest activity for police officers. More than two thirds of these traffic-related deaths were due to automobile crashes. In order of decreasing frequency, the remainder of these traffic-related deaths involved the officer struck by a moving vehicle or the officer involved in a motorcycle crash.

19. C: While reasons other than intoxication cause many driving behaviors, stopping short of or beyond a traffic light or signal is one of the most common characteristics of DWI. Additional signs include staring fixedly, which indicates a lack of concentration, since the motorist should be looking at all points in the surrounding traffic. Other signs include displaying inconsistent speeds/slowing down and speeding up frequently (but not as dictated by traffic), and weaving between lanes. While sober motorists distracted by things other than intoxication also may weave, weaving is a classic sign of intoxicated driving.

20. D: Taking a breath specimen, like taking of a blood specimen, is classified as a chemical test. Seeing whether the motorist accurately can touch the index finger to the nose, walk heel to toe, and/or stand on one leg are all classified as field sobriety tests for DWI when an officer had reasonable suspicion of it to stop the driver. The Traffic Code dictates when taking specimens is/is not indicated. (Note: field sobriety tests that could cause injury should not be given to obviously intoxicated persons, e. g. standing on one leg if they cannot stand straight on both legs, etc. Also, officers must rule out other conditions mimicking intoxication, e. g. cerebral palsy, diabetes, epilepsy, shock, etc.)

21. D: Not only the individual officer alleged to have violated civil law, but also the officer's employing agency, and the government representing the officer's commissioning authority (Title 42, Section 1983, US Code).

22. C: In criminal law, the state brings action against an individual for an alleged crime, and the court finds the defendant guilty or not guilty beyond a reasonable doubt. In civil (not criminal) law, an individual plaintiff bringing action against another individual is the owner of the suit, and the officer involved must follow all laws and rules for executing civil documents. The officer is only directly responsible for filing charges in criminal (not civil) actions. In civil law, a judge or jury finds for the complainant or for the defendant (or some middle ground) based on a preponderance of the evidence (not finding guilt beyond a reasonable doubt as in criminal law).

23. B: The possession of intoxicants on public school grounds is prohibited under the Texas Education Act (TEC), 37. 122, rather than under the TABC. Consuming alcoholic beverages near schools is addressed as unlawful under TABC 101. 75. The purchase of alcohol by minors is covered by TABC 106. 02, and the attempt to purchase alcohol by a minor is also covered by TABC 106. 025;

both actions are prohibited. Selling alcohol to minors is prohibited under TABC 106. 03; giving alcohol to minors or buying it for them is also prohibited under TABC 106. 06.

24. A: In order to take administrative action under the TABC, the officer must identify the premise licensed to sell alcoholic beverages; the premise/person with a permit to sell alcoholic drinks; the dates, times, and location of the arrest or incident; and the reason for being at the licensed premises at the time of the incident, as well as identifying intoxicated persons present and a number of other forms of information needed.

25. C: The Health and Safety Code (HSC) of the Texas Controlled Substance Act, HSC 481. 134 governs punishment for violations of Texas drug laws committed in Drug-Free Zones. The Texas Penal Code (TCP), Texas Government Code, and Texas Code of Criminal Procedure (TCCP) all govern punishments for deadly weapons findings in violations of Texas drug laws.

26. B: According to Section 482. 002 of the Texas Health and Safety Code, manufacturing a simulated controlled substance (which is represented as a controlled substance but is chemically different) with intent to deliver or delivering it in the discharge of official peace officer duties is a defense to prosecution. Manufacture or delivery of such substances *is* an offense. Doing so for a licensed medical practitioner for its use as a placebo in research or practice is a defense to prosecution, as is manufacture/delivery by licensed pharmacists or other authorized medical practitioners. However, this does not mean it is not otherwise an offense. It is *not* a defense to prosecution to manufacture/deliver these believing they are true controlled substances.

27. D: Adolescents normally are affected by internal influences: they are engaged in the process of finding their own identities and separating from their parents, so they need to assert their independence. They can react to police the same as against parental control. Some teens' development of independence is more difficult and involves acting out and rebelling against authority. External influences such as peer pressure motivate them to conform to peers' actions and expectations, but not usually to respect or comply with authority figures.

28. C: One provision of the Uniform Interstate Compact on Juveniles asserts that if juvenile delinquents escape or abscond from their state of residence, other states cooperate to return them. This compact also provides that juvenile delinquents on parole or probation are cooperatively supervised by all states contracting to the agreement. It additionally provides that runaway juveniles who are not delinquent be returned by other contracting states to their home state. This compact also provides for additional cooperative measures by any two or more of the contracting states to protect juveniles and the public.

29. D: In the State of Texas, one may not be arrested for Speeding or Open Container violations. However, in situations where officers may be inclined to make an arrest, there will almost certainly be additional violations cited. In the case of excessive speeding, a charge of reckless driving is often the attached offense. With open container, the most common accompanying offenses warranting an arrest are Driving While Intoxicated, reckless driving, and Public Intoxication.

30. C: Court and other legal proceedings often use peace officers' reports and other written communications as source documents for facts and observations pertinent to the case. In evaluations of a peace officer's competence, including performance evaluations, the officer's writing is one of the factors used. Officers' written documents are viewed by diverse readers, including the officer's employing agency; anyone working within the criminal justice system; and the public. It is

common practice to use police reports to obtain statistical data and as reference materials for judicial proceedings, administrative publications, etc.

31. A: "¿Dónde le duele?" means "Where does it hurt?" in Spanish. If somebody appears injured and in pain but you don't know where, this is the most appropriate of the choices. "¿Hay alguien herido?" means "Is anyone hurt?" The test item specifies that a person appears injured and in pain, so asking this would be superfluous, wasting time. Asking "¿En qué puedo servirle?" which means "How may I help you?" is also superfluous in an accident investigation: You already are responding to an accident, plus someone appears injured and in pain. You would only ask this if police were called and you did not know why upon arrival. Asking "¿Es usted el dueño del carro?" is asking "Are you the owner of the car?" You would only ask this in an accident investigation when there is vehicle damage and a driver might be at fault, but nobody is in immediate need of medical help.

32. B: Peace officers should realize that (1) Hispanic cultures are typically more emotionally expressive than North American culture, so nothing at all may be wrong; and (2) People from Hispanic countries with repressive governments have learned to fear police for good reason, so they could be afraid of any officer they see. Officers should be aware of these cultural factors and adjust their behavior accordingly to make their jobs easier. Hispanic emotional expression per se is not generally a sign of impending violence. As long as the officer has no objective reason to see frightened Hispanic persons as threats, they should not avoid reassuring them they will not be harmed; this rarely hurts and often helps.

33. C: According to Milstead v. Kibler, 243 F. 3d 157 (US Court of Appeals, 4th Circuit, 2001), officers performing discretionary functions are immune from liability for civil damages UNLESS their conduct violates a federal statutory or constitutional right, so they are not *always* immune. This decision also stipulates that an "objectively reasonable officer would have understood that the conduct violated that right." Additionally, the case of Okonkwo v. Fernandez, 2004 WL 22227858 (North District of Texas, 2003) states that officers are entitled to qualified immunity, which protects them from lawsuits as well as from liability for civil damages, UNLESS their conduct violates statutory or constitutional rights "of which a reasonable officer would have known." Thus officers' ignorance of these rights or not understanding their conduct violates them does NOT confer immunity.

34. D: Control is reciprocal: The officer must be completely in control of himself/herself in order to control a law violator. Self-control is considered one of the officer's biggest assets in dealing with lawbreakers. The goal of officers' control of law violators is to elicit their cooperation. In physical arrest, the officer's role is deemed essentially defensive, not offensive. Defensive means serving to protect, or to prevent or resist attack or aggression. An officer's taking the initiative in confronting a lawbreaker is not deemed aggression as the officer is defending and protecting the community, not acting out hostility. Officers can get into trouble for using force with combative but unarmed lawbreakers. They can avoid this by using reasonable alternatives to force first.

35. C: Handcuffs are NOT weaponless defense strategies because handcuffs are considered weapons by the Police Force and Academy. Touching, leg blocks (as well as arm blocks and hand blocks), and hand strikes (as well as foot strikes); using pressure points, and joint-locking are all methods of weaponless defense that peace officers must learn and practice on duty as needed.

36. A: According to the Texas Penal Code (9. 32, 9. 33): "Peace officers may use deadly force to protect themselves or others when and to the degree they reasonably believe an immediate threat of death or serious bodily injury exists." Although the impending commission of a crime may

include the threat of death or serious bodily injury, the goal of preventing the crime is not in itself sufficient grounds for the use of deadly force.

37. C: The minimum firearm proficiency requirements for handguns include a distance of 15 yards using both hands. The distance of 3 yards applies to firing using only one hand. The distance of 7 yards is for two-handed firing. The distance of 25 yards specifies the use of both hands.

38. B: According to the Texas Administrative Code, "each agency or entity that employs at least two peace officers shall: (1) require each peace officer that it employs to successfully complete the current firearms proficiency requirements at least once each year." Firearms proficiency typically is not documented monthly. It would violate this provision to document officers' firearms proficiency only once every two or three years.

39. A: The first thing to do in a patient assessment during emergency medical assistance is to make sure the location is safe for yourself and the patient. Immediate danger in the area can negate rescue efforts. Once you either secure the area or move the patient, you should see if the patient has an open airway to breathe. If not, EMS techniques should be employed. If the airway is open but the patient is not breathing, you should start rescue breathing. Bleeding must be controlled, but breathing comes first.

40. C: People in shock may appear agitated or calm, a common symptom of shock. You should still reassure the victim, who may internally feel disoriented, confused, and frightened but not show it. Victims in shock should be assisted to lie down, not sit up. Unless spinal, hip, leg, neck, and/or head injuries are suspected, the victim's legs should be elevated, not lower than the heart. In the event of bleeding, you should not wait for medical help to arrive, but try to control it yourself: blood loss contributes to shock. A victim also could bleed to death if heavy/arterial bleeding is not controlled. You should NOT give food or drink to persons in shock: they may vomit and/or need general anesthesia.

41. B: There is still some disparity among the 10-codes used by individual police departments, so you may need to check with your local department. The radio services are working to arrive at uniform 10-codes for all departments, but this uniformity is not yet established. In general, the most common meaning of the 10-30 code is Danger/Caution, so hearing it *is* a reason for concern. It *could* cause serious trouble to confuse 10-22 and 10-33: 10-22 means Disregard, while 10-33 means Help Me Quick.

42. D: The names chosen to represent alphabet letters for spelling out names/words over the radio are those found to be easiest to understand over the air. However, the American Law Enforcement Phonetic Alphabet and the Military Phonetic Alphabet do not use the same words for each alphabet letter. Though most letter words differ between the two, they are NOT ALL different: both alphabets use X-RAY for the letter X and VICTOR for the letter V. Officers are instructed NEVER to say "A as in ADAM" (ALE) or "A as in ALPHA" (Military); or "B like in BRAVO" (Military) or "B like in BOY" (ALE), but ALWAYS to say "A-ADAM" or "A-ALPHA," etc.

43. A: The correct order is first the perception of danger, which influences the speed and nature of the motorist's decision or reaction and how soon and how hard the driver brakes. The driver's perception of how dangerous the situation is affects both what s/he decides to do and how quickly s/he reacts. Reaction time figures into total time. Even after reacting and stepping on the brake pedal, the car moves an additional distance before stopping; this distance depends on the vehicle's speed at the time of braking.

44. A: The S in SARA is for Scanning, which involves reviewing preliminary information to identify incidents that are related, are similar in nature, or are recurrent to define a problem with a particular type of crime or disorder; and to prioritize that problem for future investigation. The A is for Analysis, to define what problem occurs; when and where it occurs; who is responsible and whom it affects; AND why it occurs, including enabling conditions. The R is for Response, which entails not only immediate protection of crime victims, but moreover prevention of future occurrences AND long-term change for the better in the problem. The A, for Assessment, measures the impact of the response on the problem, via *multiple* sources, including measurement *before and after* implementation of the response.

45. D: By using a random patrol pattern, officers can avoid establishing any pattern of patrolling that criminals could learn and plan activities accordingly. Times and places of police arrivals within a beat are unpredictable with this pattern. The patrol pattern related to lane selection is NOT always the same. For clear observation of oncoming traffic and between buildings on both sides of the street, the centermost lane is best. For clearer views of sides of buildings, building windows facing the street, possible hiding spots, and for readily stopping at the curb, it is best to drive in the curbside lane at lower speeds. The circular patrol pattern can be *either* inward in decreasing circles from the outskirts of the beat area, *or* outward from the center of the beat area in increasing circles. The double-back pattern is for re-checking someone or something or for problem areas, *and* this pattern is useful for learning a new beat.

46. D: The National Organization for Victim Assistance in Washington, D. C., explains that some crime victims who experience trauma will regress to childlike behaviors. While some individuals with mental illnesses or intellectual disability also display childlike behaviors, these conditions are not the most appropriate or reasonable to assume when the individual is a victim of a violent crime. In this situation, trauma is more likely until you obtain information to the contrary. A perpetrator posing as a victim and trying to distract you is possible, but highly unlikely.

47. C: According to the Department of Human Services (DHS), family violence offenders typically have histories of having been victims and/or witnesses of family violence themselves. Some other common characteristics of family violence offenders include blaming others for their actions and not taking personal responsibility for anything unless it benefits them, behaving very differently in public from how they behave at home in some cases; and denying and/or minimizing how serious their violent actions really are.

48. B: Part of the paradox of CIT is that when officers use approaches that are *less* controlling and *less* authoritarian with persons having mental health crises, they attain *more* control and authority over such individuals than if they were more confrontational, more physical, etc. This is the exact opposite of traditional suspect encounter training. Another paradoxical element is that law enforcement is using CIT much more lately, despite CIT's departure from the traditional training employed by many law enforcement agencies. A further paradox is that even though law enforcement uses CIT more and CIT has averted many deaths, the funding for mental health services in Texas is consistently decreasing, not increasing. Texas is in the bottom 10% of states for funding for mental health services.

49. A: Air pollution is not classified as a Hazardous Material (though perhaps it should be!). Toxic materials include industrial materials and chemicals, agricultural chemicals, chemical warfare agents, riot control chemicals, irritant chemicals, and biological toxins. Ionizing radiation includes ˙˙ha, Beta, Gamma, X-Ray, and Neutron types from various sources. Infectious materials include ˙athogens such as bacteria and viruses, as well as animal and plant pathogens.

50. A: Post-mortem lividity is a dark purplish-blue discoloration of the body parts nearest to the ground. This condition typically appears about two hours after death. Its presence can help to establish whether the body was moved after death. Rigor Mortis is stiffening of the muscles after death. It can begin 15 minutes to 15 hours post-mortem, but in general its onset tends to be 5-6 hours after death. It takes about 12 hours for the upper body to stiffen and about 18 hours to extend to the lower body. Within around 36 hours, the stiffness goes away over 8-10 hours. Presence or absence of Rigor Mortis can help to determine time of death. Body temperature decreases after death; rates vary by body size, clothing, and air temperature. Body temperature can also help determine time of death. Putrefaction is tissue decomposition after death. Signs of putrefaction can help determine time of death as well.

Secret Key #1 - Time is Your Greatest Enemy

Pace Yourself

Wear a watch. At the beginning of the test, check the time (or start a chronometer on your watch to count the minutes), and check the time after every few questions to make sure you are "on schedule."

If you are forced to speed up, do it efficiently. Usually one or more answer choices can be eliminated without too much difficulty. Above all, don't panic. Don't speed up and just begin guessing at random choices. By pacing yourself, and continually monitoring your progress against your watch, you will always know exactly how far ahead or behind you are with your available time. If you find that you are one minute behind on the test, don't skip one question without spending any time on it, just to catch back up. Take 15 fewer seconds on the next four questions, and after four questions you'll have caught back up. Once you catch back up, you can continue working each problem at your normal pace.

Furthermore, don't dwell on the problems that you were rushed on. If a problem was taking up too much time and you made a hurried guess, it must be difficult. The difficult questions are the ones you are most likely to miss anyway, so it isn't a big loss. It is better to end with more time than you need than to run out of time.

Lastly, sometimes it is beneficial to slow down if you are constantly getting ahead of time. You are always more likely to catch a careless mistake by working more slowly than quickly, and among very high-scoring test takers (those who are likely to have lots of time left over), careless errors affect the score more than mastery of material.

Secret Key #2 - Guessing is not Guesswork

You probably know that guessing is a good idea. Unlike other standardized tests, there is no penalty for getting a wrong answer. Even if you have no idea about a question, you still have a 20-25% chance of getting it right.

Most test takers do not understand the impact that proper guessing can have on their score. Unless you score extremely high, guessing will significantly contribute to your final score.

Monkeys Take the Test

What most test takers don't realize is that to insure that 20-25% chance, you have to guess randomly. If you put 20 monkeys in a room to take this test, assuming they answered once per question and behaved themselves, on average they would get 20-25% of the questions correct. Put 20 test takers in the room, and the average will be much lower among guessed questions. Why?
1. The test writers intentionally write deceptive answer choices that "look" right. A test taker

has no idea about a question, so he picks the "best looking" answer, which is often wrong. The monkey has no idea what looks good and what doesn't, so it will consistently be right about 20-25% of the time.

2. Test takers will eliminate answer choices from the guessing pool based on a hunch or intuition. Simple but correct answers often get excluded, leaving a 0% chance of being correct. The monkey has no clue, and often gets lucky with the best choice.

This is why the process of elimination endorsed by most test courses is flawed and detrimental to your performance. Test takers don't guess; they make an ignorant stab in the dark that is usually worse than random.

$5 Challenge

Let me introduce one of the most valuable ideas of this course—the $5 challenge:

You only mark your "best guess" if you are willing to bet $5 on it.
You only eliminate choices from guessing if you are willing to bet $5 on it.

Why $5? Five dollars is an amount of money that is small yet not insignificant, and can really add up fast (20 questions could cost you $100). Likewise, each answer choice on one question of the test will have a small impact on your overall score, but it can really add up to a lot of points in the end.

The process of elimination IS valuable. The following shows your chance of guessing it right:

If you eliminate wrong answer choices until only this many remain:	Chance of getting it correct:
1	100%
2	50%
3	33%

However, if you accidentally eliminate the right answer or go on a hunch for an incorrect answer, your chances drop dramatically—to 0%. By guessing among all the answer choices, you are GUARANTEED to have a shot at the right answer.

That's why the $5 test is so valuable. If you give up the advantage and safety of a pure guess, it had better be worth the risk.

What we still haven't covered is how to be sure that whatever guess you make is truly random. Here's the easiest way:

Always pick the first answer choice among those remaining.

Such a technique means that you have decided, **before you see a single test question**, exactly how you are going to guess, and since the order of choices tells you nothing about which one is correct, this guessing technique is perfectly random.

This section is not meant to scare you away from making educated guesses or eliminating choices; you just need to define when a choice is worth eliminating. The $5 test, along with a pre-defined random guessing strategy, is the best way to make sure you reap all of the benefits of guessing.

Secret Key #3 - Practice Smarter, Not Harder

Many test takers delay the test preparation process because they dread the awful amounts of practice time they think necessary to succeed on the test. We have refined an effective method that will take you only a fraction of the time.

There are a number of "obstacles" in the path to success. Among these are answering questions, finishing in time, and mastering test-taking strategies. All must be executed on the day of the test at peak performance, or your score will suffer. The test is a mental marathon that has a large impact on your future.

Just like a marathon runner, it is important to work your way up to the full challenge. So first you just worry about questions, and then time, and finally strategy:

Success Strategy

1. Find a good source for practice tests.
2. If you are willing to make a larger time investment, consider using more than one study guide. Often the different approaches of multiple authors will help you "get" difficult concepts.
3. Take a practice test with no time constraints, with all study helps, "open book." Take your time with questions and focus on applying strategies.
4. Take a practice test with time constraints, with all guides, "open book."
5. Take a final practice test without open material and with time limits.

If you have time to take more practice tests, just repeat step 5. By gradually exposing yourself to the full rigors of the test environment, you will condition your mind to the stress of test day and maximize your success.

Secret Key #4 - Prepare, Don't Procrastinate

Let me state an obvious fact: if you take the test three times, you will probably get three different scores. This is due to the way you feel on test day, the level of preparedness you have, and the version of the test you see. Despite the test writers' claims to the contrary, some versions of the test WILL be easier for you than others.

Since your future depends so much on your score, you should maximize your chances of success. In order to maximize the likelihood of success, you've got to prepare in advance. This means taking practice tests and spending time learning the information and test taking strategies you will need to succeed.

Never go take the actual test as a "practice" test, expecting that you can just take it again if you need to. Take all the practice tests you can on your own, but when you go to take the official test, be prepared, be focused, and do your best the first time!

Secret Key #5 - Test Yourself

Everyone knows that time is money. There is no need to spend too much of your time or too little of your time preparing for the test. You should only spend as much of your precious time preparing as is necessary for you to get the score you need.

Once you have taken a practice test under real conditions of time constraints, then you will know if you are ready for the test or not.

If you have scored extremely high the first time that you take the practice test, then there is not much point in spending countless hours studying. You are already there.

Benchmark your abilities by retaking practice tests and seeing how much you have improved. Once you consistently score high enough to guarantee success, then you are ready.

If you have scored well below where you need, then knuckle down and begin studying in earnest. Check your improvement regularly through the use of practice tests under real conditions. Above all, don't worry, panic, or give up. The key is perseverance!

Then, when you go to take the test, remain confident and remember how well you did on the practice tests. If you can score high enough on a practice test, then you can do the same on the real thing.

General Strategies

The most important thing you can do is to ignore your fears and jump into the test immediately. Do not be overwhelmed by any strange-sounding terms. You have to jump into the test like jumping into a pool—all at once is the easiest way.

Make Predictions
As you read and understand the question, try to guess what the answer will be. Remember that several of the answer choices are wrong, and once you begin reading them, your mind will immediately become cluttered with answer choices designed to throw you off. Your mind is typically the most focused immediately after you have read the question and digested its contents. If you can, try to predict what the correct answer will be. You may be surprised at what you can predict.

Quickly scan the choices and see if your prediction is in the listed answer choices. If it is, then you can be quite confident that you have the right answer. It still won't hurt to check the other answer choices, but most of the time, you've got it!

Answer the Question

It may seem obvious to only pick answer choices that answer the question, but the test writers can create some excellent answer choices that are wrong. Don't pick an answer just because it sounds right, or you believe it to be true. It MUST answer the question. Once you've made your selection, always go back and check it against the question and make sure that you didn't misread the question and that the answer choice does answer the question posed.

Benchmark

After you read the first answer choice, decide if you think it sounds correct or not. If it doesn't, move on to the next answer choice. If it does, mentally mark that answer choice. This doesn't mean that you've definitely selected it as your answer choice, it just means that it's the best you've seen thus far. Go ahead and read the next choice. If the next choice is worse than the one you've already selected, keep going to the next answer choice. If the next choice is better than the choice you've already selected, mentally mark the new answer choice as your best guess.

The first answer choice that you select becomes your standard. Every other answer choice must be benchmarked against that standard. That choice is correct until proven otherwise by another answer choice beating it out. Once you've decided that no other answer choice seems as good, do one final check to ensure that your answer choice answers the question posed.

Valid Information

Don't discount any of the information provided in the question. Every piece of information may be necessary to determine the correct answer. None of the information in the question is there to throw you off (while the answer choices will certainly have information to throw you off). If two seemingly unrelated topics are discussed, don't ignore either. You can be confident there is a relationship, or it wouldn't be included in the question, and you are probably going to have to determine what is that relationship to find the answer.

Avoid "Fact Traps"

Don't get distracted by a choice that is factually true. Your search is for the answer that answers the question. Stay focused and don't fall for an answer that is true but irrelevant. Always go back to the question and make sure you're choosing an answer that actually answers the question and is not just a true statement. An answer can be factually correct, but it MUST answer the question asked. Additionally, two answers can both be seemingly correct, so be sure to read all of the answer choices, and make sure that you get the one that BEST answers the question.

Milk the Question

Some of the questions may throw you completely off. They might deal with a subject you have not been exposed to, or one that you haven't reviewed in years. While your lack of knowledge about the subject will be a hindrance, the question itself can give you many clues that will help you find the correct answer. Read the question carefully and look for clues. Watch particularly for adjectives and nouns describing difficult terms or words that you don't recognize. Regardless of whether you completely understand a word or not, replacing it with a synonym, either provided or one you more familiar with, may help you to understand what the questions are asking. Rather than wracking your mind about specific detailed information concerning a difficult term or word, try to use mental substitutes that are easier to understand.

The Trap of Familiarity

Don't just choose a word because you recognize it. On difficult questions, you may not recognize a number of words in the answer choices. The test writers don't put "make-believe" words on the test, so don't think that just because you only recognize all the words in one answer choice that that answer choice must be correct. If you only recognize words in one answer choice, then focus on that one. Is it correct? Try your best to determine if it is correct. If it is, that's great. If not, eliminate it. Each word and answer choice you eliminate increases your chances of getting the question correct, even if you then have to guess among the unfamiliar choices.

Eliminate Answers

Eliminate choices as soon as you realize they are wrong. But be careful! Make sure you consider all of the possible answer choices. Just because one appears right, doesn't mean that the next one won't be even better! The test writers will usually put more than one good answer choice for every question, so read all of them. Don't worry if you are stuck between two that seem right. By getting down to just two remaining possible choices, your odds are now 50/50. Rather than wasting too much time, play the odds. You are guessing, but guessing wisely because you've been able to knock out some of the answer choices that you know are wrong. If you are eliminating choices and realize that the last answer choice you are left with is also obviously wrong, don't panic. Start over and consider each choice again. There may easily be something that you missed the first time and will realize on the second pass.

Tough Questions

If you are stumped on a problem or it appears too hard or too difficult, don't waste time. Move on! Remember though, if you can quickly check for obviously incorrect answer choices, your chances of guessing correctly are greatly improved. Before you completely give up, at least try to knock out a couple of possible answers. Eliminate what you can and then guess at the remaining answer choices before moving on.

Brainstorm

If you get stuck on a difficult question, spend a few seconds quickly brainstorming. Run through the complete list of possible answer choices. Look at each choice and ask yourself, "Could this answer the question satisfactorily?" Go through each answer choice and consider it independently of the others. By systematically going through all possibilities, you may find something that you would otherwise overlook. Remember though that when you get stuck, it's important to try to keep moving.

Read Carefully

Understand the problem. Read the question and answer choices carefully. Don't miss the question because you misread the terms. You have plenty of time to read each question thoroughly and make sure you understand what is being asked. Yet a happy medium must be attained, so don't waste too much time. You must read carefully, but efficiently.

Face Value

When in doubt, use common sense. Always accept the situation in the problem at face value. Don't read too much into it. These problems will not require you to make huge leaps of logic. The test writers aren't trying to throw you off with a cheap trick. If you have to go beyond creativity and make a leap of logic in order to have an answer choice answer the question, then you should look at the other answer choices. Don't overcomplicate the problem by creating theoretical relationships or explanations that will warp time or space. These are normal problems rooted in reality. It's just that the applicable relationship or explanation may not be readily apparent and you have to figure things out. Use your common sense to interpret anything that isn't clear.

Prefixes

If you're having trouble with a word in the question or answer choices, try dissecting it. Take advantage of every clue that the word might include. Prefixes and suffixes can be a huge help. Usually they allow you to determine a basic meaning. Pre- means before, post- means after, pro - is positive, de- is negative. From these prefixes and suffixes, you can get an idea of the general meaning of the word and try to put it into context. Beware though of any traps. Just because con- is the opposite of pro-, doesn't necessarily mean congress is the opposite of progress!

Hedge Phrases

Watch out for critical hedge phrases, led off with words such as "likely," "may," "can," "sometimes," "often," "almost," "mostly," "usually," "generally," "rarely," and "sometimes." Question writers insert these hedge phrases to cover every possibility. Often an answer choice will be wrong simply because it leaves no room for exception. Unless the situation calls for them, avoid answer choices that have definitive words like "exactly," and "always."

Switchback Words

Stay alert for "switchbacks." These are the words and phrases frequently used to alert you to shifts in thought. The most common switchback word is "but." Others include "although," "however," "nevertheless," "on the other hand," "even though," "while," "in spite of," "despite," and "regardless of."

New Information

Correct answer choices will rarely have completely new information included. Answer choices typically are straightforward reflections of the material asked about and will directly relate to the question. If a new piece of information is included in an answer choice that doesn't even seem to relate to the topic being asked about, then that answer choice is likely incorrect. All of the information needed to answer the question is usually provided for you in the question. You should not have to make guesses that are unsupported or choose answer choices that require unknown information that cannot be reasoned from what is given.

Time Management

On technical questions, don't get lost on the technical terms. Don't spend too much time on any one question. If you don't know what a term means, then odds are you aren't going to get much further since you don't have a dictionary. You should be able to immediately recognize whether or not you know a term. If you don't, work with the other clues that you have—the other answer choices and terms provided—but don't waste too much time trying to figure out a difficult term that you don't know.

Contextual Clues

Look for contextual clues. An answer can be right but not the correct answer. The contextual clues will help you find the answer that is most right and is correct. Understand the context in which a phrase or statement is made. This will help you make important distinctions.

Don't Panic

Panicking will not answer any questions for you; therefore, it isn't helpful. When you first see the question, if your mind goes blank, take a deep breath. Force yourself to mechanically go through the steps of solving the problem using the strategies you've learned.

Pace Yourself

Don't get clock fever. It's easy to be overwhelmed when you're looking at a page full of questions, your mind is full of random thoughts and feeling confused, and the clock is ticking down faster than you would like. Calm down and maintain the pace that you have set for yourself. As long as you are on track by monitoring your pace, you are guaranteed to have enough time for yourself. When you get to the last few minutes of the test, it may seem like you won't have enough time left, but if you only have as many questions as you should have left at that point, then you're right on track!

Answer Selection

The best way to pick an answer choice is to eliminate all of those that are wrong, until only one is left and confirm that is the correct answer. Sometimes though, an answer choice may immediately look right. Be careful! Take a second to make sure that the other choices are not equally obvious. Don't make a hasty mistake. There are only two times that you should stop before checking other answers. First is when you are positive that the answer choice you have selected is correct. Second is when time is almost out and you have to make a quick guess!

Check Your Work

Since you will probably not know every term listed and the answer to every question, it is important that you get credit for the ones that you do know. Don't miss any questions through careless mistakes. If at all possible, try to take a second to look back over your answer selection and make sure you've selected the correct answer choice and haven't made a costly careless mistake (such as marking an answer choice that you didn't mean to mark). The time it takes for this quick double check should more than pay for itself in caught mistakes.

Beware of Directly Quoted Answers

Sometimes an answer choice will repeat word for word a portion of the question or reference section. However, beware of such exact duplication. It may be a trap! More than likely, the correct choice will paraphrase or summarize a point, rather than being exactly the same wording.

Slang

Scientific sounding answers are better than slang ones. An answer choice that begins "To compare the outcomes..." is much more likely to be correct than one that begins "Because some people insisted..."

Extreme Statements

Avoid wild answers that throw out highly controversial ideas that are proclaimed as established fact. An answer choice that states the "process should be used in certain situations, if..." is much more likely to be correct than one that states the "process should be discontinued completely." The first is a calm rational statement and doesn't even make a definitive, uncompromising stance, using a hedge word "if" to provide wiggle room, whereas the second choice is a radical idea and far more extreme.

Answer Choice Families

When you have two or more answer choices that are direct opposites or parallels, one of them is usually the correct answer. For instance, if one answer choice states "x increases" and another answer choice states "x decreases" or "y increases," then those two or three answer choices are very similar in construction and fall into the same family of answer choices. A family of answer choices consists of two or three answer choices, very similar in construction, but often with directly opposite meanings. Usually the correct answer choice will be in that family of answer choices. The "odd man out" or answer choice that doesn't seem to fit the parallel construction of the other answer choices is more likely to be incorrect.

Special Report: Additional Bonus Material

Due to our efforts to try to keep this book to a manageable length, we've created a link that will give you access to all of your additional bonus material.

Please visit http://www.mometrix.com/bonus948/tcleose to access the information.